D0457604

WILD ANIMALS AND SETTLERS ON THE GREAT PLAINS

Wild Animals and Settlers on the Great Plains

BY EUGENE D. FLEHARTY

UNIVERSITY OF OKLAHOMA PRESS : NORMAN AND LONDON

Library of Congress Cataloging-in-Publication Data

Fleharty, Eugene D.
    Wild animals and settlers on the Great Plains / by Eugene D.
Fleharty.
        p. cm.
    Includes bibliographical references (p.   ) and index.
    ISBN 0-8061-2709-0 (alk. paper)
    1. Human-animal relationships—Great Plains—History—19th
century. 2. Human-animal relationships—Kansas—History—19th
century. 3. Human ecology—Great Plains—History—19th century. 4. Human ecology—Kansas—History—19th century. 5. Prairie ecology—Great Plains—History—19th century. 6. Prairie
ecology—Kansas—History—19th century. I. Title.
QL85.F58 1994
304.2'7'097809034—dc20   94-23240
                                                               CIP

Book design by Bill Cason

The paper in this book meets the guidelines for permanence and durability of the Committee on Production Guidelines for Book Longevity
of the Council on Library Resources, Inc.♾

Copyright © 1995 by the University of Oklahoma Press, Norman,
Publishing Division of the University. All rights reserved. Manufactured in the U.S.A.

1 2 3 4 5 6 7 8 9 10

PL
85
F58
1995

TO MY FAMILY:
Jo Ann
Debra, Kevin, Ann, and John
Chris, Donna, Renee, and Kristen

Contents

Illustrations

MAP

Preface

In *The Roots of Dependency*, Richard White (1983) points out that all peoples "live in a physical world which is not only natural but is also historical—a creation of their ancestors and themselves. Environmental constraints set certain boundaries on human creations, but they only limit; they do not dictate. Ideally, such human-dominated ecosystems produce food and shelter for human beings without degrading the natural systems upon which society depends" (p. xiii).

The nature of interaction between humans and "natural systems" varies depending on how people perceive their own place within the total environment. In hunting and gathering societies, individuals usually see themselves as a part of the environment—existing in it and using it to sustain themselves, much as any other animal does. In such societies people live more or less in harmony with the total system, and their activities have little effect on the integrity and stability of the entire ecosystem.

But as humans began to domesticate plants and animals, a development that culminated eventually in the agricultural revolution, the fundamental relationship between humans and the environment changed. People began to view nature as adversarial, something to overcome so that crops and livestock might flourish. Farming techniques that made life less difficult developed quickly, and technology resulted in new and better weapons to protect both individuals and their livestock. As humankind's ability to alter the environment increased, people began to view themselves as distinct from nature rather than as a part of it, capable of manipulating and controlling it. For example, by the time Kansas was settled, steel plows, reapers, barbed wire, and firearms were available. All gave the settlers a sense of power and a degree of control over the environment whence they desired to wrest their living.

Interactions between the settler and native animals were many and varied. As the grassland was broken, crops planted, and livestock introduced to the native prairie, significant changes were wrought in the environment. Environmental constraints did not dictate to these early Kansas settlers, but in the process of creating an agriculturally based society, degradation of the prairie ecosystem adversely affected many populations of native animals. Conversely, however, there were other species of native animals that benefited from these same changes. The purpose of this book, is to examine the reciprocal interactions that occurred between the settlers and the native fauna.

My interest in human/animal interaction stems from my ecological research conducted on populations of small mammals in western Kansas. This research has involved mammals living in a habitat mosaic of croplands, roadside ditches, remnant prairies, riparian woodlands, and pasturelands—the primary habitats available for occupancy in western Kansas. From a cursory glance at the miles of croplands and rangeland, one initially assumes that the intrusion of industrial agriculture into the prairies probably had a pejorative effect on all species of the native mammalian fauna. After all, the buffalo, antelope, gray wolf, black-footed ferret, and other species that once occupied this land have all, at one time or another, been extirpated from Kansas. One might assume that the smaller species of animals suffered the same fate as did their larger counterparts.

Results of my research, however, suggest otherwise. Rather than having a negative impact on these small vertebrate species, modern agriculture has actually facilitated population growth of many species of small mammals and in a couple of instances has helped increase the total number of species present. Agricultural crops not only provide a source of food and cover for some species, but the physical arrangement of agricultural land is important. Land laid out in sections of county roads and adjacent borrow ditches, which often contain a luxuriant growth of grasses and forbs, has helped immensely in providing dispersal routes for many species of small mammals. Without agriculture the number of small mammals probably would be considerably less than it is today.

In one of my studies small-mammal populations were simultaneously sampled from the previously mentioned major habitats in western Kansas for a period of two to three years, in an attempt to determine which habitat was most representative of the prairie habitat that existed during the preagricultural history of western Kansas. As one might guess, the rangeland is most similar to the prairies of 1865. However, an ancillary question remained. Is the rangeland of today, grazed by domestic cattle, significantly different from the prairies of 1865, grazed by vast herds of buffalo, antelope, elk, and deer? The few manuscripts written during that time by explorers who had some scientific knowledge provide no adequate answer. In a further effort to determine the impact of these large grazing mammals, I examined primary information sources in the form of diaries, letters, and newspapers written by settlers, for any pertinent information they might provide.

Although I did not find adequate answers to the ancillary question, I did locate a wealth of information concerning buffalo, as well as many other kinds of wildlife that occupied western Kansas in the latter half of the nineteenth century. These articles and anecdotes are written in a style that vividly portrays frontier life, with few editorial remarks, interpretations, or inferences drawn by secondary writers. They are told with such clarity and simplicity that the color and nuances of those times come alive. As I read the accounts of those early settlers struggling to adapt to such a harsh environment, I felt almost as if I were there—that I was a neighbor, experiencing the same successes and suffering, the same hardships and losses. This experience is what I hope to impart to the reader.

From this somewhat serendipitous beginning I began to look more closely at how those early settlers utilized the abundant fauna of the grasslands and how they reacted to the dangers posed by some species. I was struck by the curiosity shown by some, the concerns for the wildlife exhibited by others, and the expressions of awe and wonderment voiced by still others at the animals present in this land. Grasslands have an assemblage of animals unlike anywhere else—animals that are adapted to open areas. Large grazing mammals such as deer, elk, antelope, and the omnipresent buffalo, along with many smaller creatures such as prairie dogs and jackrabbits, were crucial residents because they helped maintain the structure and integrity of the prairie ecosystem.

I chose to study the grasslands of Kansas for a variety of reasons. I have lived and worked in this ecosystem for over thirty years and am thus familiar with it. My teaching and research interests have allowed me to spend many days in the hot summer sun of the prairies and many cool nights under the stars. I have also experienced the bitter cold and north winds of Kansas winters.

In addition, Kansas is representative of the Great Plains in general. Most vertebrates present in Kansas occurred elsewhere on the Great Plains, and there is no reason to believe that the encounters between those animals and the early settlers in Kansas differed in any substantial way from what took place in surrounding areas of the Great Plains.

My attachment to the prairies developed in early childhood. I was raised in southern Nebraska in the Platte River valley and remember listening as a child to my grandfather relate incidents involving Indians and settlers in that region. My family had a small farm just a mile or so south of the Platte River, and I came to cherish the wide-open spaces, the high sky, and a horizon that extended for miles. I delighted in the large flocks of sandhill cranes that passed through the area on their spring and fall migrations. Many was the time I sat astride our small Ford tractor and watched the cranes circle higher and higher in those endless skies until they were almost out of sight, the sun reflecting off their great wings as they circled ever higher.

During those early years I acquired an affinity for unobstructed views, the openness and vastness of a plain unbroken save for a few trees. Even today I get somewhat claustrophobic in the mountains, where horizons seem to close in upon one, and the vista narrows. The same sensation descends upon me in large cities, where tall buildings block my sight and the horizon is measured in feet rather than in miles. One of my life's greatest thrills is topping the Rocky Mountains and, looking eastward, beholding the unending expanse of grassland. Over the years I have returned to this experience many times, and the view never fails to overwhelm me. The greatness of the plains humbles me and affords me perspective about human life in relationship to nature.

I chose to study the fifteen-year period from 1865 to 1879 because during this time the prairies of Kansas were being settled and the resident wildlife had perhaps its greatest influence on the Kansas pioneers. Those were also the years when the two great railroads—the Kansas Pacific and the Atchison, Topeka, and the Santa Fe—were completed, increasing the flow of immigrants westward and providing the means by which products from the plains could be sent to eastern markets. Admittedly, the dates chosen (especially the latter) are somewhat arbitrary, but by 1879 the bison/settler coaction was completed, and the other highly visible species of wildlife had been impacted greatly. During this time agricultural practices began to impact negatively many species of wildlife. Perhaps the foundation was laid for the extinction of grassland creatures within the borders of Kansas. In an attempt to include the prairie areas of the state, I examined thirty archival newspapers published from all parts of Kansas, as well as letters, diaries, and manuscripts written during the period from 1865 through 1879. I made a conscious effort not to use reminiscences, or hand-me-down stories from relatives, as there is a tendency for time to fade memory and retelling to alter detail. Therefore, I relied almost entirely on stories and anecdotes recorded firsthand during those years.

I have tried, as well, to describe interactions between the settlers and *all* species of animals present. Volumes have been written on the buffalo and how they were hunted for meat and hide and the role they played in the colorful lives of famous individuals such as Buffalo Bill Cody. However, this is *not* another buffalo book! I do not mean to denigrate the importance of the buffalo in either its effect on the native prairie or its role in providing sustenance to the pioneer. Buffalo were certainly important. However, at the same time, interactions that took place with the smaller, less obvious animals were probably at least equally important if not more so to the survival of the average settler. Buffalo were driven from the immediate frontier rather quickly, and the average settler did not have the time, resources, or perhaps the inclination to pursue the dwindling herds that were forced farther and farther from the settlements. The majority of farming families turned to smaller game animals to supplement meat from domestic livestock and to hunt and fish for recreation. In my opinion, the interactions between these smaller animals and the settlers allowed many immigrants to survive during the formative years of agricultural development and during episodes of drought, grasshopper infestations, and economic depression. By omitting, or giving scant detail, to the interactions with lesser animals, we have an incomplete picture of the immigrant and his relations with the native fauna.

By relating events exactly as they were reported in newspapers and diaries during that fifteen-year slice of time, I hope to present to the reader a more balanced picture of the coactions that occurred between the settler and the native fauna. It is a varied picture, ranging from happiness to tragedy, laughter to tears. It is a picture that portrays members of all the major vertebrate groups and the ways in which they interacted with the newest member of the prairie ecosystem—the Kansas settler. It is a story that illustrates wanton waste, but also curiosity, concern, and creativity. I found these articles to be enlightening and in many cases touching. I hope you do too.

I would like to acknowledge several people. First and foremost is my wife, Jo Ann. She not only supported me through the many hours of gathering data, but spent a great deal of time at the keyboard entering that data into the computer. She also filed all photocopied material and helped me read the final version to copy. Her many hours are greatly appreciated. I thank James D. Drees, a local historian, who not only provided encouragement and lent articles from his research files but also critically read the manuscript and provided many helpful suggestions. Personnel at Forsyth Library—Karen Cole, director; Mac Reed, documents; Esta Lou Riley, archives; Carolyn Herman, interlibrary loan; Phyllis Schmidt and Judy Salm, reference department—were always supportive in fulfilling my requests for help. Staff at the Kansas Historical Society were equally helpful.

Fort Hays State University provided a Graduate School Research Grant and a sabbatical leave. One of my colleagues, Dr. Jerry R. Choate, read some of the early drafts and provided beneficial suggestions. Joseph Collins (The University of Kansas, Museum of Natural History), Mark Eberle (Fort Hays State University, The Sternberg Museum of Natural History), and Randy Rodgers and Keith Sexson (Kansas Department of Wildlife and Parks) provided helpful current information. I am appreciative of the efforts of Kim Johnson who did a major portion of the preliminary typing and helped me with the word processing. Finally, I thank Kim Wiar, University of Oklahoma Press, for her efforts on my behalf.

EUGENE D. FLEHARTY

Hays, Kansas

WILD ANIMALS AND SETTLERS ON THE GREAT PLAINS

Introduction

The native wild animals that inhabited the prairies of the Great Plains during 1865–79 evoked a variety of responses from the recently arrived immigrants, ranging from terror to the sublime. Examples of both can be found in the following two excerpts from newspapers of that time:

IT IS OUR TASK TO RECORD ONE OF THE MOST PAINFUL INCIdents that has ever come within our knowledge, resulting in an agonizing death to a young lady from the effects of a bite by a snake. A daughter of Mr. J. G. Briery, who resides on Twin creek, aged some thirteen or fourteen years, went with her brother, last Saturday morning, to his claim, some five miles distant, where he was doing some work, and the two expected to return together in the afternoon. They changed their plans, however, and about three o'clock the girl set out for home on foot and alone, carrying a pail in which to gather some wild berries on the way. Later in the evening her brother returned home, and great was the surprise to find that the girl was still absent. Search was immediately instituted, but went on without any avail till two o'clock Sunday. The pail she carried was found by the roadside about two miles from home, partly filled, which seemed to confirm beyond a doubt the great fear that some awful fate had delayed her return. Mr. Ward and another party who were engaged in the search, at last heard a call, and proceeding in the direction from whence it came, beheld one of the most shocking and heart-rending sights the imagination is capable of picturing. There, sitting upon the ground in a nearly denuded state, they found the poor girl by a pool, where she had found her way and endeavored to extract the poison which the fangs of a hateful rattlesnake had buried in her foot, by burying it in the soft mud. All this time she had remained there alone and experienced the symptoms of a horrible death approaching, for the venom was working in her system, and she must have suffered the most intense agony. Although sufficiently conscious to discern and call for help when it was near, her denuded state indicated that her sufferings had at times at least driven her to frenzy. One of the party who found her went at once for her father who came with a team and she was conveyed home. Nothing, however, could be done by human hands to relieve the sufferer—it was too late, and in the evening the great panacea, death, which always comes to the relief of the sufferer when anguish is too great to be borne, rescued her from her terrible misery. (*Osborne County Farmer*, 6 July 1877)

SOME DAYS SINCE WE . . . STARTED SOUTH FOR A GRAND BUF-falo hunt.

At first sight of buffaloes I should be almost ashamed to let an old hunter know what a fever of enthusiasm that far off glance communicated to my blood. I felt as happy as a green boy, and trembled all over. Buffaloes—indubitabl[y]e buffaloes—feeding on that vast, sunny, fenceless mead. In ten minutes after we separated one from the main herd which we gave a lively chase for a few minutes, but after receiving some thirty or forty shots he gently passed in his "checks." Again we made an attack on the main herd. The ground was in splendid order for running; the lay of the land as favorable; my horse had acquired his "second wind," and his enthusiasm fully equaled my own. I never knew the ecstacy of the mad gallop until now. Like young Lochinvar, "we stayed not for brake, we stopped not for stone." Some draws that we crossed made me shudder afterward as I thought of them.

Now we were plunging with headlong bounds down bluffs of caving sand, ten and fifteen feet high, and steep as a fortress glacis, while the buffalo, crazy with terror, were scrambling half-way up to the top of the opposite side. Now we were on the very haunches of our game, with a fair field before and no end to pluck and bottom for the rest of the chase, the buffalo laboring heavily, and their immense fore-parts coming down on their hoofs with a harder shock at every jump. Now we saw a broad, slippery buffalo wallow just in time to keep it clear; now we plunged into the very middle of one, but Nig dug himself out of the mud with a frantic tug, and kept on. Still we came closer to our buffaloes; and I just made up my mind to ride as long as my horse would ride in the line of the stampede, while in the meantime the artillery had been playing its part to perfection; killing and wounding several. I made for a mound, reached its summit, and to Nig's great disgust, though he was fearfully short breathed and trickling with sweat, halted him instantly to await the rear column. I had not many minutes of anxiety. The herd saw me 200 yards off, but, as I expected, paid no more attention to me than if I had been a grass blade. Nor could they if they would. All stampedes are alike—whether of men or animals. As the herd got within fifty yards of the mound, I delivered one steadily aimed ball at the fore-shoulder of the nearest bull. He gave a single wild jump and began limping on three legs. I had done for him. For a few seconds, fear of his pressing comrades gave him enough extra speed to keep up with the rest; but before the line reached the foot of the mound he had tumbled, and the whole host was rushing over him. Once more . . . the front line came so close that I could almost have jumped my horse on to their backs, [and] I fired my pistol again. The bullet did no damage to any but itself, flattening like putty on the thick matted Gibraltar of one old bull's frontispiece. They divided just in time to avoid being crowded over the mound, and in a moment half our party was standing on a desert island in a sea of billowing backs, flowed around on either side by a half-mile current of crazy buffaloes. Here was abundant opportunity to shoot, but not the least anxiety to do so. I had such a view of buffaloes as I never could have expected, never would enjoy again. This was all sufficient for me. I stood and studied the host with devouring eyes, while my horse snorted and pulled at the bridle in a passion of enthusiasm. Yes, there beyond peradventure, in my plain sight grazed the entire buffalo army of Southern Kansas. As far as the western horizon the whole earth was black with them. The desire to shoot, kill, and capture utterly passed away. I only wished to look, and look till I could realize or find some speech for the greatness of nature that silenced me. (*Ellsworth Reporter*, 15 August 1872)

To many settlers the prairies of the Great Plains were a dangerous place, in which lives could be lost because of some tragic, unforeseen occurrence. To others, however, the environment presented an awesome spectacle where one could experience an uplifting, even spiritual feeling and be almost overcome by the vastness and the beauty of the prairie.

The information herein is particularly valuable in helping to determine past geographical distributions of the native fauna. Reliable historical documentation of the presence of specific species of animals in specific localities is invaluable to biogeographers in their attempts to reconstruct the recent history of animal species occupying Kansas. For example, few locality records exist for some species of mammals such as mountain lion, otter, and porcupine. Newspaper accounts of these animals help fill gaps in our knowledge regarding the distribution of these species. Information herein should also prove valuable to environmental historians as they attempt to reconstruct a complete and realistic picture of the development of the pioneer society on the Great Plains.

But this book should be intrinsically interesting to anyone who enjoys reading about life during frontier times or who desires to know about the fauna that existed then. It provides insight into the day-to-day life of the settlers and their creative interaction with the various animals around them. Concern for these animals was clearly evident. Some of the early settlers attempted to halt the wanton destruction of wildlife long before the animals became scarce. Many settlers truly appreciated wildlife for its intrinsic worth. Many, it seems, were awed by nature and marveled at its numerous faces. Quite a few of the anecdotes are humorous, and many illustrate the heart and soul of these immigrants, revealing in detail how they viewed themselves and their surroundings. The fact that they were able to laugh at themselves and poke fun at others is testimony to the strength of the bond between neighbors. These articles also provide insight into the many tragedies that occurred on the frontier and the ways in which the immigrants confronted and overcame them. Tragic deaths due to rattlesnake bite or hunting accidents are reported with a straightforwardness and clarity that elicits empathy. In the face of these hardships the Kansas settlers continued to break the sod, plant their crops, and raise their livestock. The fact that they carried on despite such adversity is silent testimony to the tenacity and steadfastness of these people. Not all persevered, of course, but many did.

Readers familiar with the landmarks and place names of Kansas should particularly enjoy reading about those areas most familiar to them. Many differences exist between the immigrants' descriptions of certain regions and the appearance of those same areas today. Names of the settlers that appear in some articles will often be familiar to the longtime resident of a given area because family descendants often remain in the area today. I believe those who read these firsthand, unedited accounts will develop an empathy and kinship with the settlers in their struggles to survive on the Kansas frontier from 1865 through 1879.

In chapter 1 I have provided a thumbnail sketch of the natural history of the region along with a brief description of the major habitats, and the components, of the vertebrate fauna found within each. As the chapter indicates, the impressions that these vast, open prairies made upon the early settlers were mixed. Some looked forward with great anticipation to another day full of new adventures, while others found each new day almost unbearably wearisome.

Chapters 2–5 contain documentary information in the form

of excerpts from diaries, magazines, and newspaper articles written between 1865 and 1879. In chapter 2 the reader will discover that vertebrate fauna were principally regarded as game animals for hunting and fishing. Family members spent considerable time in these endeavors and met with varying degrees of success, and occasionally abject failure. However, many viewed these abundant resources as a source of income, or at the very least as a way of supplementing the meager income derived from early agricultural production. Consequently, many enterprising individuals hunted and fished to sell game to other settlers, to local eating establishments, and to markets in the east, which were now easily reachable with the recently completed railroads.

Market hunting became the principal occupation for professional hunters. This business was quite lucrative, at least for a brief time. Some animals were hunted for reasons other than food: Hides were taken from buffalo for robes and leather, and furs were sought from wolves, otter, beaver, muskrat, and skunk. Often only the tongue and hams of the buffalo were taken for food, and when the hide hunters were active, the hide alone was usually all that was utilized. Carcasses were left on the prairies to be consumed by scavengers.

Vast quantities of bones—the only remains of millions of buffalo, deer, antelope, elk, and domestic cattle—were gathered by "bone pickers," hauled to the nearest railhead, and sent to eastern markets. The trade in bones was active for a few years and helped many a farmer through a lean winter.

"Pest" species such as coyotes and wolves were hunted by many settlers for control purposes as well as for sport and recreation. Many of the immigrants had fought in the Civil War and knew how to use firearms. Firearms were, of course, a necessary accoutrement for life on the early frontier; they were needed for protection from Indians and from dangerous animals such as rattlesnakes. Not surprisingly, hunting became one of the chief modes of recreation. Hunters generally found at least some waterfowl available throughout the year, but numbers increased greatly during the spring and fall migrations. Turkey, quail, prairie chicken, and sharp-tailed grouse all provided the nimrod with abundant game. "Grand hunts" were regularly scheduled for the big game, such as buffalo and antelope. Hunting was so popular that hunting clubs were formed in various communities, and shooting contests often held. The prowess of some hunters, whether fact or legend, was widely reported. Rivers and streams harbored abundant fish for the angler as well.

Chapter 3 relates the feelings of the early settlers toward animals never before encountered. As the immigrants pushed into the Great Plains, many of them confronted new species of animals. They were often impressed by the size of animals, be they rattlesnakes, elk, or birds such as eagles and geese. The settlers tried to make pets of some, and domestic beasts of others. The keen observations of some writers regarding how the creatures interacted stimulated many questions, and provided some answers, for curious newcomers.

Not all native animals were appreciated by the early settlers. Some were a threat to their very lives; others destroyed property. Chapter 4 describes how, for many settlers, the frontier was a risky place to live. Not only did the pioneers have to put up with the vagaries of weather, but they also confronted very real dangers from some of the animals, often resulting in death. The rattlesnake and the skunk were the primary culprits—the snake produced venom and the skunk harbored rabies. Treatment of animal bites consisted of a bizarre mixture of common sense and folk remedies that often hastened the demise of the victim. Accidents involving firearms were commonplace. The book graphically portrays the deaths of loved ones and provides insight into familiar, everyday dangers.

The concern for the dwindling numbers of some species of wild animals is examined in chapter 5. While hunting and fishing for both market and recreation were prevalent, wildlife habitat was being altered. The degradation of habitat was a necessary precursor to the preparation of the land for agriculture. As the immigrants pushed westward in Kansas, wood for building materials and for fuel was at a premium; consequently, the small amount of timber that made up the riparian communities was quickly cut, thereby removing a vital habitat for some wildlife species. The result was predictable. The double-barreled impact of excessive hunting and fishing coupled with habitat degradation resulted in a rapid decline in numbers of many of the native species of wildlife. This loss caused a few voices of concern to be raised among the pioneer citizenry. Eventually legislation was introduced and passed that restricted year-round hunting for some species. Other laws regulated the methods by which fish could be captured. A state fish commissioner was appointed who implemented policies of restocking as a method of managing declining fish fauna.

The final chapter briefly summarizes the efforts of the Kansas Department of Wildlife and Parks to respond to the desires of those who simply wish to enjoy nature, and of others who wish to be able to hunt at least some of the same species their ancestors hunted. Some species that were extirpated because of the activities of the immigrants—such as the turkey, antelope, otter, and elk—have been successfully reintroduced within the state. Habitat improvement and conservation measures have augmented the populations of deer, prairie chicken, and quail. Buffalo will never be brought back to levels that would permit even a limited hunting season, but a few herds are maintained by private individuals, state institutions, and the Kansas Department of Wildlife and Parks for the enjoyment of Kansans. This official state policy of preservation and reintroduction is testimony to the enduring concern that first prompted the writing of this book— the interactions of people and wildlife on the Great Plains.

CHAPTER 1

History, Ecology, and Impressions

The relationship of a people to the environment in which they live is a product of both the history of the region and the environment itself—in particular, the flora, fauna, and climate. The writings of previous inhabitants will influence those who come later, and the environmental conditions will place constraints on what can and cannot be done. Before the settlers ever set foot on the Great Plains, they harbored certain beliefs about the area. Upon arrival in the Great Plains their impressions were surely modified, with relief in some cases and with dread in others.

The first white men to find their way into what is today western Kansas were not settlers. Several Spanish explorers as well as French fur traders passed through the region that was to become Kansas during the sixteenth, seventeenth, and eighteenth centuries. However, not until the early nineteenth century were any detailed natural-history notes recorded. In 1803 the United States purchased the Louisiana Territory from France. At that time the fledgling government of the United States had no reliable information about the territory. On 24 June 1806 Zebulon Montgomery Pike was ordered to lead an expedition onto the plains, to establish friendly relations with the Indians and to note the natural history, geography, and geology of the area. After counseling with the Indians, Pike traveled southward, reached the Arkansas River, and followed it westward into Colorado.

Shortly thereafter in 1820 Stephen H. Long led an expedition that was devoted primarily to scientific observation and study. His group consisted of Dr. Edwin James, who functioned as botanist, geologist, and surgeon, and Thomas Say, zoologist and ethnologist. The group was to follow the Platte River to its source, then drop southward and find the origins of the Arkansas and Red rivers and follow these back to Fort Smith, Arkansas (Nichols, 1980). By 5 July 1820 the expedition reached the location of Denver, and by 21 July the location of today's La Junta, Colorado. Here Long divided the expedition, taking James with him down the Cimarron and Canadian rivers and sending Say down the Arkansas River.

These explorations were followed by those of John C. Frémont. In 1840 he was commissioned to map the route from Fort Leavenworth to Oregon to find the most suitable locations to establish a series of forts. Frémont made expeditions in both 1842 and 1843 and on both occasions crossed Kansas. On 10 July 1843 he camped near the present town of Wallace and by 16 July was near Page Creek, which now flows into Cedar Bluff Reservoir (Frémont, 1845, pp. 288–89).

Prior to Frémont's exploration, overland trails had been established to allow trade with the Spanish in Santa Fe. Although many traders were involved in efforts to establish such a trail (see Zornow, 1957), William Becknell is generally acknowledged as the "Father of the Santa Fe Trail"—the first person to use wagons rather than packhorses. He left Missouri on 1 September 1821 and by 16 November arrived in Santa Fe (Zornow, 1957).

In the early 1850s, stories of gold discoveries along Cherry Creek in the Rocky Mountains were brought back to the East, and overland trails were established to reduce travel time to the goldfields. These trails included the Leavenworth and Pikes Peak Express, established in 1859, which carried heavy traffic for a few months but then faded away, and the shorter, more direct, but more dangerous Smoky Hill Trail, which was also founded in 1859. The Smoky Hill Trail was used only sporadically because there were no forts west of Fort Riley / Fort Larned to protect travelers.

In 1865 the Butterfield Overland Despatch resurveyed the route, established stations, and began passenger and freight operations. Forts Harker (1864–73), Hays (1865–89), and Wallace (1865–69) were established to protect Butterfield Overland Despatch traffic. Because of Indian activity and financial problems the Butterfield Overland Despatch halted operations on the Smoky Hill Trail in May 1866.

The Union Pacific Railway, Eastern Division (Kansas Pacific after 1869) announced in 1866 that it would build along the Smoky Hill route instead of following the Republican Valley. The Kansas Pacific Railroad began in Wyandotte in 1863 and reached Leavenworth in 1865, Topeka and Junction City in 1866, Hays City in 1867, and Sheridan in 1869. The forts were then given the responsibility of protecting the railway crews. The Smoky Hill Trail continued, albeit shortened, as the railway pushed westward until it reached Denver in 1870. Along the Santa Fe Trail, which the Atchison, Topeka, and Santa Fe Railroad would closely follow, were Fort Zarah (1864–69), Fort Larned (1859–78), and Fort Dodge (1865–82) (Zornow, 1957). The Atchison, Topeka, and Santa Fe Railroad began in Topeka in 1868, reached Emporia in 1870, Newton in 1871, and Hutchinson, Great Bend, Larned, and Dodge City in 1872.

Although there was a significant amount of travel across the High Plains by traders and trappers, there were few permanent residents, let alone settlements, until the railroads began to push westward (Forsythe, 1977; Miner, 1986). The importance of the railroads to settlement in this region cannot be minimized. First and foremost, through the Pacific Railway Act of 1 July 1862, railroads were granted lands to sell to help pay the costs of construction. In Kansas this amounted to nearly four million acres (Self, 1978). The railroads advertised their lands heavily in eastern newspapers and provided excursions to the West for potential buyers. Experimental plantings were undertaken by the railroads to illustrate that western Kansas was not part of the "Great American Desert"—that it could be as productive as farmland in the eastern states. As a result of the needs of farmers and railroad-building crews, towns sprung up as the railroads forged corridors into western Kansas (Forsythe, 1977; Miner, 1986). Trains provided the means for transporting farm produce, buffalo meat, and hides from western Kansas to the East, and needed goods and the "sportsmen" to the West.

Once the rails were laid, Texas cattle were driven north to the progressing railheads. The Chisholm Trail led from extreme southern Texas to Abilene and Ellsworth on the Kansas Pacific Railroad, and later to Newton, Wichita, and Dodge City on the Atchison, Topeka, and Santa Fe. The Western Trail, also from Texas, stretched northward to Dodge City and Ellis, Kansas, into Nebraska and points northwest. More than five million cattle were driven to these railheads (Self, 1978). Unfortunately, the Texas cattle brought with them Texas or Spanish fever, which could be easily transmitted to local herds, with the result that quarantine lines were established by the state legislature (Self, 1978). As immigrants continued to arrive, there was growing competition for land, and increasingly less "free land" existed for the Texas herds. Finally the land was fenced, and there no longer was continuous open range for grazing and driving cattle.

ECOLOGY

To better understand the interactions between the settlers and the native wildlife, a general understanding of the ecological components and their role in an ecosystem is helpful. Most of Kansas is rolling plains, notwithstanding some stretches in the western portion of the state in which relief is almost totally absent, or in the east, where elements of the eastern deciduous forest encroach and extend westward along river courses as riparian communities. Kansas can be divided on the basis of rock substrate, landforms, and climate into physiographic provinces and subprovinces (Self, 1978). Approximately two-thirds of the state (i.e., essentially areas west of the Flint Hills) lies in the Great Plains province, whereas the remaining eastern third occupies a portion of the Central Lowland province (Fenneman, 1931).

The Great Plains province is in turn subdivided into five subprovinces: Great Bend Prairie, Wellington Plain, Red Hills, Smoky Hills, and High Plains (Self, 1978). The Great Bend Prairie is found immediately west of the Flint Hills just south of the great bend of the Arkansas River and extends westward to Dodge City. The Wellington Plain is south of the Great Bend Prairie to the east. The Red Hills subprovince is west of the

Wellington Plain along the southern border of Kansas. The Smoky Hill subprovince occupies north-central Kansas, north of the Great Bend Prairie. Finally, the High Plains covers approximately the western third of the state. The Great Plains province in Kansas and the wild-animal/human interactions that occurred therein are the focus of this book.

Kuchler (1974) illustrates the potential natural vegetation of Kansas as short-grass prairie in the western third, mixed-grass prairie in the west-central region, and tallgrass prairie in the eastern third, with oak-hickory forest on the extreme eastern border and flood-plain vegetation along the rivers. The High Plains, floristically dominated by buffalo grass and blue grama grass, have an average annual precipitation from seventeen to twenty-two inches. They make up the most arid subprovince. Because of this aridity, the High Plains were essentially treeless in the years 1865–79. The principal rivers and streams that drain this region are the South Fork of the Republican River, Beaver Creek, Sappa Creek, and Prairie Dog Creek, all of which flow northeastward into Nebraska and the Solomon, Saline, Smoky Hill, Pawnee, Arkansas, and Cimarron rivers and Walnut Creek, which flow in an easterly direction. Elevation ranges from about two thousand feet on the eastern border of the High Plains to more than four thousand feet in the west. What trees were present in 1865 were located in narrow riparian communities along the rivers. Farther west running water became less reliable, and trees became fewer and fewer until they disappeared altogether.

To the east, on the Great Bend Prairie, Wellington Plain, Red Hills, and Smoky Hills subprovinces, the mixed-grass prairie is located, which consists mostly of bluestem grasses and grama grasses, though buffalo grass is present on the upper reaches of the bluffs and hills. Precipitation is greater than that on the High Plains, ranging from twenty-two inches on the west to thirty-two inches on the east. East of this prairie is the Flint Hills subprovince, which is dominated by tall grasses, such as big bluestem.

It should be noted that the junctures between these prairie ecosystems—that is short grass / mixed grass and mixed grass /

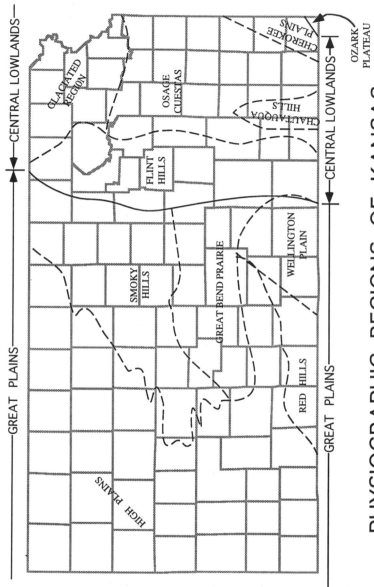

PHYSIOGRAPHIC REGIONS OF KANSAS

tall grass—are not abrupt. Because of local variation in precipitation, grazing intensities, runoff, and other environmental factors, the place where two prairie ecosystems meet is a gradual transition, a mosaic, or an interdigitation of the two, rather than an abrupt demarcation.

Broadly speaking, when settlers entered the western two-thirds of Kansas, there were three different ecosystems available to fulfill the necessities of food and shelter. Grasslands made up the largest area—tall, mixed, and short grasses—from east to west. These grasslands were dissected by a riparian ecosystem of trees and shrubs that grew adjacent to the dendritic pattern of rivers and streams that drained the grassland. As the rivers and streams decreased in size in their westward extensions, so too did the riparian communities until, in the far west, they disappeared altogether. The third ecosystem was aquatic and existed in the form of rivers, streams, springs, and a few small lakes.

These habitats also provided a place to live for a variety of wild animals. Each ecosystem has its foundation in the green plants, which through photosynthesis provide nourishment for the herbivores; they, in turn, are preyed upon by carnivores. When an organism dies, other organisms, such as bacteria and fungi, decompose it into nutrients that can be used again by the plants. Herbivores interact with plants in a variety of ways—the most obvious is the grazing of grasses and forbs and the browsing of leaves on shrubs and trees; undigestible waste in the form of fecal matter adds nutrients to the soil. Other herbivores excavate burrows and thus aerate the soil and permit increased percolation of water, whereas the hooves of large grazing mammals trample plants and compact the soil, thereby affecting the types of animals that can live there. Carnivores exert a positive influence on herbivores by controlling their population numbers but in turn can be adversely affected when populations of herbivores are reduced. Physical factors—precipitation, temperature, and wind—will affect the growth of the vegetation. This growth in turn directly influences the food, cover, and mating areas of the animals.

This overly simplified description is illustrative of the fact that an ecosystem is integrated, interconnected, and interdependent.

As changes in the physical and biological parameters occur, fluctuations within the living components will occur, but always within limits. Ecosystems are in a dynamic equilibrium.

Most of the settlers in Kansas came from the midwestern states of Ohio, Missouri, Pennsylvania, New York, and Kentucky (Richmond, 1992). Some came from overseas—mostly German or German-Russian—but goodly numbers also came from Ireland, England, and Sweden (Richmond, 1992). With a few notable exceptions (German-Russians), most of these people brought with them a historical perspective of deriving their livelihood from lands representative of a forest ecosystem, where precipitation was more plentiful, temperatures somewhat cooler, and winds less violent than what they found on the prairies of western Kansas. It is safe to say that the early pioneers did not understand the ecology of the area in which they settled.

As the immigrants settled in western Kansas, they interfered with the balance among the components of the ecosystems. They degraded and sometimes destroyed a portion of the habitat upon which the overall ecosystem was sustained, and they overharvested some of the animal components. Riparian habitat was altered almost immediately as trees were cut for fuel and building material. But the loss of trees did not constrain the settlers, as they creatively used buffalo chips for fuel and built sod houses and dugouts from the earth. However, some new habitats in the form of buildings, croplands, and weedy areas along the borders of fields were established. These habitats attracted new species as well as altered the relative abundance of others.

The early settlers interacted with a large number of vertebrate species. Animals provided meat for personal consumption and for the market, as well as hides and furs for the market. They were also a means of recreation or sport, and some were domesticated as pets or to serve some other useful purpose. Animals believed to be dangerous to the settlers and their livestock were eliminated. Probably to one degree or another recreation was involved in all these instances, and hunting and fishing endeavors became social events eagerly anticipated by the immigrants. These activities involved a variety of species. However, despite the reports of early explorers and naturalists who commented about animals they encountered, no exhaustive survey of fishes, amphibians, reptiles, birds, and mammals occurred until much later. The richness of the fish fauna in the area was relatively low. As one moves westward in Kansas, the amount of water decreases and the harshness of the physical environment increases. There were approximately thirty species of fish in the region during 1865–79 (Mark Eberle, 1994, personal communication). Most of these were nongame fishes comprising a variety of species of chub, shiner, minnow, and darter as well as stoneroller, carpsucker, stonecat, and killifish. Fish that were used for sport and food included the American eel, black bullhead, channel catfish, flathead catfish, largemouth bass, and green sunfish.

In the grasslands of the western two-thirds of Kansas, amphibians were represented by one species of salamander, seven species of frogs, and five species of toads (Joseph Collins, 1994, personal communication). Many species of amphibians are either secretive or nocturnal or both. Consequently, the early settlers may have been ignorant of the variety present. However, two species—the bullfrog and plains leopard frog—were frequently encountered. Reptiles were probably represented by seven species of turtles, ten species of lizards, and twenty-nine species of snakes (Joseph Collins, personal communication). Turtles were hunted for food; most species of snakes when encountered were likely eradicated, simply because of the dislike that humans seem to hold generally toward snakes. The horned lizard was frequently mentioned, primarily as a curiosity.

The precise number of mammalian species once present is difficult to determine. Many species are small, secretive, and nocturnal and therefore not easily detectable. However, historical information about the geographical distribution of mammals, as well as current life-history data, suggests that sixty-eight species of mammals probably were present in the western two-thirds of Kansas during 1865–79. Newspapers of the time mentioned the following mammalian species: feral horse, buffalo, antelope, elk, mule deer, prairie dog, striped skunk, muskrat, mink, otter, raccoon, beaver, rabbit (mostly jackrabbit), bobcat, mountain lion, opossum, fox squirrel, ground squirrel, gopher, mole, badger, bear, coyote, gray wolf, gray fox, and swift fox. This rather impressive list represents approximately 40 percent of the mammalian species actually present.

In the area of the Great Plains of Kansas during 1865–79 there might have been as many as 407 species of birds that either nested in the various available habitats, migrated through on a more or less regular spring-fall schedule, were resident winter species, were relatively uncommon, or were rare and present only on an irregular basis (Thompson and Ely, 1989, 1992). Resident nesting birds probably were represented by 178 species. The groups that nest on the High Plains with the number of species in each include new-world flycatchers, 9; larks, 1; swallows, 7; crows, ravens, and jays, 5; titmice and chickadees, 3; nuthatches, 2; wrens, 6; kinglets and gnatcatchers, 1; thrushes, 4; thrashers, 5; shrikes, 1; wood warblers, 7; tanagers, 2; cardinals and grosbeaks, 8; towhees, sparrows, and longspurs, 10; blackbirds and orioles, 9; finches, 3; old-world sparrows, 1; loons and grebes, 2; cormorants, 2; herons, 9; ibis, 1; geese, 1; ducks, 15; vultures, 2; kites, 1; hawks and eagles, 13; grouse and prairie chickens, 4; turkey, 1; quail, 2; rails, 4; gallinules, 2; plovers, 3; stilts, 1; avocets, 1; sandpipers, 3; phalaropes, 1; terns, 2; pigeons, 2; cuckoos, 3; owls, 7; goatsuckers, 3; swifts, 1; kingfisher, 1; and woodpeckers, 6. Interactions with prairie chicken, bobwhite quail, wild turkey, cranes, and various species of geese, ducks, plovers, eagles, hawks, pelicans, and owls as well as a variety of songbirds occurred.

The early Spanish, French, and American explorers, those who traded with the Indians for furs, and those who crisscrossed the High Plains on the various trails to goldfields in Colorado or to the markets in Santa Fe had negligible impact on the prairie ecosystem. They were relatively few in number, never established permanent settlements, and, like the hunter-gatherer Indians, largely used only the natural resources needed to survive. However, in the case of fur trappers, whose activities led to the capture of as many furbearers as possible, the numbers of certain species such as beaver and otter might have begun to decline. The final extirpation of these animals did not occur, however, until permanent settlements were in existence.

IMPRESSIONS

This land, largely devoid of forests and water and with a harsh climate, generated varied impressions among the early explorers and settlers as they entered the seemingly endless plains and prairies of western Kansas. Early accounts of the settlers' reactions to the Great Plains province often include the adjective "monotonous." As newcomers traveled down one hill of the rolling prairie and climbed to the crest of the next, the view was the same—more rolling hills, more prairie. The sameness and expansiveness of the plains, with their broad horizon and high sky, were overwhelming, and many an early traveler felt a loneliness that left one weary and longing for the place whence he came.

Zebulon Pike in his journal of 1806 stated, "These vast plains of the western hemisphere, may become in time equally celebrated as the sandy deserts of Africa; for I saw in my route, in various places, tracts of many leagues, where the wind had thrown up the sand, in all the fanciful forms of the ocean's rolling wave, and on which not a speck of vegetable matter existed" (Pike, 1810, appendix part 2, p. 8).

Major Stephen H. Long, as he left the Rocky Mountains and began to move eastward along the Arkansas River in 1820, noted, "More than one hundred thousand miles of dreary and monotonous plain lay between us and the enjoyments and indulgences of civilized countries" (Long, 1823, p. 50). Eight to ten miles later he wrote, "Here the barren cedar ridges, are succeeded by still more desolate plains, with scarce a green, or living thing upon them, except here and there a tuft of grass . . ." (p. 51). Elsewhere he stated, "We do not hesitate in giving the opinion, that it is almost wholly unfit for cultivation, and of course uninhabitable by a people, depending upon agriculture for subsistence" (p. 361).

Although concluding that the area was unfit for cultivation, both Pike and Long believed that these inhospitable lands could be advantageous to the budding nation. Pike in 1808 stated, "But from these immense prairies may arise one great advantage to the United States, viz: the restriction of our population to some certain limits, and thereby a continuation of the union.

Our citizens being so prone to rambling and extending themselves, on the frontiers, will, through necessity, be constrained
to limit their extent on the west, to the borders of the Missouri
and Mississippi, while they leave the prairies incapable of cultivation to the wandering and uncivilized aborigines of the country"
(Pike, 1810, appendix part 2, p. 8).

In 1823 Long, after his travels, reached the same conclusion as
Pike: "This region, however, viewed as a frontier, may prove of
infinite importance to the United States, inasmuch as it is calculated to serve as a barrier to prevent too great an extension of our
population westward, and secure us against the machinations or
incursions of an enemy, that might otherwise be disposed to
annoy us in that quarter" (Long, 1823, p. 361). One wonders to
what degree Long was influenced by Pike's comments.

Whatever the case, Pike was probably the originator of the
idea that these High Plains should be considered a desert. However, in his writings, and specifically on his map entitled "Country Drained by the Mississippi Western Section," Long labeled
the area of western Kansas the "Great American Desert" and
thereby popularized the idea (Zornow, 1957; Nichols, 1980).

Horace Greeley, the noted eastern newspaper man, was on
the first coach of the Leavenworth and Pikes Peak Express that
left Leavenworth on 18 April 1859 for the goldfields of Colorado.
Ten years later he wrote the following observations:

> FOR HUNDREDS OF MILES, THERE IS NO FENCED FIELD, NO GROW-
> ing grain, no tolerable house, and only the merest spot of
> garden by some military post or mail station, some Indian
> agent's lodge, many a weary day's journey from any other.
> Nature's ruggedness and man's indolence, or impatience
> of meagerly rewarded labor, combine to render this pre-
> eminently the region of rude living, discomfort and a preva-
> lent despair or disdain of anything better. Yet, even here,
> this shall not always be.
>
> I have said that the predominant impression made on the
> stranger's mind by the Plains is one of loneliness—of isola-
> tion. For days, if with the mail, for weeks by any other con-
> veyance, you travel westward, with never a mountain, and

scarcely a hill, with never a forest, with seldom a tree, with rarely a brook or spring, to break the monotony of the barren, mainly grassless, dewless landscape, out of which the sun rises at morning, into which it settles at night. God's works are around you; but those of men, save the trail beneath your feet, the wagon which conveys you, are absent." (Greeley, 1869, p. 793, 794).

The establishment of the railways did not change the impressions of some early travelers. John Putman described the country he passed through on a journey by rail in the summer of 1868:

STARTING FROM TOPEKA WE PASS GRADUALLY FROM ONE EXtreme of fertility to the other. From rich farming lands rolling in native wealth we come to a region where we lose sight of man and beast and vegetable life; to dreary reaches of level sand where there are no hills, no water! not a tree nor a bush, nor a blade of grass; not a green herb, not a living thing, not one trace of any one of the multifarious forms of life which God has filled the Earth appears to break the unending monotony of the dreary Expanse. There is not one barrier to break the force of the dry, hot wind, for the traveller, nothing to protect his head from the broiling heat of the sun" (A trip to the end, 1944, p. 201–2).

J. R. Tice in 1872 described the area in these words. "On and on we go to the westward passing a road station every twelve or fifteen miles, Walker, Hays, Ellis, Ogallah, Park's Fort, Cayote, Buffalo, Grinnel, Monument, Gopher, Sheridan, Wallace, Eagle Tail, Monotony, etc. Otherwise the scene is as monotonous as that viewed from a ship on the ocean" (Tice, 1872, p. 52).

Not all viewed this area as monotonous, dreary, and inhospita· ble. Some saw in it the potential to provide a good living. In many instances the transient visitor who spent little time on the prairie was the most eager to denigrate its qualities. Those that remained became familiar with the many redeeming qualities of the Great Plains. They came to appreciate the great vistas unimpeded by forest or mountain, the pronounced seasonal changes from hot, windy summers to bitterly cold, clear winters, as well as the abrupt, almost daily, changes that can bring a cool thunderstorm in the summer, and warm, almost springlike, days in the dead of the winter. There was not only a variety of wildlife but also a diversity of wildflowers from early spring through late autumn, basking in tranquil, clear sunrises and glorious sunsets. Not a few settlers formed a strong attachment to the land and passed this bond on to their descendants, many of whom remain today, proud to call themselves "flat-landers."

Horace Greeley pointed out that

A NEARER, STEADIER, MORE FAMILIAR GAZE REVEALS SYMPTOMS of life which you at first overlooked. At intervals, the fleet antelope looks shyly down on you a moment from the crest of a "divide," then is off on the wings of the wind. The gray wolf more rarely surveys you deliberately from a respectful distance, and, seeing no opening for speculation, slinks off in quest of more available game. The paltry cuyota [sic], to which the name prairie-wolf has universally been given, since it has in its nature nothing of the wolf but his ravenous appetite, and would hardly be a match for a stout fox or raccoon, lingers near you, safe in his own worthlessness and your contempt. The funny, frisky little prairie dog—a condensed or foreshortened gray squirrel—barks with amusing alarm at your approach, then drops into his hole, which, for mutual defense and advantage, he shares with an owl and a rattlesnake, and is silent as the grave till you pass out of hearing. Ten or twenty thousand of these little imps, with their odd partners, cover a square rood [sic] or two together with their holes, dug irregularly at distances of ten or twelve feet apart, but I think rarely communicating underground, as one may be drowned out by pouring in upon him twenty or thirty pails of water. (1869, p. 794)

In the early 1860s J. R. Mead, an early hunter, trapper, and trader, described the area along Paradise Creek as

THE MECCA OF THE HUNTER'S DREAM, AND THE INDIAN'S DE-
light. The beautiful valley, clear, cool water, plenty of wood
for camp fires, abundance of game of the grandest sort in
the world! Well might we say, here roamed the grand buffalo and slothed the noble elk, the timid deer, antelope, lordly
strutted the turkey gobbler and skulked the wolf, coyote,
the lynx, the coon, possum, skunk, porcupine, beaver and
other game in abundance. The ducks, geese, prairie chickens,
and the quail here found their home, seldom disturbed by
man, and now for the first time to hear the report of white
man's gun." (Mead, 1859–75, p. 95–96)

On the Saline River just to the north and west of Salina,
Mead wrote:

WE NOW DEVOTED OUR TIME TO HUNTING, IN WHICH WE WERE
quite successful, as buffalo were very plentiful in the immediate vicinity, as well as antelope and other game. There
were hundreds of turkeys along the timbered streams which
were easily killed, and the woods were full of fox squirrels.
The river and its tributary streams were alive with beaver
and otter, and in the brush along the river were an abundance of quail. . . . There was also numerous prairie chickens
of two varieties; the ordinary ruffled grouse of Iowa and Illinois, and another bird, not so large, which was called the
pin tail chicken" (Mead, 1859–75, p. 60).

Dixon (1867) described the abundance of wildlife as follows:

WE ARE NOW, BETWEEN BIG CREEK AND BIG TIMBER STATION,
in the very heart of the wild game country; a country of
long, low, rolling hills, covered with a short sweet grass—
bunch-grass—on which the buffalo loves to feed. We have
ceased firing at rattle-snakes and prairie chickens; reserving
our cartridges for the nobler uses of self-defence; though we
are tempted, now and then, to try a shot at some elk, or
antelope, or black-tailed deer. The great game being buf-

faloes, against the tough hides of which our small six-shooters are of no avail, we sit quietly in our waggon watching the herds troop by; in lines, in companies, in droves, in armies, the black and shaggy beasts go thundering in our front; sometimes from north to south, sometimes from south to north; but always scudding in our front, and always across our line of march. The plains are teeming with life; most of all with buffalo bulls and cows. For forty hours we have now had them always in our sight; thousands on thousands, tens of thousands after tens of thousands; a countless host of untamed animals; all of them fit for human food; enough, we should think, to stock Arapahoe, Comanche, and Cheyenne wigwams to the end of time. Once or twice the driver tries a shot; but fear of the red-skins commonly checks his wish to fire. (p. 30–31)

The publishers of the *Smith County Pioneer* of 27 July 1876 attempted to attract settlers with the following description of wildlife:

SPORTSMEN WILL FIND IN THIS COUNTY, IN THE WAY OF FEATHered game, wild turkey, quail, grouse, prairie chickens; and in the fall and spring of the year millions of prairie pigeons, or snipe, cover our prairies, and the lakes and streams are alive with wild ducks, geese, brants and swan. The countless numbers of jack rabbits, (an animal about three times larger than the ordinary brush rabbit, and an animal that can run with the speed of the wind), affords an excellent substitute for the old time fox chasing in the woodland states. The sportsman must be armed with a pack of fleet greyhounds in order to get any fun out of this part of the programme. Herds of antelope graze, during the summer season, in the brakes of the Republican, within five hours ride from the county seat. Buffalo are occasionally found in this county during the summer months, and herds of elk feed in the sparsely settled portions during the winter time. Fish are found in all the streams of the county.

Lieutenant Colonel Richard I. Dodge (1877, p. 118) wrote:

THE MOST DELIGHTFUL HUNTING . . . I HAVE EVER HAD WAS in the country south-east of Fort Dodge on the small tributaries of the Cimarron River. I append the record of a hunt of twenty days in the section, in October 1872, in which one officer besides myself and three English gentlemen participated. Everything bagged was counted as one, and an idea of the spot can be formed from this list:—

127 buffalo.	6 cranes.
2 deer (red).	187 quail.
11 antelope.	32 grouse.
154 turkeys.	84 field-plover.
5 geese.	33 yellow legs (snipe).
223 teal.	12 jack snipe.
45 mallard.	1 pigeon.
49 shovel-bill.	9 hawks.
57 widgeon.	3 owls.
38 butter-ducks.	2 badgers.
3 shell-ducks.	7 racoons [sic].
17 herons.	11 rattlesnakes.

143 meadow larks, doves, robins, &c.
1 blue bird for his sweetheart's hat.
Total head bagged: 1,262.

The next year nearly the same party diminished by *one*, went over nearly the same ground with a bag of like variety, numbering 1,141.

Into this land, perceived as monotonous by some, and bountiful by others, poured the immigrants. In their struggle to survive they encountered, utilized, and enjoyed many of the native animals, but were victimized by others.

CHAPTER 2

Hunting and Fishing for Food, Market, and Recreation

It is difficult to categorize hunting and fishing by purpose—such as food, market, and recreation—because categories often overlap. Hunting and fishing to supply one's table with food, or to sell game to others, frequently provides recreation as well. Likewise, hunting and fishing for sport often puts food on the table. Newspaper articles of the time indicate that the settler hunted and fished throughout the year, which suggests that people were in need of, or at least desired, a continual supply of fresh meat.

The abundance of animals as a source of food on the High Plains of western Kansas was a godsend to the early settler. Of the wide variety of animals present on the prairies that could easily satisfy the fresh-meat requirements, the large game animals—buffalo, antelope, deer, and elk—come to mind as the most likely choices. Of these the buffalo appear to have been favored. After all, buffalo occurred in vast herds and were seemingly everywhere. However, the herds of buffalo migrated over great distances as they searched for the best pasturage and so were not, on a day-to-day basis, readily available to the sedentary settler. Furthermore, buffalo were for the most part extirpated from Kansas by 1873. Consequently, the average settler had to purchase buffalo meat either from local meat merchants or from professional buffalo hunters who sold directly from their wagons. After 1873 even the professional hunter had to travel southwest into Texas and Oklahoma, or northwest to Colorado and southeastern Wyoming, to locate the large herds. As buffalo herds diminished, the average settler did not possess the wherewithal to travel long distances each winter to obtain buffalo meat—

much of which might spoil if the weather warmed unexpectedly. Even the relatively inexpensive meat sold by the professional hunter might have been too expensive for many pioneer families. Many could not afford meat at any price after the grasshopper plague of 1874 left them destitute.

Historians have written volumes about buffalo and their importance to the development of the West. They were the focal point in the confrontation between Europeans and the Plains Indians. The presence of buffalo also was important in the development of the railroad and early settlement in the region. However, I believe the average settler and his family did not rely to any great extent on large game mammals for their meat. When it came to a desirable source of fresh meat throughout the year, the smaller, less obvious animals were more important. Settlers were almost always assured of the availability of some sort of small game animal—often a rabbit—which could be totally utilized in a day or so, thus obviating concern about spoilage. Another rabbit could be shot another day.

Game birds presented a second ready source of food that was present throughout the year. Prairie chicken, quail, and wild turkey were all available in appropriate habitats. In addition, waterfowl and shorebirds (ducks, geese, cranes, plovers, and snipes) were present in bountiful numbers, especially during the spring and fall migrations.

If the settler resided relatively close to a permanent river or stream—and many did—fish provided a source of food as well. Since there were no regulations on method of capture until 1877 (see chapter 5), it was relatively easy to catch large numbers of fish with little effort by using nets and seines. Consequently, many households were supplied fish caught by a family member.

The presence of wild animals and fish provided the frontier families with not only a source of food but also, for some, a source of income through the marketplace. Those who were especially proficient at hunting and fishing sold game to local meat shops or directly to customers. Newspapers frequently advertised various types of game available for sale in local meat markets. Market hunting was most prevalent in connection with the buffalo, but skunks, wolves, and coyotes were also hunted for their pelts. Buffalo meat—often just the tongues—was sent to the eastern markets, primarily during the winter to avoid spoilage. Other hunters would save the hams, then smoke, salt, or dry them as jerky before shipping. Thousands of buffalo were shot, and tons of meat were shipped to the eastern markets.

When factory techniques were developed to tan hides, buffalo hunting for hides alone became a flourishing business; skins were made into valuable robes and rugs. After the buffalo were skinned, the carcasses were left to the scavengers of the prairie—for example, wolves, coyotes, and ravens. The hide hunters hastened the demise of the buffalo, but buffalo, with their migratory habits, required large areas and were doomed from the moment that agriculture and ranching became feasible on the plains. Ultimately only the bones of the buffalo remained, and they too became a valuable commodity in the manufacture of fertilizers and other items for eastern markets. A lucrative but brief business of gathering the buffalo bones strewn over the prairie occurred in the 1870s. Many destitute farmers survived the trying times following the grasshopper plague of 1874 by "picking bones."

The capture of wild horses provided an income for a few hardy souls. Horses were not native to North America but were brought from Europe by the conquering Spanish. It was the Pueblo revolt against the Spanish in 1680 that put large numbers of horses into the hands of the American Indian. By 1690 horses had reached the Red River. By 1719 the Wichita Indians in Oklahoma had horses and the Pawnee had them before 1714 (Haines, 1938a, 1938b). Over the next century and a half some horses escaped and established free-roaming herds. When the settlers pushed into western Kansas, there were not only herds of wild horses but a ready market for them as well. These wild horses were pursued (often for weeks), captured, broken, and sold as domesticated livestock to farmers and ranchers.

Recreation on the early frontier was limited, but native animals provided recreational hunting and fishing. All of the previously mentioned species were hunted for sport by the local settler. In addition to the permanent settlers, sportsmen came west for the sole purpose of hunting the bountiful wildlife. Railroads scheduled spectacular excursions for the express purpose of hunting, either from the train itself or via short side trips from selected train stops. Both men and women came from the East, and a few, like Duke Alexis of Russia, came from foreign countries. Buffalo hunts, whether for sport or meat, required days if not weeks to complete. These trips were often fraught with difficulty under less than ideal conditions, but the hunts in which those difficulties had been overcome were remembered most fondly by the participants. Certainly the outings, whether buffalo, prairie chicken, rabbit, or other game were hunted, provided camaraderie and adventure that were recalled throughout the visitors' lives.

Dogs were helpful and in some cases almost indispensable to those who hunted. Purebred greyhounds were the breed of choice and were regularly used in hunting deer, antelope, rabbit, raccoon, coyote, and wildcat. These dogs, often expensive, were at some risk when they attacked wildcats, but more often they succumbed to heat exhaustion brought on from extended chases on warm days.

Sporting clubs were a direct outcome of recreational hunting and led to the hunting of game by larger groups of people. Sometimes this group hunting took the form of hunting contests in which participants split into smaller groups to see which was the most proficient in killing specified animals. In other instances a group would participate in a "circle hunt." Hunters formed a large circle and converged toward a central point, driving the game before them, eventually shooting, or more often clubbing, all game that was frightened from cover. These sporting clubs usually had twenty or more members, and hunts became social events that included posthunt dinners and dances. In some instances the clubs became the center of social activity within the community.

Not all hunting and fishing excursions had the intended results. In many cases humorous incidents occurred, though whether the individuals involved joined in the laughter remains an open question. Newspapers printed these examples of ineptitude (some of which follow), and those who were the butt of the joke most surely became the "talk of the town."

The killing of buffalo peaked during 1872 and 1873 but rapidly declined thereafter. Populations of many other game animals were also diminished. However, at least some animals representing species that were present during 1865–79 remained in western Kansas until late in the nineteenth century or early into the next.

Eventually the gray wolf, mountain lion, deer, elk, grizzly, black bear, and wild turkey were extirpated from Kansas (Choate, 1987).

Before 1873 many farmers turned to hunting buffalo when the cold weather approached to secure meat for their families. Some newspaper editors tried to discourage this activity by arguing that farming activities required the full attention of the home-steader and that farmers should not be spending valuable time hunting.

> A GENTLEMAN FROM THE SOLOMON VALLEY INFORMS US THAT those who have attended closely to farming have an abun-dance of everything, but that those who hunt buffalo to the neglect of their farms, are the ones who are hard up. He reports that the scarcity of buffalo caused by the Indian trou-bles, has induced everybody to settle down to farming, and that as a consequence a vast amount of land is being pre-pared for crops. This has always been the case. We want set-tlers who will give their attention strictly to farming. (*Junc-tion City Weekly Union*, 17 April 1869)

The second-most-abundant large grazing species of mammal was the antelope. Although antelope might, at one time, have been as common as buffalo, they were more wary and traveled in small herds; consequently, there were no "grand" antelope hunts in the same sense as buffalo hunts. Apparently antelope were never taken in large numbers on a single hunt. Rather, they were taken singly, or by twos and threes. No news articles mentioned large numbers of antelope killed, but reports were often made if even one was taken by a local hunter:

> JIM GOODWYN WAS OUT HUNTING TUESDAY. HE BROUGHT home a large antelope which was found ten miles north of the city. (*Ellsworth Reporter*, 7 May 1874)

> YOUR CORRESPONDENT WAS ANTELOPE HUNTING LAST WEEK and succeeded in bagging three of the wavy animals. (*Larned Optic*, 28 August 1879)

Anrelope on the plains. *Harper's New Monthly Magazine.*

Two kinds of deer could be found in the state. The white-tailed deer was more an eastern deciduous forest dweller, preferring wooded habitat; it occurred primarily in eastern Kansas and extended westward in riparian habitat. The black-tailed deer, or mule deer, was a western species occupying more open range in western Kansas, often far from any wooded habitat. Deer in western Kansas were not particularly common; the shooting of a few was deemed newsworthy:

THE GYPSUM CREEK PEOPLE ARE HAVING ALL THE SPORT THIS season. Having captured the wolves, Mr. Johnathan Tinkler and the Teel brothers have been having considerable sport chasing deer and antelope. They succeeded in capturing five deer and two antelope, and will soon start after more. (*Saline County Journal*, 24 January 1878)

ANTELOPE AND ELK RANGE OVER THE HILLS IN LARGE NUMbers. (Mulberry Creek Items.) (*Ellsworth Reporter*, 27 May 1875)

Waterfowl were particularly abundant during spring and autumn migrations. During these seasons newspapers throughout western Kansas heralded their location. The Kansas River was outstanding habitat for a variety of waterfowl and shorebirds, as indicated by the following excerpts:

THE KANSAS RIVER, WHICH RUNS PARALLEL WITH THE LINE OF Railway for upwards of three hundred miles, with its tributary streams, marshes and lakes, abounds with all kind of water fowl, viz: Swans, Pelicans, Canada and Brant Geese, Cranes, Bitterns, Mallard, Gadwall, Red-head and Blue-bill Ducks, Spoon-bill, Teal, Widgeon, Pintail, English or Wilson's Snipe, and a numerous variety of the genus Sand-piper or Plover, of which latter are found on the up-lands, countless flocks of the Golden Plover, the Prairie or Up-land Plover and Curlew—these last chiefly in the spring. The geese sit on the sand-bars of the river during the day, and at night repair to the adjacent corn-fields to feed. For duck shooting, the principal requirements are—a heavy ten-bore gun and a good retriever. (Weston, 1872, p. 130)

A PARTY OF HUNTERS, CONSISTING OF B. F. EVANS, GEO. W. Cartwright, and some others, went down the Arkansas to the mouth of the Walnut a few days ago, and returned heavily loaded with game, geese and ducks principally. This reminds us that there are a good many geese in this part of the country this fall, all of which are as fat as possible. (*Larned Optic*, 21 November 1879)

Goose hunts were also popular. However, as the following articles indicate, hunters shot any game that came within range; ducks, snipe, cranes, and quail were all fair game:

WE HAD HEARD OF W. R. GEIS AND PARTY SHOOTING SO MANY ducks on the pond west of town. In fact, the report had traveled and traveled until it came to us that they had killed 27 at one shot. Of course, we thought we would try our luck at duck shooting, too. We persuaded Mr. C. Post to furninsh [sic] a team, gun, ammunition and do the shooting. We went with him last Monday afternoon out to the duck country. As we approached that region, we could see along the brow of the hills a long line of white something. This something was construed by us to be—in quick succession—buffalo bones, water, sand hill cranes and, finally, wild geese. How we were astonished when the latter prediction proved to be true. They were geese—although some of the town boys labored hard to make us think (and they almost succeeded in doing so) that they were nothing but brants. We gave up duck hunting. What was such small sport compared with a wild goose hunt. The prairie was literally thick with them. Never was there a finer army of birds. We advanced upon them. Just as we were in hailing distance, the grand army of beautifully feathered and comparisoned [sic] birds arose all together, and the clapping of wings and the squawking of many hundreds was almost deafening. One detachment flew low over us and Post leveled his gun and brought one down. The legions swung southward. They settled again just behind the hills and we "deployed as skirmishers." A ravine was handy, and by crawling carefully up this, Post managed to come within fifty steps of them unobserved. Bang went his gun, and over went a goose, while its fellows rose again as before and continued in their southern flight. East of that locality we saw another division of geese, and we hastily made for that point. Another ravine was conveniently near them, an [sic] up it Post crawled. Another shot and over went another goose, while its companions made off in the direction in which ourself was "camped." As they passed over, we saw a goose falling—falling—and we were satisfied that Post's last shot had called two instead of one to an "account of their stewardship." The goose fell and scrambled off in good order, pursued by the team and ourself across the roughest kind of ground—buggy springs being in the greatest amount of danger. We captured it at last. It was now dark, and we hauled up for Post, who was the proudest man that ever shot a gun. He was now the champion goose hunter. As we made into town we felt as if we went at the head of a conquering army. The goose hunt is the common talk of today. Others have tried their luck, but have not succeeded as well as we did on Monday. Verily, we are at the head of goose slayers, and are happy—especially ourself. (*Saline County Journal,* 29 October 1874)

THE SALINE COUNTY HUNTERS WHO WENT TO THE MCPHERSON ponds last week in search of game, return with glowing accounts of the various experiences. It seems that ducks and geese and snipe were never before so abundant in that region as now. The Chapman party report the result of their hunt as follows: 213 ducks, 8 geese, 40 quail. The Kesler-Silsby party report: 200 ducks and 100 snipe. The boys stocked the markets with a grand supply of game. (*Saline County Journal,* 30 October 1879)

Although there was relatively little open water on the prairie, what there was attracted large numbers of waterfowl during the annual spring and fall migrations. It was not unusual for hundreds to be shot in some hunts:

THE BOYS WHO WENT ON THE BIG HUNT TO THE SALT MARSH below the Arkansas river, Bell, Nunamaker, Sheriff, Maclean, Davis, Shock and Baumaster, returned home last Friday in good spirits. They had good luck, having shot 121 geese, 60 duck, 20 jack snipe and 5 cranes. They had a good time. (*Ellsworth Reporter,* 13 November 1879)

MR. NOBLE TOOK US DOWN IN HIS CELLAR AND SHOWED US A sight the other day that was truly interesting. It was nothing more nor less than a hundred and five wild geese, laid out in regular rows and covered almost the entire floor of the cellar. They were the result of Mr. Huntley's two days' hunt on the Rattlesnake, made a few days previous. The game was shipped both east and west. (*Larned Optic,* 28 November 1879)

Sandhill cranes also were hunted, though no records of large numbers taken were reported in the newspapers:

COUNTY ATTORNEY HODGKINSON SHOT THREE LARGE SANDHILL cranes last Wednesday afternoon. (*Saline County Journal,* 18 September 1873)

Shooting plover also provided food and sport. Because there were several species of plover that occurred in Kansas, it is difficult to know which species was being taken. Any bird that had long legs and a relatively long bill would often be referred to as a plover. Hunters, like those named in the following excerpts, actually may have been shooting killdeer, snipe, sandpipers, and curlews—as well as the true plover.

ON THURSDAY LAST GEO. T. HINKLE, CHAS. E. BASSETT, A. B. Webster and Judge Marshall went out in the afternoon for a glorious hunt, and we believe they had it. They returned in the evening of the same day with sixty-five plover and about half a dozen snipe. We got a snipe. (*Ford County Globe,* 23 July 1878)

CAPT. GEO. HINKLE, SENATOR BASSETT AND MAJOR THOMPSON, three crack shots, made a nice game on Tuesday. In two hours' sport they bagged forty-seven plovers. (*Dodge City Times,* 16 August 1879)

Prairie chickens. Kansas State Historical Society, Topeka.

There were two kinds of prairie chickens in Kansas—the greater and the lesser. Both were hunted for sport and as a source of sustenance. From 1865 to 1879 prairie chickens were reasonably common, and many were taken. News reports such as the following regularly reported the numbers acquired. A poor hunt killed only twenty-five or so.

> OUR SUPERINTENDENT, J. LOOMIS, SPENT LAST SATURDAY WITH us, and had a chicken hunt with conductor Warner and Major Anderson of lightning fame. They bagged sixty four chickens, and every agent from here to Wallace got a brace of nice birds with compliments of Superintendent L.—*Brookville.* (*Ellsworth Reporter,* 31 August 1876)

> THREE WAGON LOADS OF CHICKEN HUNTERS, DULY EQUIPPED with fire arms, ammunition, sedlitz powders, etc., started for Gypsum creek last Tuesday morning, to be chaperoned by Mr. Frank Wilkerson upon the stamping grounds of the fes-

tive chickens. They killed some 60 chickens, notwithstanding "thunder, lightning storm." (*Saline County Journal*, 17 August 1876)

Prairie-chicken hunts usually lasted an entire day and were less demanding than buffalo hunts. Often there was a friendly competition among hunters as to which group could bag the most birds:

THE NEXT THING UPON OUR PROGRAMME WAS A DAY'S SPORT with the prairie chickens, and the objective point Sterling, in Rice county. Having had so enjoyable a taste of the companionship of the Topeka Nimrods, they were cordially pressed to continue lending the light of their countenance upon the party, and after much sighing they ne'er could consent, consented—at least three of the four did—Judge Brockway being so closely confined to county matters demanding his attention as to find it imposssble [*sic*] to leave.

A nine-hour ride, a cordial welcome from Ricksecker, the land agent of the Santa Fe at Sterling, a comfortable tucking in our little bed, and the general turning out at daybreak, each and every one declaring that to lie longer in bed on so glorious a morning would be positive sacrilege.

The prairie chicken, as all Kansans term it, is, as is well known, the same bird familiar to ornithologists as the pinnated grouse, the most conspicuous of all the American grouse family. Though hardly a handsome bird from its rather dusky feathering, [it] is still attractive from its spirited bearing, the delicate pencilings of its feathers, and its bars of different shades of yellow and brown across the breast. It is a larger bird than the ruffed grouse, its flesh quite dark, and as many an epicure knows of exquisite flavor when "cooked to a turn." The pinnated grouse or prairie chicken has the power of inflating the two yellow sacks which he carries on the side of his neck, and during the mating season the cocks are often seen, as the writer of an exceedingly interesting and graphic article in one of the popular monthlies puts it, "strutting and swelling in mimic grandeur, with expanded wings and tail, and making a trumming noise with their wings, striving to please by their pompous ways." At these times they court conflict, and two cock birds never meet without having it out. They spring into the air, striking at each other with feet and wings and continue the animated condition of things generally until the one proves his claim to first choice, and the other sadly concludes to put up with what may be left. The writer hitherto referred to gives so keen and inspiriting a description of a scene quite familiar to old residents in the west, but evidently one of greatest novelty to him, that its substance is here given largely in his own words. One day, while upon the prairie, he noticed some objects on the summit of a knoll, and by careful watching discovered they were prairie chickens. Moved by curiosity, he carefully approached, and soon saw fifteen prairie fowl apparently dancing a minuet. They were scattered about on the short line twenty yards apart, nodding their heads to one another, and presently two would run out, and perform the figure which in a country dance is known as "cross over and back," all the while uttering a soft note of "coo-cooe," the last syllable being much elongated. Then followed "salute your partners," and "dos a dos." This scene of merriment was sustained for half an hour or more and until a shot from a neighboring gun caused the birds to run into the tall cover of the reeds. The bright sunshine of autumn, and the conspicuous group of native birds, impressed the scene vividly on the spectator's mind, and subsequently on relating it to a farmer, near by, the good old son of toil remarked, "Yes, them same birds do skye round there mostly every day."

No sooner were we robed and ready for the fray than Rick, as every one hereabouts calls Ricksecker, had his team at the door, and hardly were the suburbs of Sterling reached before we had a taste of something in the way of the wagon locomotion, Rick letting his ponies out until they plunged forward on a dead run. Over the perfectly smooth race-track like road we dashed like a whirlwind, and we had the sensation of a runaway without its dangers, for a [sic] at a word and the tightening of the reins, the ponies came down to a jog, and the dogs were thrown out to their work. It could not have been possible to make a finer hunting ground than the grand expanse of swelling prairie, the thickly matted buffalo grass, just high enough to afford excellent cover for the chickens and not too high for the dogs to work in, to the utmost satisfaction both as to themselves and the men folk behind them. Morton had his favorite pointer Bang, and Burlingame his crack setter, Ranger, and the constant bantering between the two as to the respective merits of setters and pointers bid fair to receive new impetus from the day's doings. While never agreeing on the dog question, there was no disputing judgment as to character of ammunition used by these old hands at chicken shooting. Four drachms of powder with No. 6 shot, in August and September, and after than No. 4 and 5, owing to the longer range at which the chickens must be reached and heavier feathers as they attain maturity.

Hardly had the dogs been commanded to "hie on" before Bang struck the faint scent where a covey of the birds had recently been hiding, and, in an instant reached them with every vein in his sleek brown body standing out like whip-cords. The birds were running in the grass, and hardly had Bang come to a full point, before Ranger, some fifteen yards distant crouched in the tangled growth carpeting the prairie until his long, fleecy and brilliant coat, looked like some bunch of autumn verdure. The weather was warm and clear, and, with a grandly proportioned cornfield near at hand, the fowl were loth to exert themselves. They laid close, and so many steps did we advance ahead of the dogs, that to one not conversant with the cunning of the prairie chicken, the conviction would almost, if not quite, force itself upon the mind that both pointer and setter had played us false. Just as something of this kind was creeping over your most obedient, swish! flashed an old cock bird so close to my nose that I involuntarily made a lunge at him with my gun, so bewildered that I never dreamed of shooting. The Judge, not daring to shoot owing to my being in range, held up until the bird flew beyond his reach, but Burlingame let fly, shot clean over, and thus the laugh was on all three of us. Auter, in the meantime, bagging a young 'un with that cool and satisfied bearing so dreadfully provoking to those whose powder but scented the open air. "Look sharp!" hoarsely ejaculated Morton, "the hen bird is here with a covey, and we'll get 'em up one at a time." Sure enough, up popped a youngster not twenty feet distant, and he was my meat. It had not touched the grass before the Judge flushed a pair and nipped them both in exceedingly pretty style. Another chick up only to go back to mother earth again, when the parent bird broke cover, and, making a sudden dart almost in Burlingame's face, gave that gentleman a chance for a difficult shot which he accomplished with a grunt of satisfaction that demonstrated his keen desire to get even with the Judge. Only the first bird breaking cover escaped in the entire covey of thirteen, and then onward we moved for new fields to conquer. In the meantime Rick had marked down a large flock flying from the feeding ground to the open prairie, and, speeding his ponies to us, made the new field for sport in a jiffy. Out on the long sweeping prairies of Kansas, one drives at will, there being no fences but such as are easily circumvented, and streams so readily forded as to offer no obstacle to the driver's desire to go anywhere and everywhere. As my companions were starting off behind the dogs, Rick, who remained in the wagon, called me and suggested that I try him and the team as pointers, and promising me three or four fine opportunities for "single" birds rising one at a time. Nothing loth, I assented, and walking at the horse's heads, soon had the satisfaction of seeing a cock bird break cover with a rush, and, taking my time, brought him to the grass at fifty yards.

Following on a few steps another took wing and, flying directly in the line with the team, I had another chance for distinguishing myself. Of the seven birds Rick had marked down I bagged six and knocked feathers out of the seventh. In the meantime the rivalry between Burlingame and the Judge waxed exceedingly warm, and upon picking them up for the return to town for dinner, we found Morton had twenty-six, Burlingame twenty-six, and Auter, who had talked least of all, thirty-one; the sum total of the morning's sport reaching ninety-seven.

Somewhere about three o'clock in the afternoon we went south of the river for a change, and had the best of luck, especially as night approached, the birds becoming almost as tame as domestic fowl as the twilight fell over the beautiful valley. On the way home we had some of the jolliest sport imaginable with jack rabbits, one of which would make a half dozen of the ordinary breed of long ears. They, like the chickens, are fond of the road just at nightfall, and often, when waked up to a fitting sense of the situation, would shoot ahead of us on the road as if greased, and sent bounding into futurity by some ponderous arm of warfare. Their jumps are something astonishing, and to take them in the air is the pride of old hunters who, by the way, never confess to shooting them but for the mere fun of the thing.

The chicken season, the present year, is of such glorious promise as to fairly make the boys ache over the enforced delay until Aug. 1. The season throughout southwest Kansas is fully a month in advance of previous years, and the young birds are growing so rapidly and are in such remarkably large numbers that it does appear hard that we should have to wait so many weeks yet before taking the field. But it is this very adherence to the letter, as well as the spirit of the game laws, that has led to the amazing increase of both quail and chickens, old settlers declaring they never before saw anything like it. Last year very many—thousands upon thousands—of the young birds were drowned or so weakened by the continued wet weather as to die long before reaching maturity. There has been much rain this season, but mostly in hard showers followed by warm, sunshiny days, thus enabling the birds to seek dry quarters and to recuperate and grow fat upon the unstinted abundance of grain. The young birds are plumper and heavier than ever before known at this stage of their growth, and the opening day of the shooting season—Aug. 1—will, unquestionably be one long to be remembered in the game annals of Kansas. (*Osborne County Farmer*, 9 August 1878)

As with waterfowl, the locations of upland game birds—prairie chicken, quail, and turkey—were noted by the various newspapers in western Kansas. Quail and prairie chicken were particularly abundant along the more eastern portions of the Kansas Pacific Railroad:

TO THE SPORTSMAN WHOSE CHIEF DELIGHT IS IN HIS BREECH-loader and his pointers or setters, the very finest sport may be had by getting off at any of the stations along the line from Kansas City to Salina. The whole of that country swarms with quail and prairie chickens. The abundance of quail may be estimated by the fact that they are sold in the markets at one dollar to one dollar and a half per dozen, and prairie chickens at two dollars and a half per dozen. In the season a good shot can bag his fifteen to twenty brace of quail per diem with ease. (Weston, 1872, p. 130)

LARGE FLOCKS OF WILD TURKEYS REPORTED IN THE VICINITY OF Wichita. (*Ellsworth Reporter*, 18 November 1875)

PRAIRIE HENS ARE NUMEROUS IN THIS COUNTY AND THEY WILL make chickens plenty next fall. (*Ellsworth Reporter*, 19 April 1877)

Wild turkey and quail were common in the forested areas of eastern Kansas and extended westward along the rivers and streams.

Hunting prairie chickens. Kansas State Historical Society, Topeka.

Hunters were frequently able to take large numbers, as is evident in the following excerpts:

TWO HUNDRED WILD TURKEYS WERE CAPTURED IN A SINGLE day's hunt, recently, by some of the soldiers at Fort Larned. (*Hutchinson News*, 10 April 1873)

THE MANHATTAN NIMRODS, HAVE HAD A CHAMPION HUNT. One party killed 616 quails, chickens, rabbits, &c., and the other party 431. (*Ellsworth Reporter*, 18 December 1873)

Buffalo were the dominant vertebrate species on the open prairie and the herds were immense. It is almost incredulous, and difficult to grasp fully, the tremendous size of these herds. In some cases the herds were so large that trains had to stop while they passed:

Endless herds of buffalo. *Harper's New Monthly Magazine.*

FIVE MILES WEST OF FORT ELLSWORTH WE WERE FAIRLY IN THE buffalo range, and, for miles in every direction as far as the eye could see, the *hills* were *black* with these shaggy monsters of the prairie, grazing quietly upon the richest pasture in the world. Should I estimate the number of buffalo to be seen at one view at a million, it would be thought an exaggeration, but better authority than myself has estimated them at *millions*, or, as being greater than all the domestic cattle in America.—Lieut. Julian R. Fitch's Report of the Survey's Expedition for Butterfield Overland Despatch (*Junction City Union*, 9 September 1865)

PERSONS WHO HAVE NEVER SEEN THE VAST HERDS OF BUFfalo moving can have but little conception of the almost irresistible power of such a living mass, and the difficulty of turning or breaking the herd when once it is in motion on a certain course. The countless thousands press forward, overwhelming any but the strongest barrier. Wagons have been overturned in this way, and teamsters have saved themselves and the stock only by flight.

An army officer who with a strong force crossed the Plains by the Smoky Hill route in 1865 was forced to "corral" his train of wagons and order his men to fire volleys into a herd which threatened to march over his train. This is, however, infrequent. A party may be on the Plains, or even on the Buffalo Range, for years and never see it; still such instances have occurred.

I have frequently been amused at the calculations made by wise old hunters whom one finds on the Range. They settle within a million or so the exact number of buffalo that are yet wandering about. One old fellow is convinced that there is something like seventeen millions, and that this is the exact number required to keep up the present stock. (Davis, 1869, p. 152)

The most famous professional game hunter in the Kansas region was the buffalo hunter. Dodge City and other early towns owed their primary reason for existence to supplying hunters and later shipping the bounty eastward. These big-game stalkers gathered only the bare necessities when preparing for the hunt:

WHILE SEATED TO WRITE ANOTHER RAMBLING LETTER THERE passess [sic] through Main street a half dozen wagons which the experienced observer at once identifies as belonging to "Buffalo Hunters."

It is easy enough to distinguish such a party from the snugly rigged outfit of immigrants. The latter travel with closely drawn wagon covers, and their loading is arranged with care. But the hunter's outfit is simple enough. Into an ordinary two horse wagon he tumbles a little hay, a little corn, a little wood, a little flour, a little bacon, a little sugar and baking powder and other luxuries of camp life according to his means, a coffee pot, a long handled frying pan, a roll of blankets or perhaps a bed quilt or two, lariat ropes, picket pins and ax to drive them, and with his trusty gun and amunition [sic], a box of matches securely stowed away, our hardy prairie farmer is ready for a cruise into buffalo land. I am not now speaking of spruce city chaps who leave us with such magnificent preparations and return with wonderful stories, and a beggarly display of robes and buffalo meat, but I am talking about the pioneer settlers of this famous Arkansas Valley who go to the hunt not for fun but for profit, not for the sake of slaughtering the noble game but for the hides which they sell and the meat which they eat. C.C.H. At Home, October 28, 1872. (*Hutchinson News*, 31 October 1872)

The best method for hunting buffalo was on foot. Hunters would lie downwind of a herd and shoot the buffalo one after another. The buffalo in the herd seemed to be more puzzled by the death of their members than afraid and would usually remain in the area. Often dozens of buffalo could be killed in one place in this manner. This method was referred to as "getting a stand":

WE HUNTED ON FOOT. IN LOW COUNTRY WE COULD GET A stand on them, from ten to forty in a place. Charlie and I killed fifty-four in one place. It didn't take only five minutes to cut the hams off and the tongue. We left the rest. We could load a wagon in thirty minutes. As soon as we got two loads we would send them to Hays so they could get them salted. George tended to the smoke houses most of the time. We killed several thousand on the Saline and also on the Smoky Hill river. (Diary of Matt Clarkson, 1867, in Hill, 1938, p. 65)

ONCE WHILE OUT ON A FLAT NEAR THE CIMARRON, WE SIGHTED a fine herd of buffaloes at some distance to our left. Stopping the team lest they should hera [sic] the rattle of the wagon, I started on arun [sic] to gain a position in their path. The wind was blowing to the west and they were moving liesurley [sic] to the south, so I had no fear of them getting wind of me. It was summer and there was a mirage which made the buffalo seem to be walking on stilts as they advanced straight towrads [sic] me. They looked to be eight feet high with legs no larger than a broom handle. This of course made it very difficult to shoot with any degree of accuracy. As they drew near, I got a good chance for a broadside at the leader, a huge bull, and knowing by the sharp "spat" of the ball when it struck, that the shot was a good one. I lay motionless for a time until he had succumbed to his fate. The others ran off a few paces at the report of the gun, and are moving slowly around each other, unceratin [sic] which way to proceed, with their leader gone. The hazy atmosphere, and the mirage making the smoke invisible, not having faith in getting a stand out in the open, i [sic] neglected to fill my belt with cartridges, and when I had got down to the last two, was somewaht [sic] starteled [sic] to feel something grasp my heel as I lay falt [sic], trying to select the largest of the few remaining buffaloes at which to direct my two remaining shots. It was Trask, my partner, who [had] crawled up with a pocketful of cartridges. When the team came up, it was ascertained that we had 27 buffalo. (Diary of Raymond, 1872, p. 7)

The best meat was obtained from the younger animals; the larger bulls were usually targeted by the sport hunter:

THE AVERAGE GROSS WEIGHT OF GROWN BULLS IS ABOUT twenty-five hundred pounds. I once killed a buffalo that weighed over three thousand pounds gross. Old bulls are not often killed by the experienced hunter, as the beef of the younger members of the herd is far preferable as food, it being more tender and free from the decidedly disagreeable and rank flavor noticeable in the tough old bull-beef that novices are apt to select as their game. (Davis, 1869, p. 148–49)

Once shot, the buffalo had to be butchered and then prepared in some manner so the meat would not spoil. Although ice was cut from the rivers during the winter and stored, it rarely lasted through the summer. Furthermore, this ice was usually available only to those who lived in the villages close to rivers; it most certainly would not have been available to hunters in the field. Therefore, the meat had to be either salted, smoked, or dried, as described in the following accounts:

> THE APPROVED PROCESS OF BUTCHERING IS BY TURNING OVER the carcass on the belly, and commencing work down the back. The tender loins, hump, ribs, heart and tongue are appropriated, and the rest left to the wolves. The meat is cured by being cut into slices, and exposed in the dry air; it is sometimes jerked by being placed on frame-work over a slow fire; when fresh, it is juicy and tender, of easy digestion, and possessing every aperient [sic] quality; no inconvenience is suffered from over-eating; teamsters gorge themselves, like the ogre with the hundred loaves, and grow fat without pain. (Greene, 1856, p. 123–24)

> WE HAD 75 BEARLES TOO SALT MEAT IN AND THEN WE WOOD dig a hole in the ground and plug up the holes off a big bull hide and pin it too the ground it would hold about two bearls. We fixed [it] so we would salt a hundred bearls at once there was no time to play to get our smok houses fild. We saived evy tung so we . . . would know how meny we kiled. That is the way we knew in all we kiled 22 thousen. (Diary of Matt Clarkson, 1867, p. ii; with his spelling and punctuation)

Dr. Louis Watson, an early physician and part-time naturalist living at Ellis, jotted down the following recipe for dried buffalo in his diary of 1872:

> *Dried Buffalo*— For 100 lbs meat
> 4 lbs Salt (not more)

    5 " Sugar
    1 oz Soda
    2 oz Salt Petre
      Add 6 gals of water
      Let come to boil & skim
      Put on meat when almost cold
      Can keep in pickle as cooked(?)
      meat or take out after
      5 or 6 days to dry as dried meat

Fresh meat could not be shipped by rail during the warmer months of the year because it would spoil before it reached its destination. In the winter it was cold enough to ship meat to such eastern markets as Kansas City, Chicago, Buffalo, and New York City. Apparently an experimental refrigerator car introduced in 1871 was somewhat successful:

MR. WEAVER, A GENTLEMAN FROM ILLINOIS, LARGELY INTERested in Rankin's Patent Refrigerating car, returned to this place during the past week. He reports the car-load of buffalo meat shipped to New York as having resulted very successfully. It was fourteen days on the road, and was readily disposed of at good figures. They are now gathering in a second car-load. The New York Times, in an editorial on buffalo meat in New York, says that "Mr. W. S. Rankin, a mighty hunter, no doubt, has assumed the responsible position of purveyor of bison." The Times says it retails there at eighteen cents per pound. (*Junction City Weekly Union*, 4 March 1871)

[BUFFALO MEAT HUNTING] HAS EMPLOYED DURING THE LAST year or two an amount of labor and capital that would seem incredible to a person unacquainted with the facts. The meat market opens in November, when the weather becomes cool enough for its transportation, and continues until the 1st of April. During these five months as much as 2,000,000 pounds are shipped from the stations on the Kansas Pacific to all parts of the country. In the winter months, a buffalo steak can be obtained about as easily and almost as cheaply in the butchers' stalls of the leading northern cities as a beefsteak or a mutton-chop, and in Colorado and Kansas it is common as antelope. When buffaloes are killed for the meat, only the hams and shoulders are brought in, and shipments are usually made in that shape, the hide nearly always being left on to the end of the journey. The leading markets for buffalo meat "in the rough" are St. Louis, Chicago, and Indianopolis [sic], whence it is reshipped, in cleaner and more artistic condition, to cities of the seaboard. At Kansas City, too, large quantities are cured and packed for eastern use, and some successful experiments have been made in shipping direct to New York and Philadelphia in refrigerator cars. The price in the towns along the middle and eastern divisions of the Kansas Pacific ranges from $50 to $80 per ton in bulk, and the local dealers retail at six to eight cents per pound. The settlers adjacent to the stamping-ground of the buffalo procure meat enough in a day's hunting to last them through the winter; and many a poor homesteader in the valley of the Arkansas has kept the wolf from the door on this article of diet alone for months at a time.

The flesh of the buffalo is not such as gods would delight to feed upon; nor would poets find it particularly conducive to the cultivation of sweet and tender imagery. It is a prosaic sort of meat at best, having a drouthy kind of coarseness about it, and unless very young and tender, a flavor that only a very hungry man would call appetizing. It is very nutritious, however, and when properly dried, the difference between it and "jerked" beef is not susceptible to the ordinary palate. But a dog scents the dissimilarity at a single sniff, and will none of it. The Indians rarely eat it in a fresh state, but dry it in small slices, usually in the sun, and serve it up with dried plums and pulverized acorns. In some of the more luxurious tribes a gravy, in which crushed grasshoppers form a governing ingredient, is added, as a rarity, on important festal occasions. (*Daily Rocky Mountain News*, 3 December 1874)

During the later years of the 1870s huge amounts of meat were brought to Kansas from the buffalo grounds in the Texas panhandle, as the following excerpts from the *Ford County Globe* attest. The meat was measured in thousands of pounds or by the number of wagons required to haul it.

ANDY JARD CAME IN LAST WEDNESDAY WITH HIS TRAIN LOADED with dried buffalo meat, belonging to Dubbs & Stealy, of this place. They have dried this winter, the meat of 1,700 full grown buffalos, and over 300 calves, in all about 85,000 pounds. (*Ford County Globe*, 2 April 1878)

TWENTY WAGONS LOADED WITH DRIED BUFFALO MEAT, AND drawn by seventy yoke of oxen came in from the South in charge of wagon master, Gibbs, last Monday. They unloaded at the warehouse of Lee & Reynolds. (*Ford County Globe*, 14 May 1878)

Buffalo meat sold from as little as one cent per pound to as much as ten cents in 1879, when buffalo were no longer available in most of Kansas. A common price during most of the 1870s was five or six cents a pound. The following accounts give some indication of the nature of fluctuating prices:

WE BROKE CAMP AND PULLED INTO DODGE WITH WHAT HIDES we had. I loaded some hams on my wagon. I think it is stated in the diary that I could not sell the meat the day we reached there, but succeded [*sic*] in disposing of it next day at one cent a pound. (letter written by Raymond, 1934)

BUFFALO MEAT, JUST BROUGHT IN FROM THE PLAINS, LAST week, sold readily at five cents a pound. (*Ford County Globe*, 22 October 1878)

SAYS THE STOCKTON *RECORD:* TWO LOADS OF BUFFALO MEAT were for sale on our streets on Tuesday, by parties who had killed the game 200 miles northwest of here. Steaks were sold at ten cents per pound. (*Hays City Sentinel*, 12 December 1879)

Often meat was shipped great distances. At least twice it was shipped across the ocean:

ELLSWORTH IS SHIPPING BUFFALO MEAT TO ENGLAND. (*HUTCH-inson News*, 16 January 1873)

SIX CARCASSES OF BUFFALO, WITH HIDES, HORNS AND HOOFS, were put on board the cars here on Thursday. These bodies are shipped east for export to England. Only the entrails were taken from the dead bisons. (*Dodge City Times*, 18 January 1879)

Other newspaper accounts attest to the fact that deer, ante-lope, and rabbit were also hunted for marketing:

THERE IS A GREAT AMOUNT OF GAME ON THE MARKET, COMING chiefly from the plains, *via* the Kansas Pacific, but consider-able is also received from Estes and Middle Parks. It is prin-cipally antelope, black tail deer and mountain sheep. But little buffalo on the market yet. Antelope is sold to the butchers at from 2½ to 3 cents per lb.; mountain sheep 8 cents. (*Denver Daily Tribune*, 26 November 1873)

OVER 2,000 RABBITS HAVE BEEN SHIPPED FROM THIS PLACE since the first of the present month. Brush-rabbits are quoted at 5 and 6 cents, and jack rabbits at 10 to 14 cents a piece in the Smith Centre market. (*Smith County Pioneer*, 13 January 1877)

THE CHOICEST CUTS OF DEER MEAT WAS SOLD BY OUR BUTCHERS for fifteen cents a pound this week, which reminds us that it is about time for us to push on west. (*Kinsley Graphic*, 6 December 1879)

The demise of the buffalo was hastened by the hide hunters. As the following excerpt describes, beginning in the winter of 1871 hides became valuable for tanning into leather:

The hide hunter. Kansas State Historical Society, Topeka.

PREVIOUS TO THE YEAR 1871 FOR SEVERAL YEARS THERE HAD been a slaughter of domestic cattle on the prairies or pampas of South America where they had increased to fabulous numbers and had to be killed to make room for future increase and as there was no modern process of refrigeration as now the meat was a total loss as was the case with our buffalo except for three or four months of winter weather. This great source of leather hides from South America soon ceased, then the eyes of our American tanners were turned to the buffalo. But they were unable to make firm commercial leather of them, it being spongy and only fit for horse collars and such uses as spongy leather would do. But about this time, spring 1871, a Mr. J. N. Dubois, a hide and leather dealer of Kansas City, got a few bales of hides together and shipped them to his old home in Germany. The tanners there succeeded in making firm leather of them suitable for any purpose. Mr. Dubois then flooded the frontier,—there was a frontier then, —with circulars stating he would buy buffalo hides killed at any time of the year whether they had hair on them or not, and that he would pay $2.25 for cow hides and $3.25 for males if directions were followed. They must be stretched and pegged down on the ground, skin-side up, so as to keep them straight for handling, hauling and shipping. Mr. Dubois also introduced hide bug poison, he knew of its use in South America, with which one sprinkled the dry hides and effectually preserved them from moths and bugs. This together with our American tanners getting the secret of making firm commercial leather of hides sealed the doom of our American bison.

I am one of the old buffalo hide hunters that began at the beginning of hide hunting in the fall of 1871 and remainded [sic] on the range until the summer of 1876 when the great middle herd that ranged between the Arkansas River on the south and the Platte on the north was about exterminated. (Joe Hutt, in *Ellis County News*, 5 November 1925)

"Staking out" buffalo hides to dry. Kansas State Historical Society, Topeka.

The hide-hunting team usually included a hunter, a couple of skinners, and perhaps another man who stayed in camp to cook and peg out the hides to dry:

THE BOYS HAD THE TEAMS READY AND WERE SOON ON HAND to skin the buffalo. Driving in such a way as to leave the animal lying crosswise with his back towards the wagon, a rope is doubled and made fast to the middle of the axle, leaving the ends to drag. These are fastened, one to a forward, and one to a hind leg, the team is started carefu ly [sic] forward until it is turned on its back, then putting the brake on, it will hold in that position till ready to turn completely over, which is done by moving the team farther on.

The hunter, meanwhile, is off in some direction bringing down more game. Sometimes a herd will stand huddled together till the last one is killed; their leader gone, they become bewildered and will not run. One man does the hunting, sometimes for six teams, two men to the team. One or two men are left in camp to make pegs, to cook and to peg the hides down to dry. Small holes are cut around the edge, the hide stretched tightly and pegs 4 or 4 inches long driven into the ground to hold them. Smaller outfits leaving no one at camp, we often see a roll of blankets, a "grub box" bake oven and frying pan constituting someone's home.

Nixon, when hunting was at it's best, killed forty eight hundred in a little over three months. There were camps at intervals alnong [sic] the streams and many pleasant evening[s] spent visiting the neighboring camps, by singing, playing the violin and telling stories. (Diary of Raymond, 1872, p. 3–4)

Native Americans had been tanning hides long before the immigrants arrived. The procedure was a lengthy and laborious one and was conducted only by the women of the tribes:

TO TAN A BUFFALO HIDE SO AS TO MAKE A SOFT ROBE IS A long and tedious task which has never to any great extent

been performed by civilized labor. There is in this a splendid field for inventive yankee genius. The genuine Indian
tanned robe is soft even after a thorough wetting and it is
the result of protracted and tedious toil on the part of some
tired squaw, whose lazy lout of a lord smokes his pipe in luxurious ease. These robes after long soaking are sprinkled inside with the brains of buffalo, then rolled up and laid away
for a time, after which they are stretched between stakes and
rubbed and scrubbed and thumped with some iron instru-
ment, oftentimes an ordinary grubbing hoe. This process
is repeated many times over until the skin is perfectly soft
and pliable and always remains so. (*Hutchinson News,* 31
October 1872)

In 1871 the factory method of tanning created an increased
demand for buffalo hides. The demand was indeed so high that
thousands of hunters found it lucrative to take to the plains to
slaughter tens of thousands of buffalo:

THE ARITHMETIC OF THE EXTINCTION OF THE BISON OF THE
plains is terrible, and if the statistics be right it would seem
that the flush times in meat and hides cannot last long. The
railroad reached Dodge on the 23d of last September, and
since that time 43,029 hides have been shipped. . . . Each
hide counts a buffalo slain, and 43,000 hides in three
months convey an idea of magnificent butchery that fore-
casts the speedy extinction of the prairie denizen. The buffaloes that are killed in summer or early autumn in wanton
cruelty miscalled sport, and for food by the frontier residents, are not taken into this account. (*Daily Rocky Mountain News,* 19 January 1873)

HIDE-HUNTERS ALONG THE KANSAS PACIFIC . . . USUALLY FOL-
low in the wake of buffalo-hunting expeditions and roving
bands of Indian "meat-jerkers." The Indians who kill buffalo take only a small portion of the animal, and the white
men who slay them for sport rarely touch them with a knife;

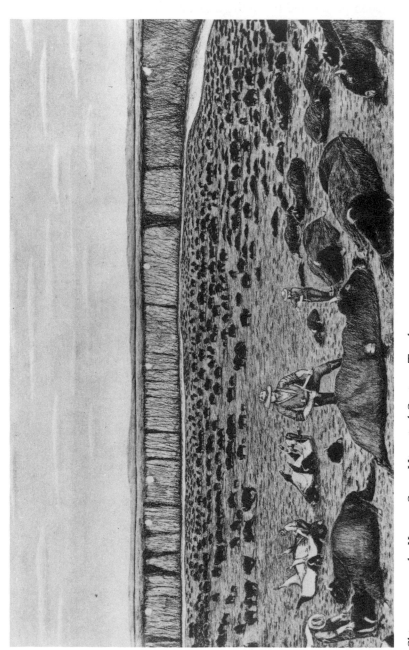

Skinners at work. Kansas State Historical Society, Topeka.

so that the hide-hunter who goes after is usually sure of his spoil, as the hide remains in good order for removal nearly a week after the killing, if the wolves keep away. When hides are not to be had fast enough or with personal safety in this way, the hide-hunters project little raids of their own out into the buffalo ranges, killing the animals simply for their hides, and leaving the meat to decay, or selling it at a nominal rate to accompanying parties of dealers. The hides are tanned and dressed by a much more rapid, but less perfect and effective, process than that followed by the Indians, and only the hides of animals killed in cold weather make really valuable robes. In a little more than three months over 50,000 of these hides were shipped from the stations on the western division of the Atchison, Topeka and Santa Fe railroad; and it is estimated that the shipments for this year over that road and the Kansas Pacific will aggregate 125,000. As each hide represents a slain buffalo, these figures convey a fair, though not a full idea of the magnificent butchery which has been going on among these "monarchs of the plains." The hides, after being dressed, are rolled up in as small a compass as possible, and shipped to the large eastern cities, where they are subjected to a process of re-cleansing and drying, and put into the market for sale. (*Daily Rocky Mountain News*, 3 December 1874)

After the slaughter and the decay of the carcasses, buffalo bones littered the prairies. These bones, as well as bones from Texas cattle, became a valuable commodity in eastern markets. Cattlemen awaiting higher prices often allowed their beef to overwinter in Kansas, thus subjecting them to cold weather that often resulted in their death. The following excerpts from newspaper articles describe the evolution and workings of the bone market.

IN CONVERSATION WITH MR. JOHN A. WOODROOF, WHO HAS been in Kansas for many years buying bones for the St. Louis Carbon Works, we heard some very interesting facts concerning bones which we beg leave to present to our readers:

About ten years ago the present manager of the St. Louis Carbon Works was traveling across these plains on the old

Santa Fe trail. He particularly noticed while journeying the immense amount of buffalo bones that covered the prairies. With a yankee's ingenuity he bethought himself that the bones might be made of practical use. He knew that in sugar refineries bones were used which were brought from North and South Carolina, and put through a steaming process to soften them and then ground. The idea occurred to him that if bones could be ground dry, the problem would be solved, as then they would retain the ammonia, which is necessary to the process of refining, and much of which is lost when they go through the steaming process. He sent to Germany and brought to America a man who was at once a chemist and practical machinist. Between them they invented and patented machinery whereby the bones could be ground dry and rapidly, and thus retain all their different valuable properties. A company was at once organized and commenced grinding bones on a large scale. Their capacity is now from thirty to fifty tons a day, and a capital of at least a hundred thousand dollars is employed in carrying on the business. After the bones are unshipped they are picked over and assorted. Of the refuse the common fertilizing phosphates are made. The other bones are ground into bone black or animal charcoal. This bone black is used exclusively for refining sugar. (*Dodge City Times*, 28 June 1879)

A LARGE PART OF [THE BONES] HAVE GONE TO WILMINGTON, Delaware, where the best are selected for combs, knife handles, &c., the next best are . . . ground into dust and used in refining sugar; and the refuse is ground into meal for fertilizing purposes. (*Hutchinson News*, 23 January 1873)

THE *INTERIOR* SAYS THE PRINCIPAL USE MADE OF THIS ARTIcle of western commerce [bones] is in the manufacture of "bone black." They are calcined until they assume a peculiar bluish color, and then are sold to the refiner to clarify and whiten sugar. Bone-black is also utilized extensively in the preparation of paints, printer's ink and even blacking. Bones are in addition a famous fertilizer, but are then only roasted and ground, not burnt as above. (*Pawnee County Herald*, 20 January 1877)

The bones that remained on the prairies following the decay of the slain buffalo helped many a destitute farmer through difficult times. Newspapers urged the farmers to gather and sell the bones as a source of income:

SINCE THE GENERAL DESTITUTION WHICH PREVAILS IN SOME OF the outlying counties along the line of the Kansas Pacific, in consequence of the grasshopper plague, hundreds of the suffering frontiersmen are making a business of picking up bones. Twenty carloads of these bones have been sent to St. Louis during the past two weeks from one station on the railroad. Contractors pay five dollars per wagon load, and it takes an industrious picker to gather a load in five days. The average bone-picker therefore earns a dollar a day . . . certainly not a very remunerative employment. He has to go out thirty or forty miles to gather his harvest, as the supply within that area is almost exhausted. The buffalo itself is rapidly disappearing, and in the course of time the enterprising bone-picker will cause all vestiges to disappear likewise. The bones sell for $20 per ton in Pittsburgh, and in Harrisburg, Pa. It costs $70 per carload or 10,000 pounds to transport them to St. Louis, and that amount brings $85. (*Daily Rocky Mountain News*, 30 December 1874)

MANY OF OUR READERS ARE UNAWARE, DOUBTLESS, THAT ONE way of making a living on the prairies is by gathering old buffalo bones and selling them. Most every man that has a team turns his attention to this business when he has no farm work on hand. These bones are found scattered around over the prairie, where they have lain bleaching in the sun for—no one knows how long. They are now worth about $7 per ton at Dodge City, and most any kind of a team can haul

Bone picking on the prairie. Kansas State Historical Society, Topeka.

from 18 to 25 hundred. It takes from one to two days to gather a load. You can now form a pretty good idea about the profits of the business.—(*Dodge City Times*, 19 July 1879)

Periodically, prices offered for bones were published in the area newspapers. The prices in the 1870s, as the following accounts indicate, varied from four dollars to nine dollars a ton.

PAWNEE COUNTY HAS GONE INTO THE "BONE HAULING BUSINESS." Four dollars a ton is what they are worth, and the people prefer to do this rather than vote bonds to relieve their necessities. So it is better, and those people are made of the right stuff and will succeed. (*Ellsworth Reporter*, 3 December 1874)

OUR MERCHANTS ARE PAYING EIGHT DOLLARS CASH OR NINE dollars in trade per ton for bones. (*Kinsley Graphic*, 16 November 1878)

Many newspapers reported that literally millions of pounds of bones were shipped from the prairies of western Kansas:

IN 1874, 3,160,000 POUNDS OF BUFFALO BONES WERE SHIPPED over the Kansas Pacific Railway and its connections. In the same year the following is the shipment of buffalo products over the Atchison, Topeka and Santa Fe Railroad; bones 6,914,950 pounds; of hides, 1,314,300 pounds; of meat, 632,800 pounds. This shows how rapidly the American Bison is passing away. (*Ellsworth Reporter*, 15 April 1875)

J. E. WOODRUFF, OF ST. LOUIS, SHIPPED TWENTY-ONE CAR LOADS, two hundred and fifty tons, or five hundred and four thousand pounds of buffalo bones from Kinsley this week. (*Dodge City Times*, 17 August 1878)

By the late 1870s newspaper articles were suggesting that the prairies would soon be free of bones and that the bone trade would cease. Initially, people transported bones to the railhead and piled them along the tracks to await shipment. However, by the late 1870s, as more and more bones were gathered, the "bone pickers" had to travel farther and farther to locate their commodity.

> THE HAULING OF BUFFALO BONES WILL SOON BECOME A MAT-ter of history. Up to the past six months it was nothing un-common to see most any day in the week from five to fifteen loads of bones being brought in. Now that many loads a week wouid [sic] be a good trade. (*Kinsley Graphic*, 8 November 1879)

> BONES CONTINUE TO COME IN, BUT THEY ARE HAULED FROM forty to seventy-five miles. (*Kinsley Graphic*, 9 August 1879)

One editor reflected with clear regret on the slaughter of buffalo that resulted in bones being strewn across the prairie. He warned that in a matter of a few short years, free-roaming buf-falo would no longer exist:

> WHERE DO ALL THE BONES THAT ARE HAULED TO THIS PLACE come from? This has been going on at the same rate ever since the town was started. Truly the amount of buffalo waste-fully slaughtered must have been large. There is now a pile of bones along one of the side tracks, which, if in their orig-inal state, would furnish meat enough to feed a multitude. Five years ago the plains were white with them. Look wher-ever you would, in valley, on hillside or plain, they were sure to meet the eye. We have seen as high as twenty eight of these skeletons lying within a radius of two hundred yards in front of some knoll behind which some "Buffalo William" had escoused [sic] himself and carried death to the ranks of some herd of buffalo. From here the bones are sent all over the country—to sugar refineries and as bone dust to enrich the lands of persons who do not have "gumption" enough to come to a country where the land needs no enrichment. Quite likey [sic], had the government taken hold of the mat-ter sooner, as it should have done, about one half of these

bones would be moving around in a different style from that in which they now travel. As it is now, the buffalo is a scarce article, and instead of being slaughtered expressly for their hides, the whole buffalo is made use of. In less than ten years they will only exist in history and the tents of the showman, and we would not be surprised if the bone business would close up. (*Hutchinson News,* 19 June 1879)

One rather famous buffalo-hunting group was that of the Clarkson brothers, though there were hundreds of hunters like them. Excerpts from Matt Clarkson's diary tell of the large numbers that they shot:

WE SAVED EVERY TONGUE SO AS WE WOULD KNOW HOW MANY we killed. That is the way we knew. In all we killed twenty-two thousand. (Diary of Matt Clarkson, 1867, in Hill, 1938, p. 65)

I WENT THAT NIGHT AND GOT OUR SUPPLIES PUT UP. NEXT day we started up the Smoky Hill river. We found the buffaloes very thick south of the Grinnell station. We made a camp on the Smoky and I went to killing just for the hides. It was the 22nd of September and was too warm to save any meat. When Charley came up I had killed 1900 buffaloes and hauled the hides to Grinnell station. (Diary of Matt Clarkson, 1872, in Hill, 1938, p. 66)

WE WENT NORTH ABOUT THIRTY MILES AND MADE CAMP FOR about forty days. We killed 2400 buffaloes and a number of antelopes. Then we went northwest over on the Republican. We camped at the Big Spring and hauled to Kit Carson. Camped there about thirty days and killed about 800 buffaloes. (Diary of Matt Clarkson, 1872, in Hill, 1938, p. 67)

Many animals other than the buffalo were killed for their pelts, from which coats, robes, and rugs were fashioned. One

The aftermath of the hunt. Kansas State Historical Society, Topeka.

such animal was the gray wolf. The use of the term "wolf" herein deserves a brief comment. There were two species of the canine family in Kansas referred to as wolves—the prairie wolf, or coyote, and the gray wolf. Editors often did not discriminate between the two but simply called them wolves. The professional hunters sought the wolves for their pelts, and poison was their method of choice. These hunters were often buffalo-hide hunters who supplemented their income by lacing the slain buffalo carcass with strychnine.

WE POISONED FIFTY WOLVES BY CUTTING SMALL PIECES OF MEAT
put in strychnine with the point of a pen knife just a little,
then take a fresh hide, turn it flesh side down and drag it for
miles over the prairies with our saddle horses, dropping a
piece of meat about every hundred yards. The wolves traveling strike the scent of the trail made by dragging the hide
and follow it up. We figured that a wolf taking a poison will
die in less than a hundred yards. (Letter of Bill, 1879, p. 4)

Another species killed for its pelt was the skunk. Two species
of skunk occurred in Kansas: the spotted skunk (or civet cat),
and the somewhat larger striped skunk. In most instances newspaper articles were probably referring to the striped variety. Skunks
were shot primarily as a pest species; however, in season some
were taken for their pelts.

A MAN DOWN IN RENO COUNTY KILLED TWENTY-SIX SKUNKS
in one day. There hasn't been any more scents. (*Newton Kansan*, 24 December 1874)

MR. R. G. COOK INVITED SEVERAL OF HIS FRIENDS IN LAST SUN-
day evening, and indulged in a pleasant skunk hunt, several
very large and juicy specimens were captured and the air
was filled with the perfume of the festive skunk for miles
around. (*Ford County Globe*, 21 October 1879)

Fishing was generally excellent in the larger rivers and streams
of the region. Until 1877 fish could be taken by any method;
seines as well as hook and line were commonly used in taking
large numbers for the market.

A PARTY OF LADES [*sic*] AND GENTLEMEN WENT ON A FISH-
ing expedition to the Saline, on Tuesday. They succeed in
catching about 150 pounds of fish. William R. Geis, one
of the party, caught a white perch which weighed sixteen
pounds—probably the largest perch ever caught in this country. (*Saline County Journal*, 27 May 1875)

A GREAT MANY FINE FISH ARE BEING TAKEN OUT OF THE SOL-
omon. At Milne's mill about a barrel were caught at one
time, and Jake Getz caught a string uumbering [sic] sixty-
three fine fellows one night this week. A party consisting of
Gillette, Honn, Gish, and others, went out Wednesday night,
but from what we can learn, their exploit panned out about
as is usual when "them town chaps" go fishing—they got a
few fish and a good deal of fishermen's luck. (*Osborne County
Farmer,* 14 July 1876)

Feral horses also offered an opportunity for some individuals
to turn a profit. One problem in having large numbers of feral
horses roaming at large was that domesticated horses often escaped from the settlers and joined the wild herd. It was usually
difficult to recover them, as they became almost as wild as the
original group:

A RECENT LETTER FROM SARGENT, KANSAS, TO THE TOPEKA
Commonwealth, contains the following; "Large numbers of
wild horses abound on the rivers. They are of all sizes and
colors, and are the wildest of all wild horses. They usually
roam in bands from six to twenty, and will run at sight of a
man two miles away. A great many domesticated horses, as
well as mules, which have strayed away from their owners,
have taken up with the wild ones. After running with them
for a while they become as wild as their untamed companions. Various methods have been adopted to catch them
but have generally proved fruitless. A scrubby colt or a broken down mule are, as a general thing, the only reward for
all the time and labor. Settlers on the frontier would hail
speedy extinction as a blessing, for when domestic animals
get with them their recovery is simply out of the question."
(*Saline County Journal,* 5 March 1874)

The locations of herds of wild horses were regularly reported,
thereby enabling hunters the opportunity to pursue and with
luck capture these valuable animals:

JESSE ELLIOT, WHO, IN COMPANY WITH OTHERS, CAPTURED ONE hundred wild horses in Lane County last season, was in the city last Monday. He says there are about one hundred head of wild horses in the unoccupied counties of Western Kansas. The center of the wild horse range is near Lake Admire, in Scott County. He says this lake never goes dry, has plenty of fish and wild ducks, and is six miles long by three in width. (*Hays City Sentinel*, 2 May 1879)

A HERD OF WILD HORSES, NUMBERING FOURTEEN, ARE RANGING about thirty miles southwest of here, on the Saline river. Parties have been endeavoring, for a week past, to capture a fine span of bays from among the herd, but at last accounts they had been unsuccessful. One young colt, unable to keep up in the chase, has been captured. (*Stockton News*, 26 February 1879)

One method employed to capture wild horses was to "crease" them. This was done with a well-aimed rifle shot that resulted in stunning the animal. Should the hunter not aim carefully, the result was a dead horse rather than a captured one.

IN THE SOUTHWESTERN PORTION OF RENO, CONSIDERABLE bands of wild horses roam. They are matchless in speed and beauty. Hunters not infrequently attempted to crease them with a view to capture by well directed shots through the upper part of the neck. The operation requires a steady nerve and good eye. A hunter a few days ago came across a splendid stallion and fired at him. The horse moved as he pulled trigger which caused the ball to strike too far back. At the second shot however the man creased and captured him, but he lived only two hours so deadly was the first wound. (*Hutchinson News*, 25 September 1873)

A more successful procedure, albeit time-consuming, was to tire the herd of wild horses. This was accomplished by keeping the herd moving continuously, thereby preventing the wild horses from obtaining needed rest. This procedure often required weeks on the open range before the herd was captured.

IT IS A WELL KNOWN FACT THAT FROM TIME IMMEMORIAL HERDS of wild horses have roamed over the plains of south-western Kansas. Their origin no man knows. It may date to the early Spanish conquest of the country. It has been exceedingly difficult to capture them, the method pursued having been to run down and lasso them with fleet horses. Lately, however, it has been found that they can be captured in herds. The method is to get up an outfit of fast walking team on a wagon carrying provisions and camp supplies, and three or four riding ponies and as many men. When a herd is found, they are kept moving, no effort being made to drive them in any particular direction. The team and ponies are not driven any faster than a walk, and every opportunity is embraced of cutting across to save distance. The wild horses are kept in motion until dark, being given no opportunity to graze during the day. At night they are too tired to graze, and will lie down.

The pursuers . . . camp[,] feed their horses from grain which they carry with them, and are up by daylight and ready to start again. This is kept up day after day. Every day takes some of the scare and wild out of them; they become accustomed to the sight of the men on horseback and team, find they are not going to be hurt by them, and leg-weary from constant travel and little feed, in from eight to ten days they will allow the men to ride in among them and drive them in any direction. They are then headed for the ranch and are quite tame and docile by the time they get in. They are of the pony order, such as are used in the cattle business, make good riding ponies, and when thoroughly broken, make good teams for light driving. (*Ford County Globe*, 10 June 1879)

Large herds often required an extended period of time for capture. In some instances it was necessary to follow a herd for several hundred miles:

MR. GEORGE YOUNG, OF STERLING, KANSAS, WHO HAS BEEN engaged in an exciting wild horse chase for the last four months with Messrs. Fulton and Stevens, called last Monday. The result of their efforts is fifty fine horses which they intend breaking for the saddle and harness. Some of these horses they followed for more than four hundred miles in a spring wagon, finally driving them into the corral and capturing them. Mr. Young says there are some fine animals among their herd, one or two of which they are now working to the wagon. They have been offered $30 a head for the lot, but refused the offer. (*Dodge City Times*, 4 August 1877)

For those hunting solely for recreation, large game animals were the most frequent quarry of choice. Herds of buffalo provided ready targets for those traveling the rails, and shooting from the train became great sport. Undoubtedly many more animals were injured than were actually killed. Trains would usually slow down or stop so the carnage could continue, or so the "hunter" could load a portion of his prize aboard. Other large grazing animals, such as antelope, were also shot, but less frequently than buffalo.

AT THIS SEASON OF THE YEAR THE HERDS OF BUFFALO ARE moving southward, to reach the cañons which contain the grass they exist upon during the winter. Nearly every railroad train which leaves or arrives at Fort Hays on the Kansas Pacific Railroad has its race with these herds of buffalo; and a most interesting and exciting scene is the result. The train is "slowed" to a rate of speed about equal to that of the herd; the passengers get out fire-arms which are provided for the defense of the train against the Indians, and open from the windows and platforms of the cars a fire that resembles a brisk skirmish. Frequently a young bull will turn at bay for a moment. His exhibition of courage is generally his death-warrant, for the whole fire of the train is turned

Hunting from the train. Kansas State Historical Society, Topeka.

upon him, either killing him or some member of the herd in his immediate vicinity.

When the "hunt" is over the buffaloes which have been killed are secured, and the choice parts placed in the baggage-car, which is at once crowded by passengers, each of whom feels convinced and is ready to assert that his was the shot that brought down the game. Ladies who are passengers on the trains frequently enjoy the sport, and invariably claim all the game as the result of their prowess with the rifle. This solution of the case is, of course, accepted by all gentlemen, and a more excited party of Dianas it would be impossible to imagine. (Buffalo hunting, 1867)

FEW LINES OF RAILWAY IN THE WORLD OFFER SUCH FACILITIES for the sportsman and hunter as the Kansas Pacific. Where else in the world can a man recline in the luxuriously cushioned seat of a Pullman Palace car, gliding over the smoothest of tracks, and look out on immense herds of that Monarch of the Plains—the Buffalo—some clumsily cantering along within one hundred yards of the train, and others still further off, watching it with a sort of lazy, stupid wonder. Not only buffalo, but herds of antelope, and the noble elk, are to be seen by passengers on the Kansas Pacific trains. It is by no means an unusual thing for buffalo to be killed from the cars, and if near enough to the track, they sometimes stop the train, take off the hind-quarters and hump, and perhaps the head of the quarry, and then proceed, having afforded a never-to-be-forgotten pleasure to travelers from the East, who have thus got their first look at the great North American Bison. This occurs frequently during the summer and early fall; in the winter they travel southward, leaving behind the aged and infirm, which form in little herds of twenty to thirty, and may be seen along the line the winter through. . . . "Still hunting" buffalo is, after the first two or three days at it, but tame sport, with but just enough spice of danger in it to make it interesting; they are easily approached by creeping on them up-wind, and will always run from you, unless too closely approached when wounded. But with a good horse between your knees, and a long navy revolver in your grasp, to single out your bull, and then dash across the velvet sward and into the middle of the herd, and bring down your quarry, has the ring of true sport about it, and requires a clear eye and steady nerve.

It is a very beautiful sight to see these animals about the time they are migrating southward, surrounding you and extending as far as the distant horizon, in dark masses, quietly journeying along to their winter quarters on the Arkansas River. They have been known to travel in such dense herds that they rubbed against the telegraph poles on the line, till they shook an insulator off, causing the wire to sag, and carried off about half a mile of it on their horns; and frequently during the migratory season the trains have to stop two or three times in a trip, to let them cross the line in front of the engine. A needle-gun or a Wesley Richards rifle are the best to use for buffalo shooting, on account of carrying a heavy ball; they are very tenacious of life, and as many as twenty-five bullets have been known to hit one before bringing him down—in fact, a shot in the heart or kidneys seems to be the only one that proves directly fatal. Parties may get off at almost any station beyond Ellis (three hundred and fourteen miles, or fourteen hours' run, from Kansas City,) and get good shooting at these noble beasts. In the northern part of Russell, Ellis and Trego counties are found elk, black-tailed deer, antelope, and wild turkeys in abundance. (Weston, 1872, pp. 128–30)

ENGLISH TRAVELERS ON THE KANSAS PACIFIC, THE OTHER DAY, were astonished to see antelope shot from the cars and the train stopped to take their carcasses in. They said that was hunting wild game luxuriously. (*Denver Daily Tribune*, 20 December 1875)

Probably the most celebrated hunt that occurred in the Great Plains region was that organized for the Grand Duke Alexis from Russia. The hunting party that assembled in Omaha was hosted by General Sheridan.

OMAHA, JAN. 11.—A HUNTING CAMP HAS BEEN ESTABLISHED near the Republican river as the basis of operations of Gen. Sheridan and Duke Alexis. Buffalo and other game is reported plentiful in the vicinity. It is expected that nearly 1,000 Indians will be collected. Reception will be given to distinguished visitors at the place to-morrow. (*Leavenworth Weekly Times*, 13 January 1872)

The preparation for the hunt was extensive. Not only was the group allowed to use a special train, but the hunting camp was plush by the day's standard. Buffalo Bill from Hays City met them at North Platte and served as their guide. Generals George Armstrong Custer, James W. Forsyth, William J. Palmer, and other officers complemented the party.

NORTH PLATTE, JANUARY 13.—THE GRAND DUKE AND PARTY arrived this morning at seven o'clock. They took breakfast on the cars. Five ambulances and a light wagon for the baggage, also a carriage for the grand duke, met the party and they started immediately for the camp. The permanent camp for the buffalo hunt on Red Willow creek is about fifty miles southwest of this post. The camp consists of two hospital tents, ten wall tents, and a tent for servants and soldiers. Three of the wall tents are floored and the duke's is carpeted. Box stoves and Sibley stoves are provided for the hospital and wall tents. The hospital tents are used as dining tents. An extensive culinary outfit is also taken along; ten thousand rations of flour, sugar, coffee, and one thousand pounds of tobacco for the Indians. Company "K," second cavalry, under command of Captain Egan are at the camp. They went out several days ago and have everything in the best shape possible. Company "E," second cavalry, under command of Lieutenant Stover, acts as escort for the party to the camp. The whole is under command of Gen. Palmer, of the Omaha barracks. Lieutenant Hayes is quarter master of the expedition. Mr. Cody *alias* "Buffalo Bill" met the duke and party here. A relay of horses is at Medicine Creek, about half way. They expect to make the trip in eight hours. The buffalo are in great numbers within ten miles of the camp. A few days ago, four hundred Indians were reported at the camp with their families, and coming in rapidly. It is expected that the war parties of Spotted Tail, Whistler, War Bonnet and Black Hat, will be there with their respective chiefs. (*Kansas Daily Commonwealth,* 14 January 1872)

THE GRAND DUKE ON THE PLAINS.
(Special Dispatch to the Kansas City Times)
CAMP ALEXIS, Jan. 16, *via* NORTH PLATTE, NEB., Jan. 16.

CLOSE OF THE HUNT.
Yesterday, the second and last day of the imperial buffalo hunt opened and closed most auspiciously in all particulars. The morning was glorious and the sun shone out in all its grandeur. The party for the day's hunt was made up as follows: The Grand Duke Alexis, mounted upon a superb black charger and dressed in a gray hunting suit, with a revolver by his side; Count Bodisco, Generals Sheridan and Palmer; Custer, who was attired in a

FULL SUIT OF BUCKSKIN,
similar to that of Buffalo Bill; Gen. Forsyth, Col. Mike Sheridan, and six or seven other officers. Buffalo Bill acted as on the previous day, as guide, but was assisted by a Sioux

CALLED FOR SHORT SHORTY.
About thirty soldiers and Spotted Tail, chief of the Sioux, accompanied by eight selected warriors. The hunters encountered a herd of buffalo after traveling about fifteen miles. Here the hunt began and was followed up in a very

exciting manner for an hour, but owing to the uneven character of the country it required harder riding and more strategy than on the previous day.

THE GRAND DUKE

killed two buffalo, the Indians eight, and General Sheridan
two in two straight shots, Shorty three, Lieut. Stevens one,
and Buffalo Bill and the other members of the party killed
forty, making about fifty-six in all for the day. Alexis had a
buffalo calf that he brought in, also the head of one of the
buffaloes that he killed, which he will have

PRESERVED AND SENT TO RUSSIA.

Everything passed off pleasantly, and nothing occurred to
mar the pleasure of any one. The day continued, as it had
begun, most beautiful. The grand duke was greatly elated
with his success, and threw off all formality and appeared as
one of the boys throughout the day. On the return from the
field of slaughter, when he caught sight of the camp, Alexis
began firing a salute with his revolver, which was taken up
by all the rest of the party, and returned by the persons awaiting their return at the camp.

GRAND POW-WOW.

The day's sport closed by a grand pow-wow and war dance
in front of the duke's tent, which was witnessed by Alexis
and all his party. After the war dance the duke presented
the various warriors, with fifty dollars in half-dollar silver
pieces twenty beautiful blankets and a number of hunting
knives with ivory handles. Previous to the war dance, General Sheridan called Spotted Tail to his tent and presented
him with

A SCARLET CAP,

ornamented with beads, a general officer's belt, and a nice
dressing gown. He gave them as a present from one chief to
another. Spotted Tail made a speech, in which he asked to
have more than one trader, as he thought his tribe could do
better where they had competition; and also asked permission to hunt south of the Platte until his farm could be made

to support his people. Col. Mike Sheridan's horse failed him
before the hunt was over, and had to be led to camp. The
animal rode by

GEN. CUSTER DIED

soon after reaching camp, from hard riding, having traveled
over fifty miles during the day's hunt. The evening was
spent at camp in hilarity until after mid night, when the
UNION was founded, and all retired in good order.

ON THE WING.

This morning the camp was active at an early hour, and
at 9 A. M. the party was moving towards this place, and the
band, which remained at camp entertained them with music until they were out of hearing. Seventeen miles on their
return trip they stopped for a lunch, and got fresh horses.
The only incident on the return was the capsizing of the ambulance containing Count Bodisco, Dr. Ash, Lieut. Tudor and
others. They were coming down a hill when the ambulance
swayed around and rolled over and over, the great wonder was
that nobody was in the least injured. The ambulance had to
be renewed. During the hunt Mr. Eaton, artist, of Omaha,
took several views of the camp, the hunting party, the

DUKE AND SPOTTED TAIL,

and other groups, and has received Alexis' order for several
hundred copies of each.

The party reached this place at 5 o'clock P. M. to-day, not
quite so fresh looking as on the start, but not much fatigued.
Gen. Sheridan and party dined with Alexis, in his car.

After dinner was over, Buffalo Bill was presented by the
duke with a large purse of money and a very valuable scarf
pin, in acknowledgment of his services on this occasion.

The excursion leaves here at 10 o'clock to-night

FOR THE CHEYENNE,

from which point they go to Denver. Generals Sheridan,
Custer, Forsyth and others accompany the duke from here.

The entire party are perfectly satisfied and the whole programme has been carried out without a thing to mar it, and

the weather has been the best that could be wished. (*Kansas Daily Commonwealth*, 18 January 1872)

When the party reached Denver, a grand ball was given in honor of the Duke. The imperial party visited Clear Creek Canyon and then boarded the train for the trip eastward to St. Louis through Kansas. On the way to Topeka a prearranged hunt was undertaken near Kit Carson, Colorado:

KIT CARSON, COLORADO, JANUARY 20. — THE GRAND DUKE Alexis and suite, with General Sheridan and staff, arrived here at 8 o'clock this morning in their special train of Pullman palace cars. They are accompanied by General Custar [sic], General Forsyth, Frank Thomson, their manager of transportation, and General E. S. Bowen, Colonel C. W. Fisher and T. F. Oakes, officers of the Kansas Pacific railway, and Dan Casement, of the Union Pacific.

For the buffalo hunt previous arrangements had been fully made. Cavalry horses had been ordered and arrived last night from Fort Wallace, and a large number of the citizens of the place had prepared horses, ambulances, wagons, etc., to participate in the hunt.

The morning was cold and cloudy and threatened snow, but about 10 a. m. the clouds cleared away and the day has been as fine as could be desired. Within a few miles of Carson the train had passed a large herd of buffalo. Upon their arrival the buffalo were in sight of town and the grand duke was impatient for the chase. At 11 a. m. everything was in readiness and the grand duke, General Sheridan, General Custar [sic], and some thirty others, on horses, made an eager and rapid start for the main buffalo range, and were followed by a number of ambulances and wagons loaded with men armed for the hunt. The grand duke was dressed in grey, and Custar [sic] in a complete suit of buckskin.

The duke took the lead in the chase. Alexis makes a magnificent appearance on horseback. General Custer says he never knew a man of the grand duke's proportions to be so fine a horseman as he is.

The buffalo were soon reached, when Alexis, in great excitement, plunged into the midst of them in advance of the whole party, and shot down the first buffalo—an enormous bull. He immediately dismounted, and General Custer was at his side instantly. The grand duke cheered, and in his great delight *clasped his arms around General Custer and kissed him.* The chase was at once resumed and continued some hours. About fifty buffalo in all were killed. Alexis shot five, General Custer three, and General Sheridan two.

Returning, the party arrived here at 6 p. m., all in the highest spirits after the greatest enjoyment of a glorious day's hunt. The imperial buffalo hunt was a grand success.

The party leave here to-morrow morning, and will reach Topeka on Monday at 10 a. m., and be entertained by the governor and legislature of Kansas and the citizens of Topeka. (*Daily Rocky Mountain News*, 21 January 1872)

Hunters came from near and far to participate in the sport of shooting buffalo on the plains of Kansas. Parties from as far away as Great Britain pursued the buffalo. Often both men and women took part in the hunt.

LAST EVENING THE NIGHT TRAIN ON THE KANSAS PACIFIC brought out a party of seventeen ladies and gentlemen, who stopped off at Wallace for a buffalo hunt. . . .

They left England only a short time since for the sole purpose of enjoying a hunt after the "American Bison." (*Denver Daily Tribune*, 14 September 1872)

Newspapers often published detailed accounts of hunting expeditions, many of which were organized for the express purpose of hunting on the vast prairie. Grand hunts were advertised widely, and hunters often traveled great distances to participate. One such hunt was assembled in Leavenworth traveling via the Kansas Pacific Railroad to Fort Hays:

A LARGE NUMBER OF OUR LEADING CITIZENS ARE MAKING UP a party to go on a grand buffalo hunt in the vicinity of Fort Hayes [sic], and propose to leave here to-morrow. All who desire to join the party are requested to call at the office of Powers & Newman, corner of Main and Shawnee streets, this morning, to perfect the arrangements. They will doubt-less have a gay time hunting the bison, unless the capricious animals should hunt them—there the fun would probably cease. We advise them to look out for the red children of our magnanimous Government, as they have just received their arms and ammunition from the kind-hearted Peace Commissioners. (*Leavenworth Daily Conservative*, 19 November 1867)

These "grand hunts" were not always as appealing and enjoy-able as the organizers would have one believe. The following article chronicles the Leavenworth hunting party. Note the acci-dents and problems encountered by the hunters.

SINCE THE INVASION OF THE BUFFALO STAMPING-GROUND BY the iron horse, parties from all parts of the East have been out at various times on a hunt, but not until the past week, we believe, has a regularly organized raid on the bison been made from this section of the country.

Last Wednesday, a party consisting of the following named gentlemen, left Leavenworth for Fort Hayes [sic], in a spe-cial car, kindly provided by Superintendent Anderson, of the U. P. R. W.: H. L. Newman, Lyman Scott, Wm. E. Cham-berlain, A. L. Baker, D. W. Eaves, W. H. Coolidge, F. S. Pinckney, T. F. Fringer, and Geo. H. Rushmore.

On arriving at Lawrence, the following gentlemen joined the party: Capt. T. F. Eckert, of Cincinnati; Judge R. G. Corwin, of Dayton; Quincy Corwin, of Dayton; and J. B. Clement; of Morrow, Ohio.

They arrived at Fort Hayes [sic] all safe and sound, where the officers of the Fort extended to them all the courtesies they could desire.

On Friday morning—Captain Graham, Lieutenants Col-
lidy, Sowders and Lee, Buffalo Bill and other scouts, having
joined the party—they started out in a southwesterly direction, on a grand hunt. The first day, and almost at the first
start, a serious and painful accident detained the party, and
dampened their feelings of pleasure materially. Mr. Newman,
who had previously been elected captain of the party, was
the victim. While riding at full speed across the prairie, his
horse stepped into a gopher-hole, and fell, dismounting Mr.
Newman, who had a severe gash cut in his forehead, and
remained insensible for twelve hours afterwards. He was taken
back to Hayes [sic] as soon as possible, and properly cared for.

The hunt was continued on Saturday, and when the party
started back to the Fort that night they could count twelve
dead buffalo, of their killing—five on Friday and seven of
Saturday.

Much anxiety was created on Saturday night by the non-
arrival of Judge Corwin, who had strayed from the party on
Friday. On Sunday, Lieut. Kennedy, of Co. G, 5th cavalry,
with a party of his men, and Buffalo Bill, with fifteen or
twenty citizens volunteered to go out and look for him. After a long ride the latter named party, found the lost man
about five miles from the Fort, nearly starved and almost
exhausted.

Sunday night at twelve o'clock the buffalo slayers started
on their return home, where they arrived at 7 p.m. last evening, in good health and spirits, with exception of Mr. Newman, whose unfortunate mishap prevented him from any
further participation in sport.

Numerous incidents occurred, which at the time caused
any amount of merriment, all of which was entered into and
enjoyed by the parties interested, with much apparent gusto.

One who had tucked himself snugly into a berth of a sleeping car on the outward trip, was most unceremoniously shaken
by a damsel who mistook him for her husband—or some

other man, and ordered to turn himself over and report from whence he came and whither was he going. All this occurred in Ellsworth, and from the well-known character of the gentleman the party attributed it to a mistake.

On the outward trip one of the party suddenly acquired notoriety by shooting from the train, while it was in motion, a prairie dog, which sat temptingly before him at the distance of one hundred yards.

The mounting of the party caused much merriment amongst the inhabitants of the lively and brisk little town of Hayes [sic] City. Some of them sat their horses like a potato with a couple of matches inserted for legs; others sat stately and mum like a stoughton bottle or a wooden man. All anxious and eager for the fray.

One party who started with the least never returned with the most, declaring that he had slain two and *could prove it.* The nearest he came to it, however, was one bison which old hunters claim had been skinned twice. If a sudden change in the weather had not froze him out, he would have had heavy additions to his tale of killed and wounded.

One of the party, whose ponderous form came looming in the distance, rode into town about noon on Sunday, mounted astride a Gothic steed, and riding against a terribly cold north wind, with the stern of his corduroy unmentionables split from side to side and at least a yard of boiled shirt streaming in the wind and cracking a merry chorus to the chattering of a good set of teeth. It was laughable and ludicrous in the extreme.

Another youth with auburn locks, who surprised the natives by numerous stories of his "straight shot," and the hair breadth escape of chickens and other barn yard game, on the first day found out from experience that he could neither hit the side of a barn nor a buffalo. The second day he got a good steady and trained horse of "Bill," and sailed in; after trying some time he seperated [sic] a poor little forlorn calf, and went for him. The calf, however, proved himself the better horse of the two, and after a chase of about six miles, our "hero" returned to camp and concluded to practice.

We regret that our space, and the lateness of the hour, will not permit us to enter into more elaborate details of the affair, some of which were decidedly "rich, rare and spicy."

To Superintendent Anderson, of the U. P. R. W.; Superintendent Geo. Noble, of the First Division of the road, and Superintendent B. Marshal, of the Second Division, the entire party desire to return their hearty thanks for the liberal and substantial courtesies shown them, and which they will always remember with pleasure. Also, to the officers of Fort Hayes [sic] for innumerable acts of hospitality and generous courtesy enjoyed at their hands. These gentlemen omitted nothing that could contribute to the comfort of their guests, and the visit will always be remembered by the amateur bison-killers with pleasure. (Leavenworth Daily Conservative, 26 November 1867)

Although most recorded hunts for buffalo were successful to one degree or another, the following article not only describes the areas through which the hunters traveled but also points out many of the hardships and difficulties that they faced. It should be noted that this hunt, undertaken in December 1876, required the hunters to leave the state in order to locate the herds.

MY FIRST BUFFALO HUNT. I LEFT HOME ON THE MORNING OF December 15th, 1876, in company with Messrs. Mark Malory, Samuel A. Ward, and his son, Royal Ward, our destination being what is called the "pan-handle" in Texas, distant about two hundred miles. The first day we made about twenty miles and camped on the South Ninescah [sic]. Nothing occurred that day except a few shots at prairie chickens and the capture of a little mouse, by Mr. S. A. Ward, who proposed in a few minutes after, to turn it loose, but I told him not to do it. The old maxim says always to hold on to the first game caught, and you will have good luck. He took my advice and turned him loose in his wagon where he had a lot of corn in sacks and the result was he cut the sacks all to pieces, and he was glad to get clear of him.

The second day we passed through Sun City, a small town in Barbour county, on the Medicine river, some fifty miles from our homes. We camped that night on the Medicine about one mile west of the city and remained there until the afternoon of 17th, when we were joined by Messrs. Gilbert Champion, George Stedman and Samuel Powell, as had been arranged. We traveled about five miles that afternoon and went in to camp for the night on Elk Creek. The next morning Mr. Ward suggested that the party load their guns as we would be sure to see game that day. I had traded guns with him the day before we left home, but had not shot since, so I told him I would have to try it before I got where the game was. I loaded up and got ready to shoot but could see no target. Mr. Ward proposed to let me shoot at his hat, saying I could not hit it. I told him to set it up and I would try and see what I could do, so up went the hat about one hundred yards distant, and I banged away, plugging it right through. Mr. Ward ran up and took the hat down saying, "confound your picture, I didn't think you could hit it. If I had, I wouldn't have set it up for you." We saw some antelope that day but killed none. That night we reached Big Mule creek, in Comanche county, and passed through the county seat, Smallwood, a flourishing little town with a single house in it. All that is left of Smallwood is an old dilapidated, double log cabin of the rudest kind, supposed to have been the hotel.

That day we killed two rabbits and five quails, and at night we camped two miles west of Smallwood. After supper we organized and elected our officers. Mr. Gilbert Champion was unanimously elected captain and Mr. S. A. Ward lieutenant and managed the business of the company the balance of the trip. On the 19th we reached Bluff Creek and camped on its banks. In crossing Buzzard creek that day,

Capt. Champion came near losing a pair of mules. It is a deep muddy little stream, so deep that when the mules were in it only their ears were visible. Here we killed three quails. These not being enough for a mess for the entire company a proposition was made to gamble for them which we did, Capt. Champion being the winner. Next morning we left camp pretty early and had not gone far before we saw a herd of antelope. Capt. Champion and Mr. Stedman went after them, but came back without any. That afternoon near Big Sand creek, we saw our first buffalo, all in a herd by himself. Lieut. Ward and myself and a stranger who had fallen in with us, took after him. It was one of the oldest bulls on the plains. After about two miles I gave up the chase but Ward and the stranger followed on about ten miles and only got three shots at him. They returned to camp about ten o'clock that night. On my return I ran into a herd of antelope and got four shots but no meat. We had had no meat for five days.

On the 21st we traveled through a very fine antelope country and saw a great many antelope. We did our best to kill them, but in vain! As usual all hands came into camp without meat. Six days and no meat. On the next morning I confess I left camp somewhat disheartened. The captain assured us that we should have meat that day. We had traveled but a short distance when we ran into a big nice herd of antelope. The captain got several shots at them and ran them round near the wagons where we all got shots at them, but killed none. That evening we reached the south bank of the Cimaron [sic], about one hundred and fifty miles southwest of our homes, and where no one goes but the buffalo hunter. We had not more than reached the south bank of the Cimaron [sic] till we saw another fine herd of antelope. Seven days without meat, away we went and it was not long until we returned with two, Capt. Champion killing one and I one. As there was [sic] several older hunters in the company than myself, you may believe I felt somewhat proud. Capt. Champion told the boys the charm was now broken and we would have plenty of meat from that [time] on, which proved to be true.

We went into camp that night and awoke on the morning of the 23d and found ourselves covered with about six inches of snow, and the snow still falling. The wind was blowing a perfect gale[;] it "snowed and blowed" the entire day and all night. We had some spades and shovels, and one pick which we used in turn during the day to keep ourselves from freezing. On the morning of the 24th the snow was about two feet deep. We had dug holes in the ground the day before and crawled into them and by that means kept ourselves very comfortable. After laying [sic] in our holes in the ground sixteen hours we crawled out to find the snow from eighteen to twenty inches deep on a level and in many places from two to five feet deep. By the time we got out in the morning the storm had abated and the sun was shining although it was still intensely cold. Notwithstanding the weather Capt. Champion and Mr. Stedman concluded they would go out and try and kill something. They returned in the evening with two antelope. While they were out the rest of us prepared ourselves better quarters. On the morning of the 25th, the sun rose clear and cold, and it was decided that Ward and myself might go hunting, Capt. Champion and Stedman staying in camp. Ward and myself traveled all day in the snow up to our knees and only killed one rabbit. Mr. Ward got two shots at a deer but did not hit it. On our return to camp, we found the rest of the boys had killed twelve rabbits and six quails. We found two strangers in camp who lived about six miles southeast from where we live. They told us they had killed two buffalo and were going to attempt to go home. They said they had washed and dressed themselves the day before so that if they were . . . found dead their friends might recognize them as they never expected to see home again. They remained with us all night and the next morning started home where I hope they arrived safely.

On the next morning I visited their deserted camp and found that they had left most of their meat, only taking with them one hind quarter and the hide of one buffalo. No one of our party attempted to hunt, except Mr. S. A. Ward, who was bound to have what he had shot the day before, but he never brought it in. On the 27th we broke camp and moved about six miles south to where we could have plenty of wood. On our way Capt. Champion and Mr. Stedman killed four antelope. After killing the antelope they found a herd of four buffalo and killed three of them. Mr. Malory and I went and hauled in the antelope, but it was too late to dress the buffalo and we had to leave them until next day when we went back, skinned them and cut them up in quarters and left them on the ground, where they lay for six days in the snow about one foot deep. When we returned for them we found them spoiled. We killed one antelope. It was a very stormy day.

On the next morning we started out, Capt. Champion, Lieut. Ward and Royal Ward going in one direction, and Mr. Stedman, Mr. Malory and myself in another. We were not out long before we saw a single buffalo and gave chase. We soon lost sight of him but ran into a fine herd of antelope at which we got some shots, but killed none. Capt. Champion and the Wards found a herd of buffalo and wounded one which ran in our direction. We gave chase but did not come up with it. On our return we met Mr. S. A. Ward who had wounded one and he and Mr. Stedman went after it and soon came up with, and killed it. After skinning it we started towards camp and on our way we killed one antelope. We got into camp about one o'clock in the morning. We left camp next morning in two parties. Capt. Champion, Stedman, and Royal Ward, in one, going south, and S. A. Ward, Malory and myself, in the other going north.

We had gone but little over a mile when we saw a large herd of antelope which we followed all day, occasionally getting a shot at them. Ward is one of the most persevering men I ever saw. We had followed the herd about twelve miles when I began to talk about giving up the chase, but Ward said he would have one of the antelope and about four o'clock in the afternoon he got a shot in that stopped one. We followed it about a mile and caught it. I then went back to where Mr. Malory was with the wagon and loaded in the first one killed and while I was doing so, Ward followed the herd and got three more. It was now getting dark and we were at least eight miles from camp. If we had had two hours more of day light I have no doubt but we would have got the entire herd of about fifty for we had them very nearly run down, but we started for camp and got in about nine o'clock, to find that the other party had not yet arrived. We enquired of Mr. Sam'l Powell, who had been left in charge of the camp, and he said he had heard about forty shots in a southwest direction and supposed they had either ran into a herd of buffalo or had been captured by the Indians. It was then after nine o'clock at night and we began to think that something serious had happened [to] them, but it was not long till Mr. Malory, being out attending to his horses heard them coming in. The[y] tried to look very sober, Capt. Champion saying he was ready to leave as there was no buffalo in that part of the country. I saw in his face a kind of a pleasing smile. I then let my eyes drop towards his feet and saw that he was bloody up to his knees and fresh blood at that. I said to him, "Come, Captain, tell us about it." He made a clean breast of it, and told us all about their days work. After leaving camp that morning and going about six miles they came in sight of a herd of about two hundred buffalo, when they opened fire on them at a distance of about two hundred yards. This was kept up for some time and when, the battle was over there was found thirteen dead buffalo on the ground. Perhaps there would have been more if it had not been for an old cow. After the boys had got down the thirteenth, this old cow made a charge on them and soon cleared the field. The next morning we started after the thirteen buffaloes. When we got to them, Capt. Champion and his party thought that they would follow up the herd and get any wounded ones that might be in the way. They overtook and killed one that they had wounded the day before. The rest of us dressed and brought in the thirteen. We arrived in camp about nine o'clock in the evening got our supper and went to bed after twelve o'clock. On the morning of Jan. 1st, 1877, just about nine o'clock a strange man came into camp and said he had just seen a herd of about thirty buffalo. We got our breakfast over as soon as we could and Capt. Champion, Stedman and S. A. Ward, started in pursuit of them. Mr. Ward killed three and the others none. The day before while out after the buffalo I lost my overcoat and gloves and this morning I had to go after them. I did not take my gun with me not deeming it necessary, but before I got back I wished I had. When I got to where I left my things I saw a very large herd of buffalo and could have killed some of them if I had had my gun, but I had n't [sic] and they were safe. We determined to start home the next morning. January 2d, we loaded up and started but did not get over a mile from camp before we saw a herd of sixteen buffalo. Capt. Champion led off and we all followed him in single file[;] we did not go over half mile until we opened on them at about one hundred yards distance. The firing was like that of a skirmish line of an army. We kept up the fire for about fifteen minutes and the result was eight buffalo laying dead on the field. I had the honor of killing one. We skinned them and loaded them up and the next morning, January 3d, started home. On the 5th, Capt. Champion killed one more. We loaded six teams with the meat. On the way home I killed a wolf that was following our wagons. We got home on the 9th of January, after being out twenty days of the worst weather ever seen. The result of our trip was thirty buffalo, fourteen antelope, one wolf and some rabbits. None of the party was sick and no accident happened [to] us during the entire trip. W. A. W. HOUSER. (*Hutchinson News*, 15 February 1877)

Wolves were also hunted. Newspaper accounts were probably intended not so much to call attention to potential hunters and trappers as to alert local farmers of the potential danger to livestock:

A FEW OF THE HUNTERS, FOR WHICH GYPSUM IS JUSTLY FAmous, went on the chase with horses after wolves last week. Several were seen, but only two were captured. John Kingman was the lucky man, as he got both of them. The wolves— both coyote and grey—are doing considerable damage. They double discounted the holidays in their ravages in the turkey roost and hen house. Several more hunts are on the tapis. (*Saline County Journal*, 11 January 1877)

COYOTES AND WOLVES ARE UNCOMMONLY NUMEROUS IN THIS section this winter. This is regarded as an indication of an extreme hard winter. We have had remarkably pleasant weather thus far, but there is time yet. (*Smith County Pioneer*, 5 January 1878)

Occasionally the den of a wolf was found; the wolf could be dug out, though with some danger to the hunter:

TWO LITTLE SONS OF JAMES TULLY, AGED NINE AND ELEVEN years respectively, while herding cattle came across a wolf den. One guarded the hole while the other went for a pick and the dogs. When the digging had made considerable progress, the mother wolf assisted on evacuation, which she accomplished at a side hole from the den. She went for reinforcements and soon returned with the last year's family, but the boys and the dogs "held the fort," and finally killed four young wolves and captured three others alive, making seven wolves at one haul, in spite of the mother and all her friends. (*Hays City Sentinel,* 6 June 1879)

Various techniques were used to hunt wolves. One of the more sporting methods consisted of a chase on horseback:

FRIDAY EVENING WE WERE ALARMED BY SEEING MAJ. HOUSTON making 2:40 on a pony over the prairie through ravines and up and down the banks of the Pawnee; and what made the scene more exciting was the vociferous and repeated noise of the Major. Wishing to relieve our anxiety we hasten-to [*sic*] the nearest possible place for information when lo and behold, we saw, fifty yards in advance, a wolf making his best time to keep out of danger. The Major had nothing but a halter to rein his pony, yet he managed to keep on track and every bound of the pony shortened the distance be-tween him and the wolf. The wolf seemed to understand that the broken banks of the ravines was his safest retreat and therein tried to effect his escape; but to no avail. The Major and pony were as expert as the wolf in every spot and soon worried him down, after which the Major borrowed a gun of his neighbor Williamson, and finished the race. If the Major was as persistent in routing the enemy as he was the wolf, we judge he made it hot for them. (*Pawnee County Herald,* 28 May 1878)

One animal that provided the settler with both food and recreation was the bullfrog. The more common grass frog was probably used most often for the "target practice" mentioned in the following items:

I HEAR OF A GOOD MANY FROGS BEING SHOT NOWADAYS, WELL, they are good eating if cooked right, but I guess the sports-men are only practising [*sic*] on the frogs until such time as it is lawful to shoot chickens, when that time comes, dear boys remember me. (*Ellsworth Reporter,* 3 August 1876)

BULL FROG-HUNTING IS A FAVORITE AMUSEMENT OF THE b'hoys. (*Hays City Sentinel*, 11 May 1877)

Hunting jackrabbits was the sport for many, often with the aid of horses and dogs. The following article describes the rabbits, their behavior, and habitat. Dogs were not always successful hunters. Even though greyhounds could run faster than jackrabbits, they could not turn as quickly and therefore eventually lost their prey.

OUT IN KANSAS WE HAVE RARE SPORT HUNTING JACK-RABBITS. Eastern boys can hardly guess how much sport there is in it. We have other game, of course. Deer and antelopes are quite common in Edwards and other soutwestern [sic] counties; and the wolves that prowl over the prairies are worse for our sheep and calves than bears are, or ever were, in New England.

But the greatest sport of all is hunting jack-rabbits. We hunt them on horseback, with greyhounds. All the settlers in our section keep one or more greyhounds on purpose to hunt jack-rabbits. I went fox-hunting twice, with hounds, in Maine, and did not have half the fun that I have had out here, in Kansas, hunting "jacks."

Our jack-rabbit, I should say, is no such little scrub as the Massachusetts rabbit, or even the Maine hare. Jack is quite a beast, and makes roast or stewed a pretty good dish. Many a settler's family lived on jacks, after the grasshoppers came. Our rabbit has black legs and black ears, and a blackish head. When he stands up on his haunches, for a look around, he is nearly three feet tall. His tail is long, and that is black, too. But the body is a brownish gray. I have seen jacks almost as large as a small goat. Now, and then one comes across a tremendously large one,—so big and tall and long-eared, and so awfully clumsy-looking, as fairly to make a fellow stare, even when he is used to jacks. Generally, however, they do not weigh more than fifteen or twenty pounds.

These jack-rabbits live right out on the open prairie and

along the shallow river-valleys, where there is not a bush, nor a tree, anywhere in sight. Most of the grass, except by the streams, is buffalo grass,—a short, curly, fine grass; but scattered about are seen bunches, or rings, of taller grass, two and a half or three feet high. These rings of high grass are commonly not larger across than a bushel-basket, but quite thick. And right inside of the grass rings is where the jacks hide. They hide in there, curled up; cuddled warm out of the prairie wind, and well out of sight, too. You scarcely ever see a jack stirring on the prairie in day-time, even in places where they are really very numerous. Those grass bunches are so thick that you may pass close to one and not see the jack cuddled up in the middle of it; and if he sees you he will not stir, unless you kick or strike into the grass. Then out he goes, ten feet at one jump, and clumsy as he looks there is nothing that runs which can catch him, if he gets twenty yards start—not even a greyhound. Away he flies like an old felt hat flopping along the ground before the wind; and you think that the hound will catch him in no time; but he doesn't. Jack keeps just about two jumps ahead, and will run one mile, or two, or all day, just as you like. There is no such thing as tiring one down, when once he has had a good fair start, and has had a chance to get his eyes fairly open and catch his wind. The only way we ever catch jack-rabbits with hounds is to take them by surprise, before they have time to lay themselves out for good steady leaping.

I have often laughed to see a wolf hunt jack-rabbits. The wolf will sneak along, crouched close to the ground, and work up to a ring of grass, then give a sudden jump right into the midst of it. About one time in fifty he will manage to seize the sleeping jack. But commonly the rabbit will, in some mysterious way, leap out from under the wolf's very nose, and go twenty or thirty feet, as if propelled by a single kick, then stop and look. The wolf knows that the game is up. I once saw a wolf sit down and look hard at the rabbit, and sniff him longingly; and the jack, not yet half awake, sat and winked. But the wolf turned away and went to another bunch of grass. He knew better than to waste his strength chasing a jack-rabbit.

The way we used to hunt jacks was to start out—eight or ten of us—on our ponies (and there are no horses in this country fleeter than some of those Texas ponies), with all the greyhounds we could muster—sometimes fifteen or twenty of them. Riding out on the prairie, we would now string out in a line, with the dogs all running close beside the ponies, and go at a gallop for those rings of tall grass. Just as some pony's feet were going into a bunch of tall grass, out would leap a rabbit. The greyhounds would be close hauls, not two yards from the rabbit's tail; and everybody knows how a greyhound will buckle down to the ground and run, without so much as a *yip*.

The jack, waked up so suddenly, would not have time to straighten out for long leaps, and would tack, first right then left. In that way he would dodge one hound, but in dodging one another would grab him. That was the way we used to hunt them. Sometimes we would by this plan catch eighteen or twenty in an hour. O, it was live sport! Such shouting and cheering on! Three or four jacks going at once, and all crazy after them, at a dead run! The ponies would chase as eagerly as the greyhounds. Why, I have seen more excitement and more downright, laughable fun in a jack-rabbit hunt than in anything, else I ever witnessed. (*Osborne County Farmer*, 25 December 1879)

There were two species of jackrabbits in Kansas at this time. The black-tailed jack occurred primarily in southwestern Kansas, and the white-tailed jack occurred in open prairie habitat in west-central and northwestern Kansas. Most of the jackrabbits portrayed herein were probably whitetails, though this is never directly stated.

There were, in addition to the two species of jackrabbits, two species of cottontail. The eastern cottontail prefers woodland with brushy areas and the desert cottontail is at home in the short-grass upland. Newspapers sometimes specifically mentioned "jackrabbits" whereas at other times they would simply state "rabbits." It remains unclear which species they were referring to.

> TUESDAY WAS A SORRY DAY FOR RABBITS. THESE LITTLE ANI-mals are very plentiful this winter on the prairie, and the white covering on the ground Tuesday exposed them con-spicuously to view as they moved around. Severeal [sic] per-sons went out and brought in several, Wes. Tally and Pret Gillette doing the best, the former bagging twenty-eight and the latter ten. In the evening, it being very light, numerous parties sallied forth with shotguns, and a large number of the little pests were slaughtered in the moonlight gambols. Rabbit potpie has been a staple article of diet all the week. (*Osborne County Farmer*, 10 March 1876)

> BILL KELLAR, THE BOSS HUNTER, LAST SATURDAY, TOOK IN forty-one jack-rabbits, and still he did not have time to take a good hunt. (*Larned Optic*, 18 December 1878)

The circle hunt was a popular method of hunting some species of native animals, including wolves, coyotes, and rabbits. Circle hunts could rid an area of an animal species that many farmers regarded as undesirable and were considered both social and sporting events as well. These hunts had to be well orchestrated, with cooperation from all those involved, in order to be success-ful. Details of one such organized circle hunt for wolves follows. In order to prevent accidental shootings of the participants, firearms usually were excluded from use by all but a few.

> THE FOLLOWING IS THE PROGRAMME ARRANGED FOR THE grand wolf hunt to take place on Saturday, January 15th:
> Starting in four straight divisions, the west line will form on road running from Chauncey Bliss' to Osborne City at 9 o'clock a.m. C. M. Bliss will superintend the right, E. M. Jones the right center, T. H. Rigby the left center and John Tallentire the left. L. A. Weeks marshal of west line.

The results of a coyote hunt. Kansas State Historical Society, Topeka.

South line will form on section line two miles south of town eight at 9 a.m. Mr. Lawson superintends the left, Mr. Briery left center, Mr. Hilton right center and J. Karney the right. Mr. Reed will be general marshal of south line.

East line will form on section line joining M. M. Pickering's place on the west at 9 a.m. M. M. Pickering superintends the right, Wm. Smith right center, J. S. Farmer left center and Thomas Collins the left. C. W. Stansbury marshal of east line.

North line will form on section line joining Mr. Tindall on the south. C. M. Baldwin superintends the right, Frank Smith right center, T. Rochford left center and Mr. McCormick the left. W. F. Cochran to be marshal of north line.

At 9 ½ all marshals and superintendents will fire a salute as a signal for all to advance.

Abe Smith will be chief marshal.

The center of circle will be on the Danl. Otto claim, owned at present by the editor of the Osborne Farmer, (being the sw quarter sec. 22, T. 8, R. 12.)

All that are in the enclosure are requested to join their respective lines in the morning, and *not wait for the line to come to them.*

When each line arrives within a mile of claim they will halt and arrange their respective lines to the best advantage, and the general marshal of each line will advance and wave his hat as a signal that his line is ready to the chief marshal stationed in the center. When all report the chief marshal will raise a flag as a signal that the lines are all in position. The marshals will then return to their lines and officers will fire a salute and advance till the circle is three hundred yards in diameter, then they will turn their dogs loose. It is desired that all dogs be tied till the time of turning loose.

No one except the officers allowed to carry fire-arms.

Start with all the horns, bells, drums, etc., and some good

long spears would not come amiss. Make plenty of noise, so that you can keep together in line.

No stopping the sport short of thirty degrees below zero.

The officers of each line should set their time by the sun, so that all will have the same time starting and coming together.

The lines are all expected to be within one mile of claim at 12½ p.m.

Come one, come all, and let us have a grand treat. Let everybody come and see what they never saw before, old and young. It is not only your privilege, but your known duty to share this sport. Start right off and help us catch those shaggy fellows that visit our hen-roosts to[o] much. MANY CITIZENS. (*Osborne County Farmer*, 14 January 1876)

In many cases hunts were devised strictly for rabbits; often there was a contest between two groups of hunters. At other times large numbers were taken in grand hunts—most certainly circular in nature.

THE HUNT IN THIS COUNTY ON THURSDAY AND FRIDAY LAST was a grand success. About 1400 rabbits were killed. The "count" ran up to about 9,000. The hunters on Aldrich's side were treated to a supper served up at both hotels at the expense of the hunters on Meadow's side. Full particulars and the "official count" and other matters relative to the hunt will be given in next week's issue. (*Smith County Pioneer*, 28 December 1876)

A RABBIT HUNT IN THE VICINITY OF RUSSELL, RESULTED 'n the death of 137 rabbits. (*Hays City Sentinel*, 12 January 1877)

Fishing was also a popular pastime during the warmer months. Just as fishing reports are published today, so too did the early newspapers announce the locations of the best fishing holes:

Displaying the results of a rabbit hunt. Kansas State Historical Society, Topeka.

TWENTY-SIX POUND FISH, IN LARGE NUMBERS, HAVE BEEN SEEN in the Smoky within a week or so passed. (*Saline County Journal*, 25 September 1873)

SOME OF THE FELLOWS ARE QUITE SUCCESSFUL AT FISHING. We hear of a number who have caught fish at our town dam. We also hear that they are being caught in great numbers near the farm of Mr. J. Peck, on the Smoky. (*Saline County Journal*, 29 March 1877)

For the true aficionados, even if fish were not caught, the experience of sitting on the riverbank was a pleasant and rewarding venture:

CALMLY THE FISHERMAN SITS BY THE RIVER'S BRINK, WATCHing intently the cork which prophesies the intentions of the finny tribe about as accurately as the barometer indicates the "intentions" of the weather. As he sits there with his head bowed, silent and immovable, we pity and yet admire him. We pity him because he looks so grief-stricken and humble. We admire him because he has the patience to sit the live long day, in the warm sun or cold wind, and fish, without getting even a bite. What if he does growl occasionally, when his hook and line is firmly lodged in an overhanging limb, or in a submerged, complicated snag! The general average of his patience and meekness will pass him safely through the trying ordeal of the criticism of his neighbors. (*Saline County Journal*, 26 April 1877)

WE INDULGED IN A FEW HOURS OF GENUINE LEISURE LAST week, by giving a whole afternoon to the shady banks of Buffalo creek, and the finny inhabitants of its clear waters. Our friend Phelps, (in whom the power to entice the fish from their native element seems inherent) induced us to visit his field of oats a few miles up the river and we could not resist the temptation of riding behind his magnificent sorrells [*sic*], on the soft cushions of his stylish buggy, so we

Sunday fishing. Kansas State Historical Society, Topeka.

looked at the oats, and we guessed at the number of bushels, until we found ourselves approaching the creek by a sort of a circuitous route home, when Phelps pulled out of the capacious side pocket of his coat, some fine cigars, and two lines, with the laconic remark, "let's go a fishing," the truth then dawned upon our minds that it was fish he started for, and not oats, taking advantage of our known love of agricultural products to inveigle us into the expedition. Well, we found ourselves in business immediately, having volunteered to "string 'em," and "string 'em" we did, but could only get even with him when he hunted for a fresh grasshopper. Fortunately grasshoppers were so scarce, that he had to forage around considerably to find one, or we should have been smothered with the fish he scattered so regardlessly all round us. We don't know exactly by actual count how many were caught, but after two hours hard work, we drove leisurely home with a buggy full. (*Ellsworth Reporter*, 15 June 1875)

Although most pleasure fishing involved a quiet afternoon on the banks of a stream, some fishing parties were more extensive and lasted for several days and nights. Often these parties included both men and women:

SEVERAL LADIES AND GENTLEMAN INTEND GOING TO THE PAW-nee on a fishing excursion, as soon as the weather becomes settled[.] They will take a tent and provisions along, and be gone two or three days. (*Kinsley Graphic*, 19 April 1879)

Dogs were important to the early settlers. To many pioneers they were not only companions and watchdogs but were valuable in hunting several kinds of game, such as deer:

MR. JOHN MCDANIEL SHOT A FINE BUCK ON HIS FARM, NEAR Tiblow station, Wyandotte county, a few days since. He chased it with dogs for about an hour, but ran it to earth and killed it. This is the only one killed in the neighborhood for years. It weighed 125 pounds, when dressed. (*Saline County Journal*, 15 February 1872)

Fishing excursion with the ladies. Kansas State Historical Society, Topeka.

A PARTY OF TWELVE GENTLEMEN TOOK A RIDE OVER THE RIVER last Monday, to have a chase with Mr. A. A. Gibson's hounds, after any game which they might start from the hills. After an hour's ride without starting any game, the party with the exception of Mr. Gibson, Wm. Wambaugh and Mr Wilson, started home. They were hardly out of sight, when a large black tailed buck deer was sighted. It was several minutes after the first shout before the hounds caught sight of the deer. They being bewildered after the first signal, in not seeing the game or striking the trail, Prince and Susie, the two pet hounds of the pack, were the first to get sight of the deer, and then a race for life commenced. To say the hounds that are kept in this country to catch deer, antelope and jack rabbits are swift, would hardly describe their capacity for running. In this case the race lasted but a few minutes. They caught the deer in a run of one mile and a quarter. Tuesday, Mr. Gibson, with the same dogs, caught another deer in a run of two miles, the dogs working at a disadvantage in the start, but took their game just about the middle of the Arkansas river. The sportsmen of this vicinity will regret to hear that Mr. Gibson has sent his noted blue hound Susie to Ohio for the winter. (*Kinsley Graphic*, 21 December 1878)

Sometimes the chase of a deer by dog and master required heroic efforts. One chase and hunt took three days and covered one hundred miles:

THE "CHASE" IS ALWAYS RARE SPORT. MR. THOS. MCHAFFIE, AN old hunter, who often indulged in such sport when he lived on the other side of the great waters, recounts a stirring adventure seldom indulged in, in any country. On the last day of December, he started a deer one mile south of L. C. Brown's farm, in Walnut township, from whence he followed it to Dennis Sullivan's place; from thence to John Ireland's place, where he gave it the shot which eventually resulted in its death; from Ireland's place to S. S. Godfrey's farm, where he left it for the night. On the second day he found the deer on Sullivan's farm, and run him with his hounds, at considerable speed, to Godfrey's farm, thence to Henry Oltman's. That night, a heavy snow storm occurred, which covered up his tracks, yet in spite of this Mr. McHaffie kept upon his trail and followed him as far as Robert Anderson's farm, east of Salina, where he left him for the night. The next morning he found the deer dead, three miles north of Salina. Mc. thinks that in the pursuit he must have traveled at least 100 miles. While upon Luther Brown's farm one of the hounds jumped from a bank 100 feet high to the ice in the river, and still kept on the deer's trail. The hound formerly belonged to Col. Alexander. The deer weighed 200 pounds. (*Saline County Journal*, 9 January 1879)

Antelope hunting with dogs was particularly popular in the Dodge City area. Mayor Kelley had dogs that were adept at capturing the fleet antelope:

MAYOR KELLEY BROUGHT IN FOUR ANTELOPE AS THE FRUIT OF his chase Sunday. He challenges any one west of Leavenworth to compete with him in the chase. (*Dodge City Times*, 9 February 1877)

A HUNTING PARTY, CONSISTING OF MAYOR KELLEY, C. M. BEEson, W. J. Miller, Fred. Singer, Neal Brown, M. F. McClean and Charles Todd, went on an antelope chase, with hounds, Wednesday, with a remarkable and successful result. Four of Mayor Kelley's grey hounds captured six large fat antelope out of a herd of twelve, four and a half miles from the city. The chase was an exciting and interesting one, and the party returned in high glee. The chase extended four miles west. Five antelope, previous to this, was the highest number caught at a single chase. The hard, crusty snow made the run rather difficult. (*Dodge City Times*, 11 January 1879)

ntelope hunters with greyhounds. Kansas State Historical Society, Topeka.

Very high prices were paid for greyhounds. According to the following article, one such dog purchased by Mayor Kelley cost one hundred dollars:

MAYOR KELLEY PURCHASED A GREYHOUND AT THE MAGNIFI-cent price of $100. The canine was brought down from Grenada by Charles E. Bassett. This dog will catch an antelope with a distance of three miles between them at the start. Mr. Kelley says it is the fastest running dog in the world. Last week he made a chase with this dog and his pack of hounds, and the former caught four antelope in a short space of time, while the latter were fatigued from the chase. The new dog is only two years old. (*Dodge City Times*, 15 March 1879)

For the serious hunter, bird dogs were indispensable. Although, as the following excerpt indicates, they were expensive, they became renowned in their own right.

WE ADVISE SOME ONE TO GO INTO THE BUSINESS OF RAISING bird dogs, as they sell here at from five to thirty dollars. We are informed that last week R. C. Bailey sold eight pups at ten dollars apiece. (*Hutchinson News*, 20 February 1873)

Hunting rabbits with dogs was great sport and widely practiced and reported in the western Kansas newspapers:

ONE AVENUE OF WINTER ENJOYMENT, THAT OF THE CHASE, IS open to the Kansas dweller. True, the deer and fox are pretty much strangers to a prairie region, but there are plenty of rabbits—jackrabbits as large as a small yellow dog—and a troop of the dashing young men of the country mounted on scrub Texas ponies, urging on a pack of a dozen curs in pursuit of a little long eared specimen of the rabbit tribe presents a spectacle calculated to excite the envy of a man who has hunted elephants in their native jungles. (*Osborne County Farmer*, 1 February 1878)

NEARLY EVERY EVENING A PARTY OF FROM FOUR TO TEN GO out a horseback with hounds a little ways from town, and give the jack rabbits a race. (*Kinsley Graphic*, 5 July 1879)

When the opportunity presented itself, exhibitions were arranged to showcase a hound's ability to capture rabbits:

WE NEVER FULLY REALIZED THE TREMENDOUS SPEED OF THIS prince of the canines until last Monday. We were loitering around S. T. Kelsey's experimental gardens, when we noticed several dogs, among the rest a Greyhound, run a hare into a pile of oak posts. Throwing several of the posts to one side we caught the hare; also a second one that had been run in before. Taking our game with the greyhound some two hundred and fifty yards into the prairie, away from any fence or house, we dashed one of the hares to the ground. It set off with the speed of the wind with its swift footed pursuer close behind. Before they ran a hundred yards the hound ran over the hare, which finding itself outmatched in speed, commenced doubling with inimitable quickness and skill. Not less than six times did the hound run over it. At length the hare found safety in a pen of corn. Whistling the dog immediately to us, we threw the other hare to the ground which ran gallantly as its mate, but with less fortune, for on one of its doubles the remorseless jaws of its pursuer crushed it to death. So much did the speed of dog exceed that of the hares, we were surprised. It must have run one fourth faster. We see nothing to hinder that dog to feast on rabbits morning, noon and night. (*Hutchinson News*, 13 November 1873)

Occasionally an unfortunate rabbit ventured into a small town, where the omnipresent dogs would give chase. Most often the rabbit was caught, though the following report suggests that at least one managed to outdistance the dogs:

A JACK RABBIT, CLOSELY PURSUED BY ABOUT TWELVE LONG-eared dogs, among the lot two gray hounds, did good work on Friday morning—getting over this town site in just about 29 seconds. The last seen of them they were putting in their best licks on the divide north of town, the rabbit leading by several rods. We judge the jack won the race. (*Russell County Record*, 22 February 1877)

A JACK-RABBIT MADE AN ATTEMPT AT CROSSING THE SQUARE last Monday, but before he had traveled one-half the distance some six greyhounds were in hot pursuit. The race continued in plain view for a distance of about two miles, when he was taken in. It is needless to say that for once a

dog after a rabbit was successful, and an excuse for not catching unnecessary. (*Kirwin Chief,* 8 August 1877)

Hunting conditions improved in the winter, as snow helped
the hound not only to find, but to capture, the rabbit. Evidently
dogs could outmaneuver the rabbits if the snow was fairly deep:

THE DEEP SNOW HAS PLACED THE FESTAL RABBIT A GREAT
disadvantage in the chase. Even the lumbering old farm dog
can pick up one now and then. (*Hays City Sentinel,* 4 January 1879)

SINCE THE FIRST SNOW, MR. S. F. TAFT AND HIS DOGS HAVE
made several attacks on the army of rabbits around his farm
and he has at times brought in from three to six. (Salt Creek).
(*Hutchinson News,* 16 January 1879)

Dogs were used to hunt raccoon as well. However, such hunts
were relatively rare in western Kansas, where raccoon habitat in
the form of forested areas along creeks and streams was sparse.

COON HUNTING IS ON THE TAPIS. LANE BROTHERS AND HONK
caught three one day last week, E. J. says it is royal sport to
see the dogs pulling one way and the coon the other. (*Kinsley Graphic,* 1 February 1879)

Coyote hunts with the help of dogs were also popular. These
hunts not only provided recreation but helped control what the
settlers perceived as a pest species.

MOUNTING, WE RODE SLOWLY TOWARD MY FAVORITE CHICKEN
ground. There we turned the hounds loose and hunted for
the coyote; I found her in the high grass of a ravine. She
looked up and smiled at me, as much as to say, "Is that you,
Frank? Good afternoon to you, but I must be going. Fare
you well, my dear;" and she trotted briskly off. I yelled, put
spurs to my horse, and a dozen hounds were in full pursuit
instantly. We drove her across the creek, then up the up-

lands, and what a blood-stirring ride we had! A big yellow hound overtook the false creature, snapped at her flank, and caught her. The coyote turned for fight. Fatal mistake, as the dozen long-jawed dogs were on her at once. Each had hold of her, and they formed a circle, the coyote the center, the hounds a living circumference that tugged and jerked savagely backward. The coyote was stretched to death in less time than it takes to tell it. After skinning madame we rode home. Roasted rabbits awaited us, and while eating them we arranged for a chase of gray wolves with our greyhounds at the ranch of the ex-Confederate in gray. So you see that agricultural life on the plains of Kansas is not without its exciting pleasures and compensations. (*Kirwin Chief,* 24 December 1879)

Hunting wildcat, or bobcat, was especially challenging for the dogs. In many cases, as the following examples indicate, the wildcats undoubtedly inflicted painful wounds upon the dogs.

A WILD CAT IN CHASE COUNTY "CLEANED OUT" A DOZEN DOGS in two minutes. (*Ellsworth Reporter,* 27 January 1876)

WES. TALLY ON MONDAY LAST BROUGHT TO TOWN A LARGE wildcat, which with the aid of his three dogs he killed just across the river south of town. Riding along on horseback he came suddenly upon the animal napping beneath some brush, when the dogs caused it to take refuge in a tree, from which by virtue of a well aimed club he made it come down and give battle. There were lively times for a few moments. The animal being nearly as large as an ordinary cur, supple, and armed with savage teeth and claws, gave desperate resistance, cuffing and clawing and combing the dogs, and sending them off protesting "'twan't I!" But they were grit, and renewed the attack till Mr. Cat was stretched out a lifeless corpse. (*Osborne County Farmer,* 10 March 1876)

Dogs, in their efforts to chase down prey, were at some risk.

Sometimes the weather was too warm and the chase too long; the result was that dogs became overheated and died from exhaustion.

THURSDAY MORNING OF THIS WEEK MAYOR KELLEY AND LIEUT. Gardner, accompanied by Mr. Wolcott, of Atchison, Dr. Howe, I. Johnson, John B. Means, E. F. Colborn, and enough others to make up a party of twelve, participated in an antelope hunt, which from its tragic termination will not soon be forgotten.

The dogs of both gentlemen are known to be among the best in the land, and were eager for the contest. The party crossed the Arkansas river about four miles east of Fort Dodge, and started two fine antelope from the lower hills that skirt the valley. Then followed a race after flying dogs and antelope, that for excitement and reckless enjoyment makes it the finest sport in the world. The antelope clearing away over the prairie with flying feet, almost seemed for a while to out-do the sleek, graceful hounds, who, with ears laid low and active muscles, dashed after the beautiful fugative [sic]. It was a beautiful sight. The antelope, the hounds and the huntsmen. A mile and a half of break neck speed told the story, and just as that wonder of modern speeed [sic] and ugliness, yelept "Old Calamity," carried this daponent [sic] over the brow of a hill, the hounds brought the tired creature to the ground. It was a victory dearly won, and the dead antelope was soon to be followed by its captors, in a chase through animal paradise. The last of the huntsmen had hardly reached the finish, when it became apparent that the faithful dogs had given their lives for the game. Unable to stand, they were taken upon the saddles before the hunters and hurriedly carried toward the river, three miles away. Poor Fly, a most beautiful animal, never reached the water. The others were taken to the river, bled and rubbed, but to no purpose. "Rowdy" soon followed "Fly," and to close the scene, Kate, and an elegant imported hound of Lieut. Gardner, both

animals that for grace, beauty and speed, have probably no
peers in Western Kansas, paid the debt of nature.

The best dogs die first, and the latter two were a very
king and queen. The loss to Mr. Kelly [sic] and Lieut. Gardner is one that their friends will readily understand.

It is not everybody that enjoys this kind of sport, but once
a participant, there are but few who will not admire the
graceful animals, and after so noble an affront, be sorry to
see them die. (*Dodge City Times*, 15 September 1877)

MAYOR KELLEY LOST TWO OF HIS VALUABLE GREY HOUNDS ON
Monday last. One the $100 dog, which he prized highly. The
dogs had been on a chase after a jack rabbit, in the excessive heat of the fore part of the week, and died from the
effects of over-heating. Several of the dogs belonging to the
pack were disabled in the chase. (*Dodge City Times*, 18 October 1879)

Sporting clubs were primarily recreational and social in function. However, some were concerned for wildlife and desired to
advance those activities that would benefit the native animals.
Some of these clubs, notably the one at Victoria, went so far as to
emulate the hunting clubs of England, including their attire:

QUITE A NUMBER OF THE MEMBERS OF THE VICTORIA SPORTING
Club, of which Sir George Grant is President, have ordered
full dress hunting coats, of the English pattern, for field sports.
The first hunt by the club will take place one week from to-
morrow, and our citizens look forward to the day with much
pleasure. (*Ellis County Star*, 15 March 1877)

LARNED NOW HAS A "SPORTING CLUB," WHICH IS A GOOD
thing, if it is well managed, as we have no doubt it will be.
Some of the members of the new club already have a standing record that will average with any in the State. Next Tuesday at 9 o'clock A.M., the club shoots for the pigeons, and
will have a pigeon supper in the evening. The club will on

that occasion classify and equalize the company, and elect officers. The company will adopt the rules for shooting as laid down in the new book by A. H. Bogardus, which will be on the ground next Tuesday, and which may be seen any day at Casper's restaurant. (*Pawnee County Herald,* 17 March 1877)

The various sporting clubs organized the Kansas State Sportsman's Association, which held annual meetings. These meetings consisted of contests and hunting events, like those described in the following announcement:

THE KANSAS STATE SPORTSMAN'S ASSOCIATION.

The second annual meeting and Tournament of this association will be held in Oak Dale Park, Salina, Kansas, October 7th, 8th, 9th, 10th, and 11th, 1879. There could not have been selected a finer place in the State than Oak Dale Park. The grounds are spacious and, outside of the half-mile race track, are covered with beautiful shade trees.

The little steamboat 'Bell of Salina' will make regular trips during the tournament so that the distance from the city will be a few minutes ride.

This is not a State but a National Tournament. The grand cash prize of $500 in gold will be open to amateur teams of ten, belonging to any regularly organized State Association in North America. This prize is donated by the citizens of Salina, and will bring from the east some of their best sportsmen. Besides this there will be about $3,000 in cash prizes and $1,000 in donations. Capt. A. H. Bogardus and son, of Chicago, the champion shooters of the world, will be here on the second day, and shoot in the afternoon. The Captain will exhibit his superior skill, with a shot gun, and his son with a rifle. They also propose to shoot a grand display of fireworks at night.

The Board of Managers have concluded to make Tuesday, October 7th, the opening day, in order to have more time in which to carry out their programme. The people of Salina are rendering the Board of Managers all the assistance in their power, and with such men as Willis Kesler, D. R. Wagstaff, and Wm. R. Geis on the Board, we may be assured that this Tournament will bring to Salina the largest crowd that has ever been seen in our city.

The programme is being printed and will soon be ready for distribution throughout the United States.

Arrangements have been made with the K. P., the M. K. & T. and A. T. & S. F. Railroads for reduced rates over their lines. Fully appreciating the situation, reduced rates will be given by our hotels, and every accommodation in their power will be extended to visitors during the Tournament.

At the close of the Tournament there will be a grand wild goose hunt to the lakes of McPherson County. Arrangements will be made with the Salina & Southwestern Railroad to carry hunters at reduced rates. These lakes are literally filled with ducks and geese every fall, and afford hunters an excellent opportunity to indulge in good shooting. (*Saline County Journal*, 11 September 1879)

Hunting contests were held in many localities. Various animals perceived as pests were allocated a certain number of points. Teams were chosen and the hunt joined. The team that scored highest, either by killing the most animals or those worth the most points, was declared the winner. These hunting contests had at least three purposes: pest elimination, recreational activity, and social activity (most were followed by a dinner).

THE SPORTING FRATERNITY OF SMITH COUNTY MET AT THE court house in this place last Saturday, and after electing Capt. W. H. Nelson, as chairman, and Will D. Jenkins, secretary, they proceeded to adopt a plan and programme for a grand hunt. After considerable discussion it was decided to select two captains, and the two captains so selected should choose 50 men on each side. It was then decided that the hunt should continue two days—Thursday and Friday, the

28th and 29th inst.,—and that each individual should bring the game killed at that time, to this place on Saturday, the 30th inst., where a count will be made, supper rendered up, and a good time indulged in generally. The result of the hunt will be ascertained as follows:

GAME.	COUNT.
Jack rabbit,	10
Gray rabbit,	5
Wolf,	50
Fox, Swift,	20
Hawk,	10
Crow,	5
Owl,	5
Pack-rat,	1

Now, let every man chosen on either side, do his utmost to make this hunt a grand success. Get all the game you can, and report on Saturday. If yon [sic] don't kill anything more than a pack-rat, bring it along, it might possibly be the one point that would turn your side to victory. The supper will be served up at both hotels, and nothing will be left undone to add pleasure to the occassion [sic].

The following, signed by Aldrich and Meadows, will give all the further information necessary.

All parties to hunt where they please. Bodies or heads must be brought in for the count. Sides to be evened at time of count by choosing from the lowest count on opposite side, and the side having the lowest count, shall pay for the supper for the entire party. The count to be made by three parties to be selected from disinterested persons.

W. P. MEADOWS.

C. S. ALDRICH. (*Smith County Pioneer*, 21 December 1876)

HUTCHINSON, NOV., 17, 1879.

Meeting was called to order by G. V. Ricksecker, president of club. On motion it was unanimously decided to have the annual hunt on thanksgiving day, the 27th. Inst. The club is to be divided into two parties under separate captains. On motion Messrs. E. H. Gregg and J. S. George were chosen captains for ensuing hunt. The following game score of points was then adjusted by club.

Deer, 100, antelope, 100, wolf (gray) 100, wolf (coyote) 75, wildcat 50, raccoon 30, jack rabbits 10, cottontails 5, Swan, 25, crane 20, Geese 20, canvasback duck 25, mallard 20, any other kind of duck 5, prairie chickens 10, snipes, any kind, 5, eagles 100, hawks 50, owls 50, gulls 5.

Messrs. French, Grayson and Langille, were appointed a committee to make the necessary arrangements for supper.

(*Hutchinson News*, 20 November 1879)

As hunters and fishermen took to the field, the results obtained were often not those intended. Newspaper editors would, with regularity, print accounts of the ineptitude, mistakes, and failed excursions of the disappointed sportsmen. Humorous episodes were reported for almost every major group of animals on the prairies. Although most were reported in fun, many a sportsman who was the object of such humor must surely have been embarrassed.

Even big-game hunting, which presented real dangers, was often treated in retrospect humorously.

ONE OF THE BEST LOOKING YOUNG MEN CONNECTED WITH THE K. P. Railway office, in this place, . . . S. Flower Rankin, "proprietor of the Refrigerator on Wheels," [started] on a trip to the plains, buffalo hunting, last Tuesday morning. Judging from the quantity of powder, shot, guns, knives and brogans they took with them, and considering that Rankin felt as happy and confident as a "big sun flower," we shall expect to see all their friends liberally supplied with choice buffalo steaks on their return. A dispacch [*sic*] from them thirty-six hours after leaving, informs us that they had killed one, and scared one more so bad that the chances for life were against him. The dispatch came from the top of a telegraph pole. We suppose the buffaloes were so thick they had to climb up there to get a chance to use their howitzers. (*Junction City Weekly Union*, 17 December 1870)

THE BUFFALO EXCITEMENT CONTINUES. AS WILL MILLER WAS putting harness on his mule today along came a buffalo. He gathered up an old musket and after it he went. I saw them pass over the hill about a mile off, Miller about two hundred yards behind the buffalo. He rode finally to within 50 yards. He cocked his gun and endeavored to get a little closer so as to give him a deadener. Just as he was going to shoot, the buffalo turned his head, rolled his eyes, stuck out his tongue, and snorted so loudly that the mule scared, and threw Miller about ten feet right over his head. I was waiting for him to come for me to help him skin the creature. He came back with his head down, and when I asked him "what for luck" he told me to "ask that d—d mule."

The buffalo passed on to section 12 by Sam Slack's, and they having some fast men and horses pursued and soon killed the creature. Directly afterwards several other buffalo came along. Giving chase they captured a calf, and were pursuing the others full of excitement, when, I understand, as Allen Watts was drawing a revolver it discharged, two loads going through the horse's neck killing him instantly. The horse tumbled end over end and fell upon Watt's body, dangerously injuring him.

My teams were on section 10 a mile and a half from the ranch. My boy had mounted a young mare to go for a jug of water, when ten or fifteen of the buffalo came right towards him. He could not hold the mare, dropped the jug, and the mare ran off before the buffalo for over a mile. My boy at length reached the ranch safely. They were the first buffalo

he had seen, and he says hc hope they will be last. Yours,
Z. T. (*Hutchinson News*, 19 June 1873)

NOTWITHSTANDING THERE IS A FAMILY ON NEARLY EVERY
quarter section, small herds of buffalo pass by frequently.
And most of our settlers being frontiersmen, are, as a matter
of course, pretty good shots, and from nearly every herd that
passes we take our toll. On the 10th of this month a herd of
about 100 passed in through here, and Mr. James Allen, and
A. Stewart, with Spencers in hand moved upon them for
their customary toll. At the crack of Mr. A's . . . rifle, down
came a large fat bull; but this was not enough, so he followed on and fired the second time, and down came another fine fellow. And when they got quite near him, he
sprang to his feet and made for Mr. S, they had no time to
shoot again, so Mr. S, exclaimed "tail him Jim," and tail
him Jim did, and held him by the tail until Mr. S, cut his
ham strings and let him down. A bystander says that James'
heels flew into the air higher than the buffalos back, the
instant he grabbed the tail. (*Kirwin Chief*, 27 June 1874)

Antelope hunters also came in for their share of misadventures:

ONE OF OUR LAND AGENTS DROVE OUT WITH A PARTY OF EN-
thusiastic "Hawkeyes" the other day to see the country and
"wing" antelope. An enthusiastic Nimrod, unaccustomed to
the effect of our pure atmosphere upon visible objects dis-
covering in the distance a supposed herd of antelope asked
permission to step to the front for a shot. "See they move.
By jove, I'll get one, perhaps two," and bang, bang, went the
Henry rifle, when the fun loving agent and companions made
the valley ring with laughter. Our confident antelopist had
been firing at the beams of the Henderson bridge on Coon
creek, three fourths of a mile distant, but then there is no
law to prevent a man shooting at a bridge that distance in
this country. (*Valley Republican*, 24 November 1877)

Prairie chicken, quail, and plover were not always easy to bag, either. Tales of hunters' ineptitude were common in the local newspapers:

THREE OF OUR YOUNG MEN CONCLUDED TO TAKE A GRAND hunt on Saturday last. So after gathering together a perfect arsenal of arms, they dashed off to the "Sand Hills," behind a span of swift horses with bright visions of buffaloes, antelopes, and prairie chickens, glinting in their fertile imaginations. After spending the whole afternoon they came back gloriously laurelled with success, having killed *six small birds*— wrens we believe. They now insist the extermination of the buffalo and antelope is a myth, they should trouble only the weak minded. (*Hutchinson News*, 8 August 1872)

MR. FULLENWIDER BECAME RESTLESS AND CALLED REPEATEDLY to the balance of the party to show him a plover; but his reputation as a marksman had evidently preceded him, for the plover, and all other game, kept out of sight. We were going in the direction of Bunker Hill, and, as we neared that burg, the grave dignity of a ground or prairie owl attracted the attention of our sportsman, and stopping the horses he leveled his gun at the sedate looking bird, (which was standing about ten feet away) and fired. The feathers flew, and so did the owl, directly upward a few feet, and then down, occupying his former ground; and gently closing one eye, he delivered himself of a bow, which would have done credit to any drawing room on Fifth Avenue, and otherwise said in as plain language as he could command: "Call again." Out of pure regard for Mr. Fullenwider's feelings the Doctor never cracked a smile, although it was quite evident that he would have given five dollars for the privilege of laughing.

Of the further exploits of Mr. Fullenwider we have not time to speak, except that ere we reached Russell, one plover, four black birds and another owl went the way of all the earth, and several acres of buffalo grass were trampled down trying to crawl up on a jack rabbit, which played lame just for the fun of it. (*Russell County Record*, 27 July 1876)

Duck and goose hunters were also the object of some light-hearted ridicule:

FOUR FOOLISH MEN WENT DUCK HUNTING LAST SATURDAY. Their lamps were not trimmed and burning; hence not much luck could be expected to accompany their frantic efforts. Our experiences at duck hunting thus far proves that ducks killed by the orthodox fashion of hiring livery teams and traveling from 20 to 40 miles in one day costs not far from $2.50 apiece. Some hunters, of course, can do better than that. But we have special reference to average and below the average sportsmen. But with reference to last Saturday's duck hunt, remarks are only in order. Robinson and Good-now got up a splendid corner on a lot of ducks in the bend of the river. When they had shot their last "random" shot, and the dying notes of ne'er a duck sounded on the breeze, they returned to the place whither the "mare and buckboard" were hitched. Lo and behold the said mare and buckboard had vanished! We have no space in which to detail the experiences they underwent in traveling many and many a "weary mile" which intervened between the hitching post and the place where the mare and buckboard had anchored for the night. And it came to pass that Foster, by the Pool of Bean, landed. He aimed long and well at that duck in the center of said pool. He shot, and over went the duck. "A splendid shot," saith Foster. Off went Foster's garments until he was as bare as Adam—except coat and shirt, which he raised up about his neck to keep them from being wetted. He waded carefully into the center of said pool—the water coming only to his ankles. Foolish man, that he should thus expose his person in ankle-deep water. He secured the duck. It was a mud hen. We have nothing more to say. (*Saline County Journal*, 12 April 1877)

Rabbit hunting also provided its share of humorous incidents:

A PARTY WHILE CHASING RABBITS A FEW DAYS AGO RUN A jack into a prairie dog hole. George attempted to go in after him, but stopped just on the outside. Dr. Stearns set the bone in his shoulder. He is doing well. (Brookville). (*Saline County Journal*, 17 January 1878)

Even hunting such dangerous predators as the gray wolf could provide grist for the humorist's mill:

A YOUNG MAN THAT LIVES ABOUT SIX MILES NORTH OF NET-tleton, saw what he supposed to be a large grey wolf playing with his dog, and wishing to pay his regards to his wolfship, took his shotgun and started out. He saw the dog and the supposed wolf run into the stable. Calling the dog out and thinking the wolf would follow, which it did, it stuck its head outside of the door when bang went the old gun, and, oh my: he had shot the head off a calf that was the wolf. (*Kinsley Graphic*, 14 June 1879)

OUR VALIENT [*sic*], CITIZEN PETER SCHOO BY NAME, WHO FIG-ured so prominently last week in the capture of the wild cats on Hog's Back, discovered another wild cat, in a tree, near town, on Tuesday morning. After he had fired twenty-three rounds at it, the owl turned around to rest on the other foot; and Peter sat down on the grass, and wondered when green apples would be ripe. (*Hays City Sentinel*, 15 June 1878)

Even in the nineteenth century fishermen had reputations for telling tall fish-tales, so it was probably particularly gratifying to report incidents such as the following:

FRITCHEY CAN RELATE HIS EXPERIENCE NIGHT-FISHING A GOOD deal better than we. It must have been interesting to wander about half the night to find the river and after finding it sit and hold a pole over the bank the whole of the balance without feeling a nibble, and we can just imagine the sickly, greenish-yellow glare the sun painted on Fritchey's countenance, when it came up and smilingly revealed to him the spectacle of a sand-bar on which he had been casting his bait, that had not been near the water since the spring rains. (*Osborne County Farmer*, 4 August 1876)

CHAPTER 3

Pleasures and Fascinations

Presumably, the early Kansas settler appreciated the variety of wildlife that inhabited both the prairie and the riparian communities dissecting the plains. Although few writings can be found that openly express such appreciation, one would assume that those people who hunted, trapped, and fished must have been pleased with the abundance and variety of wildlife around them.

Still others, however, took joy from the mere presence of the diverse animal life with which they shared the prairie. A number of the immigrants were pleased with the avifauna and rejoiced when new species were attracted to the habitats created by planting trees and shrubs. At least one person, B. B. Smyth, was a serious bird-watcher and recorded the arrival and departure dates of migrant species. Others simply enjoyed the singing of birds and calling of frogs or reveled in the thrill of being able to observe such a variety of wildlife.

Farmers were more prudential in their appreciation of animals. They recognized quickly the help that wildlife could provide in controlling undesirable, crop-infesting insects such as the grasshopper. Early settlers were beset with plagues of these pests in 1820, 1848, 1850, 1860, 1864, and 1868, with the worst recorded in 1874 (*Kansas City Star*, 22 July 1891). Although the invasions in the 1860s resulted in relief efforts in the state (Gambone, 1970), most attention was focused on eastern Kansas, because settlement in the semiarid western regions did not become widespread until after 1868. The 1874 grasshopper invasion had an overwhelming effect on many of the settlers in western Kansas (Miner, 1986).

In the aftermath of this plague, newspapers in western Kansas advocated controls to prevent future grasshopper infestations, such as planting trees to attract more birds, introducing nonna-tive species of birds to the area, and passing laws aimed at the protection of insect-eating birds (chapter 5). Neither did the fact that toads, turtles, and skunks consume numerous insects escape notice.

Most of the immigrants who came to western Kansas were from the eastern states, where trees were abundant, along with a variety of species of bird life. On the open prairie, with trees existing only along the small streams, many settlers felt a sense of desolation. When the first immigrants arrived, the few trees available were cut for construction purposes and for fuel. Conse-quently, the riparian habitat for tree-dwelling birds was degraded. Editors urged the planting of trees so that additional bird life might be attracted.

At the urging of newspaper editors, legislation at both the state and federal level was passed to stimulate tree-planting ac-tivities. On the federal level the Timber Claim Act of 1862 provided 160 acres of land free to any person who would plant 40 acres with trees. On 2 March 1868 the Kansas legislature passed a "tree bounty" law. People who were willing to plant an acre, or one-half mile of public road, with trees, and then cultivate them for three years, would receive two dollars for 25 years for each acre planted, or two dollars for each half mile planted. This law was amended on 28 March 1872 to require that each acre planted contain at least 160 trees. For many of the settlers who arrived from the east, where trees were common, such encourage-ment was probably unnecessary.

Some settlers who were delighted with the wildlife present attempted to keep animals in captivity, either as pets or simply as oddities. These included squirrels, opossums, and prairie dogs among the smaller mammals, and bears, coyotes, foxes, gray wolves, raccoons, and badgers among the larger ones. Even buf-falo, antelope, and deer were kept by some. Wild birds were also captured, ranging from the larger eagles and owls to the smaller magpie, quail, and cardinal. Some animals—prairie dogs and antelope—were sold as pets to buyers in the East.

At one time or another a number of enterprising individuals tried to domesticate antelope, buffalo, and prairie chickens. Al-though several such endeavors were made, they were relatively unsuccessful, despite the fact that the *Ellsworth Reporter* of 7 March 1872 advertised "domestic buffalo" for sale.

Many people are fascinated by animals that are exceptionally large and deem it desirable to capture them. For example, Collins (1993) lists, for each species of reptile, the largest known specimen taken within the state, and there are some herpetologists who make a point of trying to best the published record. Likewise, sportsmen avidly seek to break state records of game fish, buck deer, antelope, and so on. The settlers, however, were especially fascinated by large birds. Early newspapers made reference to seven species of birds that were habitually killed and measured. By far the most commonly reported was the eagle, followed by the pelican, great blue heron, goose, egret, owl, and swan. Unfortunately, these kinds of reports inevitably led to the killing of animals merely to best a record.

One phenomenon that fascinated the settlers was the occasional "rain" of fish and toads during intense storms on the prairie. If a tornado crosses shallow water that contains fish, aquatic creatures might be picked up by tornadic winds and dropped elsewhere. Toads, as well, can be picked up and dropped, though more likely they simply burrow into the soil during dry weather and emerge in response to the rains.

Two species of mammals, house mouse and barn rat, accompanied the settlers immigrating from the East. Settlers considered the presence of these rodents indication that civilization had arrived, as both species exhibit commensal behavior with humans. Later, however, the immigrants came to rue the presence of these particular rodents (chapter 4).

One pleasant way for the settlers to remember successful hunting excursions was to preserve a trophy. Taxidermy was practiced then, as it is today, to preserve the large or unusual animal. In fact, taxidermists traveled throughout the frontier displaying their specimens. Another way to preserve an animal was to place it in a zoo. The first zoological park in western Kansas, and probably the first in the state, was established in what is now Alton. This zoo harbored representatives of a number of different species, and people traveled from a wide area to visit and observe the live animals at close range.

Some settlers were keen observers of interaction among the

plains animals. Dramatic encounters between the buffalo and gray wolf, for instance, were recorded by several astute observers. Differences between the prairie wolf (coyote) and gray wolf were carefully noted, as was the effect of grazing by buffalo on the composition of the local flora. Generally, as the century drew to a close, the short buffalo grass was replaced by taller, more rank vegetation of forbs and grasses. The buffalo, through their grazing and trampling, perpetuated short-grass prairie; when they all but disappeared, a different type of vegetation became dominant.

People were fascinated with questions that seemed to have no answer. Where do prairie dogs obtain drinking water? How can cold-blooded animals like snakes be active in the winter? Why does it "rain" fish and toads during a storm? How can trout occur in the Arkansas River? To the immigrants from the East many prairie animals were unique. A number of animals that piqued their curiosity, though reasonably abundant, were somewhat secretive. The horned "toad," for instance, was protected by cryptic coloration. Others were primarily nocturnal (badger, gray fox, and porcupine), thus precluding observation by most settlers. Some animals were notable because of aberrant color phases such as albinism. The revered white buffalo was remarkable in this respect, though there were examples of white birds and mice as well.

Sadly, as today, some people were cruel to animals. Experimenting to see how long a snake could live without water, determining how much liquor a raccoon could be forced to drink, and subjecting a captured buffalo to a Fourth of July chase are sordid examples. Some immigrants believed that their security could be assured by killing all of the buffalo as quickly as possible. The Indians would thus be deprived of their food source and would be dependent on the white man, which in turn would bring comfort to the settler on the plains.

The plethora of articles extolling the hunting abilities of the settler suggests that there were some truly outstanding marksmen. Certainly some of those who hunted thought so. To test the prowess of these hunters, various types of shooting contests were held throughout the frontier. Turkeys were awarded to the marksman who could score the most points shooting at targets. Although these contests were called "turkey shoots," turkeys were not the target. In pigeon shoots, however, live pigeons were released at varying distances from the competitors. Hunters who killed the most were declared the winners. Eventually, glass-ball shoots were held in which glass balls were substituted for live birds. These shooting exercises became social events for the settlers and their families.

Some immigrants appreciated wildlife for its intrinsic value. B. B. Smyth of Great Bend, for instance, was a serious student of birds who kept records each spring of the first appearance of various species of migrant birds. The following notes from the *Great Bend Register* are attributed to him:

BIRD NOTES: [APRIL 1879]

On the 2nd, sparrows were plentiful; 4th, swamp or red-winged blackbirds about; 5th, plovers (*Actiturus Barthramius*) heard; 7th sand swallows about; 8th, skylarks seen; 10th, gulls going north; 12th, buzzards (*Catharies aura*) seen; 14th, slate-colored sparrows about; 19th, yellow-head blackbirds abundant; 25th, bittern heard; 26th, kingbirds about; 27th, mourning doves heard; 28th, night-hawks heard. Robins, jays, brown threshers, chewinks and cat-birds were seen toward the close of the month, first coming not noticed. (*Great Bend Register*, 8 May 1879)

The following birds not noticed in April, were seen early in the month: Yellow-throat blackbirds, red-headed woodpeckers, mocking birds, and red-birds. (*Great Bend Register*, 3 July 1879)

Settlement of the land with the concomitant planting of trees was usually given credit for the additions to the local avifauna. As trees were planted, certain kinds of birds, heretofore not present in the relatively treeless prairie, began gradually to appear. These "new" birds were noted by the local papers:

ROBBINS [*SIC*]—FOR THE FIRST TIME—HAVE MADE THEIR APpearance in the vicinity of Peabody. (*Ellsworth Reporter*, 27 May 1875)

BLUE-BIRDS HAVE BEEN NOTICED IN THIS VICINITY THIS SPRING.
It has been stated that there were none here. (*Russell County
Record,* 19 April 1877)

THE BOBOLINK HAS MADE HIS APPEARANCE IN KANSAS. (*ELLS-
worth Reporter,* 21 June 1877)

THE FIRST WREN WE HAVE EVER SEEN IN WESTERN KANSAS
was observed in Rader's grove the other day. We are not
thoroughly posted in Kansas ornithology, but we believe the
wren is found in eastern and well settled districts. Like the
robin and bluebird, it seems to have no fancy for roughing
it, but follows westward the star of empire. (*Osborne County
Farmer,* 22 May 1879)

For many of these people the song of the bird was a cheerful
occasion. Some enjoyed watching the flight of these creatures as
they crossed the endless skies. As evidenced by the following
passages, the aesthetic qualities of bird life added much to the
rather isolated life of the Kansas settler:

BLUE BIRDS, ROBBINS [*SIC*], MEADOW-LARKS, PRAIRIE CHICKENS
and other feathered harbingers of spring, are once more
heard in concert. No reserved seats! (*Ellsworth Reporter,*
15 May 1873)

MR. F. A. SPENCER, WHO HAS ONE OF THE OLDEST AND BEST
improved farms on Blood Creek, informs us that he will have
plenty of peaches this season, as well as plums and other
smaller fruints [*sic*]. Another pleasant feature of tree culture on his farm is the accumulation of birds of all kinds. He
says it is delightful to hear the sweet melodies of the birds
about his farm in the morning. Among the varieties of birds
which have made their appearance since his trees put on
their foliage, are the English mocking-bird, sparrow, blue-
jay, wood-pecker, thrush, cat-bird, oriole, and many others,

familiar to the Western States. (*Ford County Globe*, 21 May 1878)

In addition to the song of birds, a surprising number of editors enjoyed the chorus of frogs:

THE TUNEFUL FROG NIGHTLY SINGS HIS EVENING SONG. THERE are no warblers that have more satisfaction in their songs. (*Ellsworth Reporter*, 21 May 1874)

WHAT A GLORIOUS PLACE KANSAS IS TO LIVE IN, WHERE A man can plow just when he wants to and sit at the window and listen to the soul-stirring music of ye little frogs every month in the year. (*Dodge City Times*, 4 April 1878)

A few articles, indeed, suggested that pleasure could be had through merely observing some of the native animals in addition to birds, such as buffalo, antelope, mountain lion, and coyote:

IN MY RIDES I SEE ANTELOPE ALMOST EVERY DAY AND AT THIS season of the year often are near them—also buffalo and coyotes but I make no attempt to kill them, only sometimes ascertain how near I can approach them. (Watson, letter to his mother, 24 June 1873)

MR. J. KELLY, WHILE OUT ON THE SALINE, SIX MILES SOUTH-west of town, came across a mountain or Colorado lion. Not having anything to shoot with, he had the satisfaction of seeing him trot of [*sic*]. (*Osborne County Farmer*, 27 November 1879)

Farmers wanted birds to inhabit their property primarily to help control insect pests. Even before the grasshopper plague of 1874 newspapers pointed out which species of birds ate grasshoppers or their eggs and implored the settlers not to harm those species. After 1874, however, articles such as the following, concerning the importance of birds in the control of insects, became common.

Antelope on the prairie. Kansas State Historical Society, Topeka.

A PRAIRIE CHICKEN WAS KILLED A FEW DAYS AGO. IN ITS CROP was found the heads of one hundred grasshoppers. This was near sundown. At the same time the examination of a Plover or "Kill-dee's" crop discovered the heads of thirty hoppers.

My neighbors say ten hoppers will eat one ear of corn per day. This being true the chicken has saved ten ears of corn and the plover three ears. And this on the supposition that they took only what were in their crops at sundown.

I heard a sportsman boast a few days ago, that he had killed one hundred chickens already this fall. That is to say this gentleman has been the means of destroying the birds that would have destroyed hoppers that have eaten one thousand ears of corn in one day, or over eight bushels of corn per day or say sixty bushels of corn per week. Would it not be a good idea to let the birds live? A SUFFERER. (*Hutchinson News*, 7 September 1876)

THE PRAIRIES ARE LITERALLY ALIVE WITH PRAIRIE PIGEONS OR snipe. There seems to be a disposition on the part of some of our sportsmen to kill them off. This should not be done. We might, sometime, be afflicted with grasshoppers as is the case with Minnesota and Iowa, and in that event these vast flocks of insectivorous birds could do much towards routing them and keeping them out of our cornfields. So don't kill the birds. (*Smith County Pioneer*, 31 August 1876)

THE SWALLOW, SWIFT, AND NIGHTHAWK ARE THE GUARDIANS of the atmosphere. They check the increase of insects that would otherwise overload it. Woodpeckers, creepers and chickadees are the guardians of the trunks of trees. Warblers and flycatchers protect the foliage. Black-birds, crows, thrushes and larks protect the surface of the soil. Snipe and woodcock protect the soil under surface. Each tribe has its respective duties to perform in the economy of nature, and it is an undoubted fact, if the birds were all swept off the earth, man could not live upon it; vegetation would wither and die; insects would become so numerous that no living thing could withstand their attacks. The wholesale destruction occasioned by grasshoppers, which have lately devastated the west, is undoubtedly causeed [sic] by thinning out of the birds, such as crouse [sic], prairie hens, etc., which feed upon them. The great and inestimable service done to farmer, gardener and florist by the birds is only becoming known by sad experience. Spare the birds and save your fruit; the little corn and fruit taken by them is more than compensated by the quantity of noxious insects they destroy. The long persecuted crow has been found, by actual experiment, to do more by the vast quantites [sic] of grubs and insects he devours than the little harm he does in the few grains of corn he pulled up. He is one of the farmer's best friends. (*Ellsworth Reporter*, 3 May 1877)

In the latter 1900s the English sparrow was proposed by some as a solution to help control the grasshoppers. Although the sparrows would have eventually spread to Kansas anyway, they were introduced to several localities in the region:

A MOVE IS BEING MADE IN THIS STATE TO INTRODUCE THE English sparrow—which goes for insects more than any other bird. (*Ellsworth Reporter*, 26 February 1874)

ONE OF OUR CANADIAN EXCHANGES (THE COBURG (ONT.) SEN-tinel) writing of the English sparrow, says: "These pugna-cious immigrants are rapidly spreading over this Canada. The towns and cities along the seaboard already swarm with them, and from thence they have spead [*sic*] over the whole northern part of this continent, and will be a great benefit in the destruction of grubs and worms of every kind." It will be remembered that a few sparrows were re-cently brought here. It is said that they, too, are rapidly in-creasing in number. We believe it to be the duty of Kansans to take special pains to introduce these useful birds into our State. They will do more towards ridding our fine prairies of such pests as the grasshoppers than all other birds put to-gether. (*Saline County Journal*, 13 December 1877)

Some of the insect-eating birds were protected by law as early as 1868 in Kansas, but enforcement was scant (chapter 5). There were, however, those who suggested that protecting the birds would ultimately result in the birds themselves destroying the crops.

THE CRY OF SOME PEOPLE IS THAT THE "SLAUGHTER OF BIRDS" must be stopped. It is certainly a question as to what bounds the prevention of killing or trapping birds should be carried. A bill pending before the Legislature of Indiana to prohibit the killing of quails for five years is strenuously opposed by the farmers on the ground that the increase would be so great by the end of that time that all the grain in the State would not suffice to feed them. An exchange, commenting on the subject, says;

There seems to be good cause for this fear, for if there are 500,000 quails in the State and each pair produced ten chicks a year (both small quantities,) the total number at the end of two years would be 18,000,000, and at the end of the fifth year 3,888,000,000, which would require 15,000,000 bushels of grain per day to feed them.

In Kansas the cry is: "Preserve the birds; they will destroy the grasshoppers." Now, which is best—that the crops should be distroyed [sic] by the birds or the grasshoppers. (*Saline County Journal*, 15 March 1877)

In response, some editors quickly pointed out the beneficial aspects of planting trees:

TREES FURNISH A HOME FOR MILLIONS OF BIRDS, AND THUS are the growing crops protected from the ravages of devouring insects.

The joyous song of the birds makes the heart of a man happy, and thus are the burdens of life made lighter by the planting of trees.

Trees casts a welcome shade along the dusty highway, and the heart of the weary traveller is made to rejoice. (*Ford County Globe*, 26 February 1878)

Some suggested that the law protecting birds be expanded to include all bird species. This idea was eventually implemented with the 1876 bird law (chapter 5):

A CORRESPONDENT OF THE NEW YORK *TRIBUNE,* GIVES THE following advice to the people of the grasshopper devastated region: "Let the people of those Western States take better care of their birds! For years past they have waged such systematic warfare against them that the market of even the eastern cities have been glutted with grouse, prairie hens, wild turkey, etc., which if unmolested, would have kept the insects in check. We cannot derange nature's balance of power and not expect to suffer somewhere. A law to prevent the killing of any bird in Kansas and Nebraska for five years, would be better than subscribing money every winter for these sufferers." (*Hutchinson News*, 4 February 1875)

Several other species of animals, in addition to birds, ate insects. Some editors suggested that settlers would be prudent to refrain from killing these species, including skunks, toads, and turtles, as well:

THE SKUNK WILL NOW AND THEN EAT A CHICKEN—BUT VERY rarely.—What does it live on then? Beetles, crickets, grasshoppers, mice, etc. Recently much has been said about this animal—and we are glad to see mostly in its favor. The skunk is a benefit to the farmer, and not a single one should be killed, unless it gets to chicken-thieving, which, of course, is not very pleasant.—And then the chickens should be taken care of rather than the skunk. If you do not hurt it, it will not hurt you; and it will weed your garden of insects, and charge you nothing for it. One of our exchanges calls it the "farmer's friend." (*White Cloud Kansas Chief,* 5 January 1865)

THE WET SEASON HAS CAUSED FRUIT AND OTHER TREES TO make a vigorous growth as well as encourage the stay among us of insectiverous birds, and brought us hosts of toads to devour the ants and worms which have heretofore been numerous, and the former particularly troublesome to our housekeepers. We welcome these animal friends, and also hope for a rapid diminution of the various rodents which infest our prairie lands and damage our root crops. (*Hutchinson News,* 2 August 1877)

TURTLES EAT POTATO BUGS, LEAVE THEM IN YOUR GARDEN. (*Ellsworth Reporter,* 3 July 1879)

Of the small native mammals kept as pets, squirrels were popular, and the prairie dog was particularly desirable. The latter

Unafraid prairie dogs. Kansas State Historical Society, Topeka.

were usually captured by flooding their burrows and were often shipped east.

> THE FAMILY OF JUDGE BEVERLEY MOURN THE LOSS OF A PET squirrel. His squirrelship was buried with great pomp and ceremony by the younger members of the family. (*Dodge City Times*, 6 April 1878)

> A PARTY OF FOUR OF OUR YOUNG TOWNSMEN WHILE OUT UPON a buggy ride last Sunday captured twenty-three prairie dogs by turning the water from a pond near by, created by the recent heavy rains, into their holes and drowning them out. They were all brought in a sack, and are now on exhibition. (*Newton Kansan*, 22 May 1873)

HAMPSON & PIERCE SHIPPED FIFTY-THREE PRAIRIE DOGS EAST last week. (*Newton Kansan*, 29 May 1873)

One man became so proficient at capturing prairie dogs that he was known as Prairie Dog Dave Morrow:

MORROW HAD CAUGHT A COUPLE OF PRAIRIE DOGS AND TAMED to some degree. Carrying them in his pockets he undertook to deliver a lecture to a trainload of gaping tourists bound west through Hays City. He walked along the station platform orating on the lovable peculiarities of his pets when one of the tourists surprised him by offering $5 for them. The deal was completed and Dave was in the prairie dog business. It was brisk.

Morrow used a wagon to haul barrels of water out to the nearest dog-town and proceeded to stock up his pet business by "drowning" out the little creatures. Finding this too slow and difficult he put his imagination to work and conceived a prairie-dog trap, consisting of a barrel full of sand, open at the end. This was placed over the hole so that when the sand ran in, the dogs fought their way out through the sand only to find themselves trapped against the barrel head. The sand filled the hole and the animal couldn't get back into his home.

Morrow went around at his leisure, to tip the barrels and shake his captives into a sack. He soon captured so many that the prairie-dog market was glutted. The price dropped from $5 a pair to $1, then 50 cents and a quarter. Dave had competitors by this time so he dropped his business. (*Hays Daily News*, 17 March 1957)

Larger mammals kept as "pets" included bear, coyote, wolf, fox, wildcat, raccoon, opossum, and badger.

A NUMBER OF YOUNG CINNAMON BEARS HAVE LATELY BEEN captured along the creeks of the range.

Prairie dog. Kansas State Historical Society, Topeka.

Maj. Kirk captured a cub cinnamon bear near his camp last week. He took it to his home at Larned. (*Kinsley Graphic*, 31 May 1879)

BRADSHAW'S TAMED COYOTE HOWLS HIS OBJECTIONS TO THE ringing of the bell. (*Ellsworth Reporter*, 29 March 1877)

MR. JOHN MARSH, AT EDWARDS BROS. & NOBLE'S STORE, HAS a pet wolf. (*Kinsley Graphic*, 19 July 1879)

THE FIVE YOUNG FOXES CAPTURED THE OTHER DAY BY MESSRS. Samuels, Clark and Muller, after a couple of hours of hard work, are now kept as pets in their office and afford much amusement to visitors. (Spearville). (*Dodge City Times*, 7 June 1879)

CHARLIE COPELAND HAS, IN HIS WARE HOUSE, A VERY TREACH-
erous little pet in the shape of a young wild cat, which, although not larger than a domestic cat, shows a magnificent set
of teeth, and a disposition to scratch, whenever a stranger ap-
proaches him. (*Russell County Record*, 10 August 1876)

D. C. NELLIS HAS PURCHASED A PET COON WHICH SAME IS DO-
miciled in the Nellis' mansion. It will measurably compen-
sate him for the absence of his family. (*Hays City Sentinel*, 6
July 1878)

A LIVE 'POSSUM WAS THE CENTER OF ATTRACTION AT BROOK-
ville on Wednesday. It was captured by Mr. Hoss, at his farm
on the Mulberry. "Carve dat possum." (*Saline County Journal*, 6 February 1879)

TRACEY HAS A PET BADGER, A SPECIES OF ANIMAL HE HAS LONG
been yearning for. It was captured on the Saline. (*Hays City
Sentinel*, 8 June 1878)

Buffalo, antelope, and deer were also kept, though how "tame"
they became is debatable:

KRUEGER'S BUFFALO STILL CONTINUES TO MAKE DEPREDATORY
incursions to the Post, invading back yards, overturning
slop barrels, and cropping the green and tender grass on the
parade. If the owner does not soon look after him, the soldiers will doubtles [sic] try what kind of steaks this innocent
bison can furnish. (*Ellis County Star*, 11 May 1876)

A YOUNG ANTELOPE, IN A WAGON, ATTRACTED MUCH ATTEN-
tion and admiration one day last week. The pretty creature
was perfectly tame and showed the liveliest sense of affec-
tion when petted. (*Stockton News*, 2 July 1879)

HAM BELL CAPTURED A YOUNG DEER ON THE CIMMARON
[sic], and the animal has become perfectly tame and domesticated. (*Ford County Globe*, 8 July 1879)

Domesticating antelope. Kansas State Historical Society, Topeka.

A few native fish and even snakes were kept by some:

GEORGE SEITZ HAS A HANDSOME AQUARIUM, WITH GOLD FISH
and some natives from the Smoky. (*Ellsworth Reporter,* 7
May 1874)

J. W. MCNEMARA CAPTURED A SMALL SNAKE BEHIND THE
counters at Edwards Bros. & Noble's store, about a week
ago. Mac has the snake in a box and calls it his pet. These
single fellows will pet anything. (*Kinsley Graphic,* 4 October
1879)

Birds were often kept as pets, especially the cardinal and mock-
ingbird. Other species captivated were eagle, owl, magpie, and
quail:

THE COVY [*SIC*] OF QUAILS IN THACKER & COPPARD'S FRONT
window attracts universal attention. (*Saline County Journal,*
14 December 1871)

MESSRS. GILLETTE AND YOXALL HAVE A VERY FINE PAIR OF
red-birds, which they purchased from Atchison. The red-
bird is a native of Kansas and Missouri, are very handsome
in plumage, excellent songsters, and domesticate very readily.
Very seldom, however, has one been seen more than a hundred miles west of the Missouri river. (*Osborne County
Farmer,* 30 March 1877)

MESSRS, WINSLOW & ALLBRIGHT HAVE A FAMILY OF YOUNG
magpies at their stone drug store. They were brought to this
city from Colorado by Mr. John Lindsey. (*Hutchinson News,*
18 July 1878)

MIT. HAZEN, OF OAK CREEK, PRESENTED THE PIONEER LAST
Wednesday with a genuine full-grown American eagle. The
bird is a fine specimen, and will measure six feet from tip to
tip of wings. We have him caged, and will only let him out

on special occasions. Mit. will accept our hearty thanks and a promise to endeavor to capture for him a grizzly bear, in return for the eagle. (*Smith County Kansas Pioneer*, 8 November 1878)

OSKALOOSA HAS A HORNED OWL WHICH AMUSES THE PEOPLE there by killing cats as fast as they are handed him. (*Larned Optic*, 11 December 1878)

CHALEY DON CARLOS HAS THE "BOSS" MOCKING-BIRD. IT MOCKS anything from a grasshopper to a jack-rabbit. (*Kirwin Chief*, 30 April 1879)

Frequently the pioneers captured the young of antelope and offered them for sale, and at least two were shipped by rail to Boston. In other cases the owners simply appeared to appreciate the animals and wanted them about.

A COUPLE OF ANTELOPES TAKEN TO BOSTON FROM ELSWORTH [*sic*], have sold for ninety dollars. (*Pawnee County Herald*, 31 March 1877)

AYER & WENTWORTH HAVE A YOUNG ANTELOPE, CAPTURED out in the wilds of Rawlins county, which they are taming for Boston Common. (*Smith County Kansas Pioneer*, 13 June 1879)

The domestication of antelope, buffalo, and prairie chicken was advocated. Domesticated buffalo were advertised for sale, but the evidence would suggest that the efforts to tame them were somewhat less than successful:

THE KANSAS PACIFIC RAILROAD HAS MADE A PROPOSITION TO the Government which may result in a series of experiments tending toward the utilization of buffaloes. The propsition [*sic*] is, that the Government shall join the company in providing enormous "corrals" on the reserve lands, fencing and ditching so that barriers, impassable to the buffaloes should enclose large tracts in favorable localities. Into these the herds will be driven at the proper season, and shall be used as shall be deemed best; that is to say, killed for their meat and hides, or kept and permitted to breed, much as the domestic cattle are kept in Texas. Some experiments have been tried in crossing the buffalo with domestic cattle, and the result is highly satisfactory, a breed of animals being produced which retains many of the valuable properties of both breeds. The animals are large and strong, the chief objection to them being that no ordinary fence stops them for a moment, and that they love the water so much that they will swim and sport in it even when it is full of floating ice. We have heard of a cow and calf whose love for athletic exercise was such that they would jump from a bank ten feet high into deep water, when there was an easy path close at hand. These personal peculiarities are drawbacks to the introduction of buffalo-blood into the veins of the family pets; but, on the other hand, when properly cared for, these animals make most delicious beef, and their hides, when soft-taned [sic], are as much superior to the buffalo-robe of commerce as wool is to shoddy. The present writer saw the pelt of the amphibious cow, mentioned above. It was much larger than any buffalo-robe which he ever saw before, was covered with a mat of soft, short, curly, brown hair, there being none of the long, shaggy hair ordinarily seen. It is thus seen that there are advantages as well as disadvantages, in the proposed domestication; but it is beyond question that, if any use can be made of the vast herds of buffaloes, a valuable addition may be made to the wealth of stock farmers. (*Ellsworth Reporter*, 8 February 1872)

ANTELOPE ARE VERY ABUNDANT, AND FORTUNATELY THESE interesting animals are in no immediate danger of extinction. Eventually they will be domesticated for profit. (Guild, 1879, p. 465)

W. S. NEFF SELLS HIS PET BUFFALO, "DICK," TO P. T. BARNUM in New York City. There were a good many pet buffaloes in the county at this time (1873). Mrs. Ira Stockbridge and a neighbor lady each caught a calf near Bull's City, and succeeded in domesticating them until they became great favorites. They were killed by some sportsmen, who claimed that they thought the yearlings were wild, and not owned by anyone. John Fink, William Rader and other gentlemen kept young buffalo with their herds. There was no utility in them except the mere exhibition. Attempts have been made to train a pair of them to yoke. They pulled admirably, but there was no obstacle in the way of their sweet wills. In summer, they took the shortest road to water, regardless of intervening obstructions, and they thought nothing of flinging themselves over a perpendicular bank, wagon and all. (*Osborne County Farmer*, 7 October 1880)

THE GENERALLY RECEIVED OPINION THAT THE PRAIRIE CHICKEN cannot be tamed or domesticated is rather stretching the facts. Mr. Edward Van Horn, of this city, has one not half grown following one of his domestic hens around, and is becoming familiar with the premises although caught out on the prairie but a few days ago. Anyone that questions the truth of this statement are [sic] referred to Mr. Van Horn who has the chicken and is ready to make proof of the same. (*Larned Chronoscope*, 10 June 1881)

Impressive large animals captured or shot by the settlers were often reported by the local newspaper:

HENRY HOKE WRITES US THAT HE SHOT A FISH CRANE [GREAT blue heron] last week, near the Smoky, that measured five feet and eight inches from tip to tip. (*Russell County Record*, 30 September 1875)

ED. MURPHY SHOT A MAMMOTH PELICAN WEDNESDAY. IT MEASured 8 feet from tip to tip, being the first specimen of the

Shipping live buffalo by rail. Kansas State Historical Society, Topeka.

kind ever seen in this latitude. (*Kinsley Graphic*, 18 May 1878)

W. W. COLLINS OF TWIN CREEK, CLAIMS TO BE SOMETHING OF an owlist. While out gunning the other day he shot an owl that measured five feet from tip to tip of wing. (*Osborne County Farmer*, 21 December 1877)

A GENTLEMAN BY THE NAME OF SCHANTZ KILLED AND BROUGHT in a large swan Monday. The bird measured eight feet from tip to tip of its wings, and weighed about twenty-five pounds. (*Stockton News*, 5 March 1879)

J. SMITH, OF RUSH, KILLED A WHITE CRANE LAST WEEK WHICH measured 8 feet from tip to tip and weighed 25 pounds. (*Hays City Sentinel*, 2 November 1878)

H. DAVIS CAUGHT A BALD EAGLE, THE OTHER DAY, MEASUR-ing eight feet and four inches from tip to tip of wings. This is without doubt the largest eagle ever killed in the State. (*Ellsworth Reporter*, 21 December 1871)

A GOOSE, MEASURING SIX FEET AND FOUR INCHES FROM THE tip of one outstretched wing, to the tip of the other, has been shot just west of Brookville, and is the biggest goose of the season. (*Saline County Journal*, 17 April 1873)

Captures of large bear, wildcat, catamount, wolf, deer, elk, rabbit, otter, and turtle were also reported by the papers:

A 400 POUND BEAR WAS KILLED IN BOURBON COUNTY LAST week. (*Hutchinson News*, 23 January 1873)

JOHN GILBERT, OF RUSH COUNTY, RECENTLY SHOT A WILD CAT which measured 22 inches high, 3 feet long, and weighed 24 pounds. (*Hays City Sentinel*, 7 December 1878)

AN OTTER WAS TRAPPED IN CHASE COUNTY, WHICH MEA-sured five feet and seven inches from tip to tip, and weighed twenty pounds. (*Russell County Record*, 29 November 1877)

W. G. HATTON CAUGHT A GREY WOLF THAT MEASURED 2 FEET 7 inches in height. (*Russell County Record*, 24 February 1876)

N. F. DILLON KILLED LAST WEEK ONE MILE NORTH OF CEDAR-ville, an elk that dressed 362 pounds. This is undoubtedly the largest that has been killed in this county since '71. Dil-lon is entitled to the "belt" in that section. (*Smith County Pioneer*, 10 November 1877)

ALEX. BOGGS KILLED A BLACK TAILED DEER OVER IN THE breaks of the Saline, last Monday, which dressed 183 pounds. Patton & Buckius served the monster to their cus-tomers. (*Hays City Sentinel*, 7 December 1878)

A CATAMOUNT MEASURING FOUR FEET IN LENGTH AND weighing 50 pounds, was killed on H. A. Myers' place in Pawnee township last week. The animal in color was of a reddish cast. It's [*sic*] hide is on exhibition at Mr. Myers' place. This is probably the largest catamount that has been killed in this section since the settlement of the county. (*Smith County Pioneer*, 29 December 1877)

A JACK RABBIT, WITH A TAIL EIGHT INCHES LONG, WAS CAP-tured by Major Kelley's dogs this week. (*Dodge City Times*, 11 August 1877)

MRS. ZAUN AND MRS. HIGGINS CAPTURED A MAMMOTH SNAP-ping-turtle, yesterday, while engaged in angling in the briny Big Creek. It weighed 30 pounds. Patterson take a back seat! (*Hays City Sentinel*, 31 May 1876)

NATE HUDSON SHOT A TURTLE IN THE ARKANSAS RIVER LAST
Sunday that weighed about fifty pounds. It was utilized for
soup. (*Ford County Globe,* 6 May 1879)

A beaver was measured in one of two ways: The entire animal
was weighed, or the skin was removed and weighed:

ONE OF THE LARGEST BEAVERS EVER CAPTURED IN THIS SEC-
tion of country, was killed by Maj. Alcorn and one of the
Dinkle boys, one day last week, near their camp on the river
just opposite Nettleton. The skin weighed five and three-
quarter pounds just after it was taken off. (*Kinsley Graphic,*
8 November 1879)

MR. JOHN MURRAY, OF WALNUT BEND FARM, VICTORIA, KILLED
a twenty-eight pound beaver last Saturday. (*Hays City Sentinel,* 7 December 1877)

Large snakes were always of interest. The largest species reported were bull snakes and rattlesnakes.

GEORGE MCNAMER KILLED THE "BOSS" SNAKE ON WOLF CREEK
the other day. It measured nine feet and one inch in length,
and belongs to the order known as bull snakes. (*Osborne
County Farmer,* 7 June 1878)

NORTON COUNTY HAS KILLED A RATTLESNAKE WHICH MEA-
sured six feet, in length, and sported sixteen rattles. (*Hays
City Sentinel,* 29 August 1879)

Large-fish records were a must, and papers commonly reported
them:

SOME OF THE LARGEST EELS HAVE BEEN TAKEN OUT OF THE
Pawnee lately we have ever seen. One that Col. Morris had
on Tuesday measured thirty-eight inches in length, eight
and a half inches in circumference, and weighed six pounds.

J. W. Morris had one that was even larger than this, measuring forty inches. (*Larned Optic*, 18 July 1879)

CHARLEY RICKSECKER CAUGHT A CATFISH TUESDAY, THAT WAS not quite as large as he was, but it weighed fifty-five pounds and measured twenty seven inches around. It was caught with a small hook and linen line and he held it until three or four men got sticks and spears and helped him get it out. It required about forty minutes to land it. Charley is several pounds ahead and is much proud. (*Hutchinson News*, 11 July 1878)

Creatures that were rarely encountered, such as horned toads, badgers, porcupines, and gray fox, were reported as curiosity pieces:

ONE DAY LAST WEEK MR. H. C. KNOX, WHILE HUNTING, KILLED a swan on one of the ponds. He brought it to Major Probert's drug store, where it was upon exhibition for several hours and attracted considerable attention. Its beautiful plumage elicited many words of admiration from a number who had, for the first time, seen a swan. There was wondering why his swan-ship was found so far from his "native heath." (*Saline County Journal*, 20 March 1873)

WE HAVE OFTEN HEARD AND READ OF THE HORNED TOAD BUT never saw one until the other day at the salesrooms of E. Wilcox & Co. He was caught by a party of buffalo hunters and huntresses 20 miles southwest of here. He is now basking in alcohol and looks like a common toad, save that he has a tail of considerable length, and his body is covered with horns. (*Hutchinson News*, 28 August 1873)

THE CITIZENS OF THIS VICINITY GATHERED AT THE RESIDENCE of your correspondent, on new year's morning, and, in the forenoon, indulged in a circle hunt, which resulted in the capture of—not a mountain lion, nor a lynx or panther, but a gray fox; after which they repaired to the aforesaid house, where they were served to a sumptuous repast, gotten up by the ladies of Carmel. Marcus Won. (*Smith County Pioneer*, 7 January 1876)

TWO PORCUPINES HAVE BEEN SEEN NEAR KANSADA POST-OFFICE, Ness County. One of them has been killed. (*Hays City Sentinel*, 12 September 1879)

FOR A VARIETY THE SOUTH SIDE IS STILL AHEAD. RECENTLY A large Cinnamon bear has been seen in the sand hill near the bridge several times, and considerable excitement prevails among the residents. This is a fine chance for some of our gallant young bloods to get a good "hug." Go over and interview his bearship, gentlemen. (*Larned Optic*, 24 October 1879)

White animals were always a curiosity. The most famous white creature was the buffalo. Although buffalo came in a variety of colors, usually ranging from various shades of brown to black, occasionally a buffalo would be sighted that was a very light gray and perhaps albino. These "white" buffalo were revered by the Indians and brought a high price when shot.

DENVER, APRIL 7, 1873. — *EDITOR NEWS:* — I SAW THE "WHITE buffalo" of which a writer gave particulars in a recent issue of the *Tribune*. It was at Fort Larned. When I saw it it was of a bluish and brown color. I do not claim that the buffalo I have is the only one ever seen by a white man or Indian; but this I do claim, that it is the only one ever killed by a white man, and that it is the only one that has ever been stuffed. In 1864 there was a buffalo white enough to be called white, killed by a renegade Indian near the mouth of the Platte river, and it was brought into a rancho kept by myself. Anybody could see it if they would set the toddy up for the boys. There was another one run into a lake near the head of the Missouri river and killed by the Indians. These Indians are afraid to go near the lake to this day, as they say they can hear it lowing. It is to be accounted for by the whistling of the wind through a ledge of rocks near the lake.

I do know that white buffaloes are not plentiful, for I have been hunting buffaloes four years. During the last two years I have killed three thousand, and can name men who have killed more, and none of us have seen a white buffalo before this one in these four years. JAMES T. MORGAN. (*Daily Rocky Mountain News*, 10 April 1873)

PAT SUGBRUE [*SIC*] SUNDAY SHOWED US A WHITE BLACK BIRD he had killed in a flock of black birds. We had heard of white black birds, but had never before seen one. We remember once we were skeptical on white mice; but after a friend presented us with a litter of white mice we became sufficiently credulous to believe in white black birds. This bird had white tipped wing feathers, and its color was lead. The yellow feathers under the throat indicated the black bird. There is a black sheep in every flock of sheep, and we assume the rule will hold in a flock of black birds having a color contrary to its general species. (*Dodge City Times*, 14 September 1878)

MR. H. K. W. TAYLOR, OF SALT CREEK TOWNSHIP, WHILE PLOW-ing turned up a mouse which is a real curiosity. It is perfectly white and unlike our domesticated white mice which have pink eyes, this specimen has eyes perfectly black, lustrous and beautiful. Its ears are shaped differently from those of domestic mice and furthermore has a pale yellow stripe from head along back to the tail. The little fellow is on exhibition at the popular stone drug store and the proprietors Messrs. Winslow and Allbright, value it as highly as any specimen yet received. (*Hutchinson News*, 14 September 1876)

The Norway rat and the house mouse both accompanied the colonists as they immigrated to America. Subsequently, as the immigrants pushed westward into the prairie, these unwanted European rodents migrated also:

A SENSATION WAS CREATED IN TOWN TUESDAY MORNING BY the capture of a large Norway rat. This is the first ever seen in town. Another evidence of the progress of civilization. (*Junction City Weekly Union*, 8 May 1869)

A REGULAR, "BONA FIDE" RAT JUMPED OUT OF A CAR AT THE depot the other day—the first rat that has been seen at Salina, that we know of. As the star of Empire moves westward, the rats go along too. If Salina has not previously been able to show herself a second Chicago or St. Louis by any other means, she has certainly commenced to make that showing since the advent of that rat. Rats are enterprising and stick to enterprising towns in great numbers. That rat may "accumulate" to such an extent that the question may soon arise as to whether there is more rats or enterprise in Salina. (*Saline County Journal*, 3 February 1876)

Taxidermic preparation of animals was common, and owls, pelicans, eagles, wildcats, mountain lions, and the heads of elk and buffalo were all prepared as taxidermic specimens.

ONE OF THE FINEST SPECIMENS OF BUFFALO HEADS EVER brought to this country can be seen at Brown & Bigger's land office. It was a present to the firm from the soldiers at Camp Supply. (*Hutchinson News*, 18 February 1875)

A STUFFED OWL, ONE OF THE FINEST SPECIMENS WE HAVE EVER seen, is now one of the curiosities at Doughty & Bullock's drug store. (*Larned Optic*, 19 December 1879)

QUITE A COLLECTION OF STUFFED ANIMALS AND REPTILES, including young antelopes, jack-rabbits, swifts, deer head, bull snakes, &c., made their appearance in town Saturday morning, and created quite a furor among our sight-seeing people. (*Kirwin Chief*, 19 June 1879)

General Hiram C. Bull, founder of Bull's City (now Alton), appreciated animals so much that he established a seven-acre zoological park. In it he kept a variety of animals for his pleasure, and also for visitors. He later enlarged his park to fifteen acres. Today we would call it a zoo.

WHILE AT BULL'S CITY LAST SATURDAY WE MADE IT A POINT OF interest to visit the home of Gen. H. C. Bull. The general, as all [who] know him are aware, possesses a strong inclination toward the aesthetical pursuits of life, and he is giving "full swing" to his commendable taste in the home he is erecting, in which to spend the afternoon of his life. The site of his residence, a neat stone structure, seems to have been chosen with this object in view. It is situated in a picturesque nook, a few moments' walk from his place of business, in the environs of a little grove through which a clear, ever-living stream finds its way. He is enclosing the grove, some seven acres in extent, with a neat, high and substantial fence, as a park for the reception and keeping of wild animals. Across the stream at the lower end is a dam, which holds a fine pond of water for the accommodation of the pets and waterfowl with which he intends peopling the retreat. We saw a splendid large elk with as fine a pair of antlers as ever graced a stag on Highland Scottish heath, three graceful antelope, a jackass rabbit, a little cotton-tail, several prairie squirrels, a fox squirrel, and a little red-eyed white mouse, all waiting expectantly upon the completion of their fairy abode. (*Osborne County Farmer,* 1 September 1876)

OF COURSE WE VISITED HIS PARK. HE NOW HAS FIFTEEN ACRES enclosed by an eight foot picket fence, and his animals appear as contented in their small paradise as a happy family well could. He has four elk—a pair of moose-elk and a female mountain elk and fawn, and a young buffalo. Ill fate befell four of his antelope, a predatory wildcat killing them, and the other died. He expects soon to have a male buffalo and a blacktailed deer added to his collection, having obtained knowledge where the same can be procured. (*Osborne County Farmer*, 30 August 1878)

Many observers of nature reported a great variety of dramatic interactions among animals. Furthermore, as the buffalo were driven from the plains, a change occurred in the structure of the prairie itself that did not go unnoticed.

HERE NEAR SALINA, THE BUFFALO GRASS BEGINS; BUT IT IS evidently yielding to the coarser and stronger grasses of the prairie. Up about Fort Harker it predominates. The idea, that as the buffaloes are driven back the buffalo grass ceases, is one that everywhere prevails in this country. I think it is well founded. My own opinion is, that this is the only grass that can bear the heavy trampling of those vast herds. Hence, small as it is, it keeps possession as long as the buffaloes remain; but when they are driven off, the larger and coarser grasses come in and smother it. (Copley, 1867)

THE PLAINS OR PRAIRIES (FOR THEY ARE AS MUCH PRAIRIES AS the bare country of Illinois) are changing as respects their vegetation—The "Buffalo Grass" is passing away and other grasses replacing it, and vegetation in forms of weeds one, two, or three and four feet high are thick, when two or three years ago, [there] was nothing higher than the universal grass, only two or 3 inches high. (Watson, letter to his mother, 29 October 1875)

WHILE EXPERIENCING THE DELIGHTS OF A SHORT RIDE IN A "prairie schooner," or Government wagon recently, an incident occurred, which seems sufficiently curious and interesting to warrant a brief description:

It was while riding over the prairie between this post and Mr. Sternberg's farm, on the "Smoky," I saw a large hawk (whose motion a [sic] had been watching for some time) descend suddenly as if pouncing on something and commence struggling with what I supposed must be a young rabbit, prairie chicken, or some other small game, and although but a short distance away, I was unable on account of the long grass to determine what it really was, until on coming quite near, the hawk slowly and heavily arose into the air, to a hight [sic] of about forty feet, bearing in his claws a large bull snake, whose contortions and twisting embarrassed the flight of the hawk to such an extent that he remained almost stationary for some time at the altitude before mentioned—during which period the snake apparently coiling himself about the body and wings of his captor so effectively, that they started all at once for "terra firma" more after the manner of an old boat than anything else I know of.

Being somewhat anxious to see how things were going to terminate, I left the wagon and started for the scene of conflict; nearing the spot I observed the hawk industriously going for the snake, tearing him with his beak and otherwise making a total wreck of the serpent; but who on my approach rose swiftly, bearing his victim, inanimate, defunct, in the shape of an inverted letter "U," and was soon lost to sight.

It reminded me somewhat of the "coat of arms" of some nation or other, or else somebody's trade mark, I am not sure which, representing as it did an eagle or other large bird—in flight, bearing in his talons a writhing snake. (*Ellsworth Reporter*, 29 August 1872)

EARLY ON TUESDAY MORNING WE RODE OUT OF KING CITY IN route for McPherson Centre. As we passed up the creek we saw legions of prairie chickens pursued by rapacious hawks. We felt sorry for the chickens and lost no opportunity to direct a pistol shot at their pursuers. (*Hutchinson News*, 31 October 1872)

Many detailed observations were recorded that indicated the settlers' abiding interest in the environment and in native animal life; the relationship between the gray wolf and the buffalo, in particular, was frequently noted:

WE HAVE OFTEN READ AND HEARD OF A PACK OF WOLVES AT-tacking a buffalo, but not of one wolf doing so; yet such was the case near Kingman on the 31st day of May last, as we are credibly informed by our old friend, J. K. Fical. It was about a mile and a half from Kingman. The buffalo was a two-year old bull while the wolf was of the largest size. The tactics of the wolf were to worry the buffalo down. He attacked from behind. At first the buffalo tried most energetically to gore his adversary, frequently chasing him fifty yards. As soon as the buffalo stopped, the wolf would renew the attack. At length the bull was so worried that he could not turn and could scarcely turn round. Taking advantage of his fatigue his adversary would viciously bite him on the hams, evidently aiming to cut the hamstrings. After watching the fight quite a while, and seeing that the bull would be vanquished, Mr. Fical crept forward to first shoot the wolf and then the buffalo, but before he got close enough Mr. Wolf saw him and fled precipitatedly, in which maneuvre he was imitated by Mr. Buffalo, both escaping the rifle of Fical. (*Hutchinson News*, 12 June 1873)

Prairie-dog villages were often constructed far from any free-flowing surface water. This led several settlers to speculate that prairie-dog burrows were deep enough to reach water. In other words, they reasoned, the prairie dogs, like the settlers, dug wells to obtain water.

DO PRAIRIE DOGS DIG WELLS?
Last summer one of the staff of the American Agriculturist, when in Nebraska, published information furnished him by Mr. M. T. Leech, then of Ogalalla, but now of Julesburg, Nebraska, to the effect that prairie dogs dig wells, each "dog town" being provided with one. It was asserted, among other things, that no matter how far down the water might

A winter attack by wolves. *Harper's New Monthly Magazine.*

be, the dogs would keep on digging until they reached it. Mr. Leech adding that he knew of one such well two hundred feet deep. These statement [sic] have been widely copied, and they have been several times denied by, among others, one of the professors of Yale college. We met Mr. Leech last fall in Wyoming territory, where he holds a responsible position in the railway employ, and he reiterates the original statements and affirms their truth, adding that if the skeptics will come to Sidney, Nebraska, they will find convincing proof of their accuracy. There is a town of 25 or 30 pet prairie dogs, about five rods from the track northwest of the railroad hotel. The owner of the praire [sic] dogs will show the visitor the well, and will tell him that about the first move the dogs made, after being located there, was to dig for water. At a point on the Kansas Pacific railroad not far from Buffalo station, the workmen in sinking a reservoir some time ago, struck one of these prairie dog wells, and followed it down to a depth of two hundred feet. Mr. Leech's statements were verified by Prof. Aughey, the well known geologist at the Nebraska state university, who informed us at Lincoln, that he had discovered these wells while making geological explorations along Logan river in northern Nebraska. Mr. Leech, who is a frontiersman of long experience, further informs us that there is no foundation for the prevailing notion that dogs, rattle snakes and owls occupy the same holes. When for one cause or another a prairie dog abandons a hole it is taken possession of by an owl, who stops it up with rubbish at about three or four feet from the mouth, and constructs its nest. Rattesnakes [sic] infest the dog towns for the purpose of preying upon the young dogs, and the eggs of the owl. Mr. Leech states that he has several times killed rattlesnakes, within the stomachs of which he has found on dissection youg [sic] prairie dogs three or four days old. (*Osborne County Farmer*, 30 January 1879)

Settlers recognized that snakes were not active during the colder months but remained in hibernacula. Occasionally, however, snakes were encountered during the winter—an unusual occurrence and quite notable:

A BULL SNAKE WAS LATELY FOUND NEAR PAOLA, NAVIGATING through the snow as lively as he would in summer. So report his captors, two brave quail hunters. (*Hutchinson News*, 23 January 1873)

REV. MITCHELL KILLED A RATTLESNAKE ON THE 19TH OF FEB-ruary. (*Hays City Sentinel*, 30 March 1878)

The settlers also expressed wonder at the showers of animals, such as fish and toads, in rainstorms:

THE FIRST SHOWER OF FISH THAT WE HAVE HEARD OF, AND perhaps the first on record, in this state fell about a mile east of Concordia, on W. S. Townsdin's place two weeks ago this evening. We do not know how far they extend, nor how many of them fell. Mr. T. gathered about four quarts, all about the same size. Jas. Kienard tells us that Oak creek was full of the same kind of fish, after that storm, which shows that some must have fallen in the creek, as they had never been seen in it before. The fish found on Mr. Townsdin's land cannot have come from the creek, for the spot was too elevated for the water of the creek to overflow it. (*Osborne County Farmer*, 29 June 1877)

THERE WAS A SHOWER OF YOUNG TOADS ALONG WITH THE rainstorm Sunday night. Next morning in some places, the ground was literally covered with them and they appeared to hop about as happy and serene as if nothing had happened to them. (*Osborne County Farmer*, 29 June 1877)

Wolves and coyotes were known to escape a trap by chewing off the limb held by the snare. When one did otherwise, it became newsworthy:

Prairie dog town. Kansas State Historical Society, Topeka.

HARVEY REMSNYDER SET HIM A TRAP LAST MONDAY AND caught a large grey wolf. The jaws of the trap seized upon but one toe of his wolfship and his failure to escape—minus one toe, of course—strikes us as being unprecidented [sic].
(*Hays City Sentinel*, 30 November 1878)

The following article compares at some length the coyote and the gray wolf:

THE COYOTE IS MUCH SMALLER THAN HIS GRAY BROTHER. THE latter is nearly as large as a Newfoundland dog, the former about twice the size of a cat. The coyote fancies a camp fire, and sits on a hillock within sight of its place, barking for hours. The gray wolf bays at the moon like a dog. Graham says he has seen them sitting on the highest rocks gazing at the bright orb with their heads thrown back uttering unearthly howls. The wolf scorns the coyote. When the large wolves drag down an old buffalo bull the coyotes huddle in the vicinity, licking their chops and barking, as though begging a share of the prey. Should these venture too near, the big fellows utter ominous growls, and the coyotes slink away, tails between their legs and head turned over their shoulders. The coyotes quickly determine the status of a hunter. If he finds him killing wolves he keeps at a respectful distance; but if he is only hunting bears, antelope or buffalo, the little fellow becomes quite social. While a bear hunter was butchering game, coyotes patiently watched his operation, and a gray wolf loped hungrily on an outer circle. The trapper threw a piece of meat to the small fellows, who ran off and were waylaid by the big wolf. They dropped the meat and returned, but seemed to learn nothing by experience for they fed the robber as long as the hunter chucked them the meat.

Many coyotes pick up their supplies in the prairie-dog colonies. If one is lurking in the streets and sees a dog away from his hole, he steals upon him with the utmost secrecy, striving to cut off his retreat. An old dog, however, is rarely caught napping. Some of the fraternity are sure to espy the wolf, and a warning bark sends the dog into his hole, with a tantalizing shake of the tail. The coyote despondingly peers into the hole, takes away the dirt with a paw, and sniffs at the lost meal. He gets his eye on another dog, and crawls toward the hole like a cat upon a mouse. The warning bark is again heard, and a second meal disappears. Infuriated by his disappointment, the wolf frequently turns upon the little sentry, and for a few seconds makes the sand fly from the entrance of his residence. Worn out by his futile efforts, he flattens himself upon the sand behind the hole, and, motionless as a statue, watches for hours. If the dog pops out his head he is gone. The wolf springs upon him, the jaws come together like the snap of a trap, and the helpless little canine is turned into a succulent supper. One Meier, a well known buffalo hunter, was riding across a dog town some years ago, when he saw what he supposed to be a dead coyote stretched out at one of the holes. He dismounted and lifted it by the tail, intending to take the body to camp and skin it. The coyote made a snap at his leg, wriggled from his grasp and sped over the prairie more surprised than the trapper. He was in a sound sleep when caught. But the coyote's greatest harvest is in the spring of the year, when they fatten themselves on the inexperienced young dogs caught wandering from home. Whole families enjoying the cool evening breeze on the mountains above their burrows are taken unawares, and the tender young snapped up before their parents can force them under the ground. (*Hutchinson News*, 6 February 1879)

Occasionally a trout from the headwaters of the Arkansas River in the Colorado Rockies would be caught far downstream:

A MOUNTAIN TROUT, WEIGHING THREE POUNDS, WAS CAUGHT in the Arkansas river, at this point, on Monday, by Lewis

Lownsberry, a boy. He fished it out of a shallow pond. Mountain trout have not been known to descend to this point; at least they have never been caught east of Pueblo. (*Dodge City Times*, 25 October 1879)

In 1878 a rather bizarre simulated buffalo chase and kill was scheduled for the Fourth of July in Hays City:

IN THE DAYS OF YORE THE FAVORITE PASTIME OF OUR BOYS was hunting buffalo; and as the noble bison roamed over the plains in countless numbers, there was plenty of it. But with the coming of civilization, this amusement made its exit.

Next Thursday however an opportunity to indulge in the sport of a buffalo chase will be offered the young man in whose bosom slumbers the fire of days gone by. Patton and Buckius have obtained a rampant young buffalo bull, and will turn loose the same on the large flat, south of the creek and west of the Fort, on the day indicated. The chase is free to all, upon the payment of two dollars each. The conditions are these: The bull is to have 100 yards start; and the hunters are to be mounted on ponies and armed with pistols. The man who kills the bull is entitled to his carcass. As an incentive to speed, a tin pan or two and a bunch of firecrackers are to be tied to his tail—the bull's tail, we mean; and these, in addition to the natural wildness of the animal, will send him over the course like a belated locomotive. Quite a number of our sports have already entered for the chase; and from present indications, there will be at least twenty-five starters. (*Hays City Sentinel*, 29 June 1878)

THE BUFFALO HUNT DID NOT COME OFF AS ANNOUNCED. VERY few entries were made and Patton & Buckius refused to put the bison in the field. (*Hays City Sentinel*, 6 July 1878)

A number of people advocated the slaughter of buffalo as a permanent solution to the Indian problem. Without the buffalo,

"The Chase." Kansas State Historical Society, Topeka.

they argued, the Indians would cease their hunts into the prairie, thereby removing the danger for early settlers:

WE BELIEVE THE COMPLETION OF THE KANSAS PACIFIC ROAD to Denver will be a practical settlement of the Indian question, so far as Kansas is concerned. It is a patent fact to all who are acquainted with the habits and character of the uncivilized Indians, that their deadly incursions are only to be apprehended within easy reach of favorable hunting grounds. So long as the buffaloes, crossing the Arkansas in the Spring, continue to range all along our western and northwestern frontier, just so long will they be followed by roving bands of Indians, from whom, however peaceful may be their professions, danger is always to be apprehended. Make the Arkansas the northern boundary of the buffalo range and the Indians will be kept beyond that boundary far more easily than by any treaties that can be made. This is what the railroad will accomplish. With frequent through trains to Denver, and the facilities which they will offer to hunters, the buffaloes will disappear in less than twelve months. At the first glance this may seem like a trifling theory, but we know it to be one that is entertained by the clearest military minds in this nation. (*Topeka Commonwealth*, 23 November 1869)

THESE MEN (THE BUFFALO HUNTERS) HAVE DONE IN THE last two years, and will do in the next year, more to settle the vexed Indian question than the entire Army has done in the last thirty years. They are destroying the Indian's commissary; and it is a well-known fact that an army losing its base of supplies is placed at a great disadvantage. Send them powder and lead, if you will; but, for the sake of lasting peace, let them kill, skin, and sell until the buffaloes are exterminated. Then your prairies can be covered with speckled cattle and the festive cowboy, who follows the

hunter as a second forerunner of advanced civilization.
(General Phil Sheridan, in Gard, 1960, p. 215)

Sometimes animals were used in the perpetuation of practical
jokes. An unsuspecting young man who feared snakes was the
victim of one such prank:

> A COUPLE OF YOUNG LADIES ON THURSDAY LAST, KILLED A
> rattlesnake and placed it on the sidewalk of west First street,
> hiding its bruised head between two planks, then stationing
> themselves behind a window at a neighboring house in order
> to see somebody jump. They did not wait long, for in a little
> time a young gent of legal proclivities approached. His easy,
> careless step indicated that he was returning to his office
> from dinner; and that he much appreciated the cigar in the
> fingers of his left hand. Everything however is subject to
> change. All at once our friend's cigar flew into the air, and
> his pleasant saunter resolved itself into a furious bound;
> which placed him far from his snakeship, but not content
> with escape, our hero, with remarkable activity sprang over
> a neighboring fence, seized a large stick and, with unabated
> activity, again cleared the fence and attacked the dead
> snake. The passiveness of the reptile made it a matter of but
> little difficulty for our friend to appreciate and understand
> the shouts of laughter from the window. He threw down the
> stick and affirms that he will get even with those girls if it
> takes him a year. (*Hutchinson News*, 11 May 1876)

Unfortunately, as previous tales have already indicated, some
wild animals were treated cruelly by the immigrants. One person
experimented with snakes by depriving them of food and water;
others tortured a raccoon:

> D. F. SHERMAN HAS BEEN TESTING THE LENGTH OF TIME A
> snake will live without food or water. He has had two young
> snakes of the Viper species confined in a box for seven weeks,

and they have nearly doubled in size. (*Russell County Record*, 28 June 1877)

A NIGHT WANDERER IN THE SHAPE OF A RACCOON WAS CAUGHT on the street, a few evenings since, by a party of "boys" who began to experiment on it by pouring some Old Bourbon down its throat. The "coon," however had not human strength, and laid down and died. Mean whiskey killed it. (*Hutchinson News*, 9 October 1876)

Many of the pioneers were expert marksmen, and many more thought they were. To display this prowess, various shooting events were promulgated throughout the frontier. In some cases anyone could participate, and in others one community would challenge another to enter its best marksmen:

A GRAND TURKEY SHOOT TOOK PLACE ON JOHN KINGMAN'S place, on Gypsum, last Friday. The shooting was done with a rifle at a distance of forty-five yards rest, or thirty yards off hand. Free Kingman was the champion shot and won sixteen birds. The boys report an immense time and all the sport they could ask for. (*Saline County Journal*, 28 December 1876)

Frequently, these "turkey shoots" lasted an entire day and became a social as well as a sporting event:

LOVE FOR THE CHASE, HUNTING, SHOOTING, FISHING, AND other outdoor sports are getting to be almost a mania among the Americans. They have copied copiously in this respect from the fellows "across the Rhine." It is the fashion now to own a gun, a horse and a dog. Without these essentials a man cannot, in the eye of the code, stand up and call himself a gentleman. He must talk gun, horse or dog, or be denominated a thribble-X greenhorn class. We happen to belong to the thribble-X greenhorn class for we have neither gun, horse nor dog, and we cannot speak gracefully of any one of the three gentlemanly articles. However, we like to associate with gentlemen, and consequently force ourself into their company when the occasion is offered. We did this last Saturday. A turkey-shoot took place at the George Prescott farm, on Gypsum creek. We were wheeled there by one of Hilton's fast-going teams, having as companions Lieut.-Gen. Eakin and Maj.-Gen. Baker. With us, also, were two spanking greyhounds and a bird dog. Promptly at 8 o'clock in the morning we were on our way. The roads were somewhat heavy; but what was that to us when weather, scenery, conversation and spirits were cheerful. A jack-rabbit would occasionally jump from the grass, the hounds and dog after him, and away they would all go sailing with velocity over the prairies. We did not suppose that a long-eared-jack rabbit could create near the fun that a long-eared jackass does. But such is the case, when the "hounds and hunters pursue." No jack-rabbit can "play for safety" when Eakin's hounds get after him. Neither can a jackass, except with his heels. By agreement we were to meet at the Prescott place, that morning, a party of gentlemen who had gone out the night before and stopped at the hospitable mansion of Mr. Frank Wilkeson. As we rode up to the shooting ground, the party aforesaid, composed of Frank Wilkeson, J. E. Robinson, Wm. Berg, W. R. Geis, John Ryan, J. N. Schwartz and Fred Kuhner, loomed up in the south, approaching us at a rapid rate. After unhitching and properly caring for our teams, we advanced to the shooting grounds. Several parties living in the neighborhood were already practicing with their guns. It was in a grove that the match was to take place—a grove nearly as lovely as our park. The grove is surrounded by Gypsum creek, whose clear waters now murmur sweetly night and day. It is of greater length and about the same width of the park. The ground is nicely carpeted with grass, which though faded and wilted even now makes a fine resting place for tired or lazy limbs. We admire the shrewdness and tact of the man who selected such a spot for a day's sport. The targets were soon arranged, the usual distance stepped off, and everything was ready for the shooting to commence. In the first match 11 turkeys were contested for. Each man had five shots. The following gentlemen were "entered": J E Robinson, F Wilkeson, H D Baker, J N Schwartz, W R Gels, Wm Tinkler, John Ryan, F Kingman, J H Kingman, Capt Eakin and Wm Berg. F Wilkeson won the first prize. Wm Tinkler the second and J H Kingman the third. The same party of gentlemen were entered for the second match, which resulted: F Wilkeson first prize; Wm Berg by W R Geis, second prize; F Kingman, third prize. Still another match was made, but we are unable to give the result. During the afternoon, when the boys were nearly starved to death, all were invited to partake of an excellent lunch provided by Mrs. F Wilkeson. Many were the thanks tendered to this lady for her kindness toward that poor, innocent and hungry little flock. About four o'clock the marksmen commenced dispersing. We came home with a bundle of turkeys presented to us by Messrs. Ryan and Geis. We were the only staid and dignified appendage to this expedition, and of course the boys thought we were entitled to some pay for our distinguished services. The shooting was good, although some of it might have been better. Of course we make no allusion to those who did not hit the tree at all. We are ready for another trip of the kind. (*Saline County Journal*, 8 February 1877)

In other contests, live pigeons were released at specified distances and the marksmen attempted to shoot them within specified boundaries. Domestic tame pigeons were sometimes used, and in other cases pigeons were trapped elsewhere and imported for the sportsmen. One can only speculate as to whether these were the common pigeon we have all come to know or whether they might have been the now extinct passenger pigeon.

PIGEON SHOOTING IS A NEW SPORT AMONG THE SALINA hunters. A pigeon-shooting match came off on the vacant land west of Geo. C. Probert's Ninth street property, last

Friday afternoon. It was conducted by Mr. S. W. Jones—an expert in this business. He had fixed the trap and marked the boundary lines, and had some forty tame pigeons in cages. About half hast [sic] 5 o'clock the shooting commenced. There were Skancke, Garver, Fred. Wildman, Seaton, Cunningham and Clarkson—all rated good-shots. The word "ready" pronounced, and up would go the pigeon—most of the time unharmed—and away it would fly toward the neighboring church spires. All of them seemed to be religiously inclined, as those who did not "bite the dust" invariably anchored in some church tower. Frank Seaton made the largest score. Only eight birds were killed, all told; and Salina's best shots were on the ground. What was the matter with the boys? (*Saline County Journal*, 1 June 1876)

THERE WERE AT THE COMMENCEMENT OF THE TOURNAMENT 3,500 pigeons for the use of the shooters. They were trapped in Wisconsin and Michigan and purchased by Mr. Willis Kesler [sic] at Chicago. (*Saline County Journal*, 9 October 1879)

Finally there was glass-ball shooting in which marksmen attempted to hit glass balls thrown in the air. This method of displaying marksmanship has come down today in the form of modern "skeet," "blue-rock," or "clay-pigeon" shooting contests:

THERE SEEMS TO BE A GROWING INTEREST AMONG THE SHOTgun votaries of Ellis County. Last Saturday the following-named gentlemen indulged in a series of glass-ball matches at Ellis, making the total scores set opposite their names:—

Dr. Davis	29	out of possible	39
B. T. Brooks	20	" "	"
F. C. Montgomery	32	" "	"
Charley Smith	30	" "	"
William Judd	20	" "	35

F. C. Montgomery made the best "run," breaking fourteen consecutively. Charley Smith's shooting was excellent
after the first three matches, when he seemed to get down
to his work, as it were. Brooks fell far below his average
shooting, while Davis and Judd added to their reputations
as marksmen.

The boys have arranged for a match in Hays tomorrow,
when Ellis boys are expected down. A match with Wa-
Keeney is also on the tapis. (*Hays City Sentinel,* 29 August
1879)

These instances make clear that many settlers had a genuine
interest in the native fauna with which they shared the ecosystem. They enjoyed their presence, not only aesthetically but also
for the many benefits derived from the native wildlife. At the
same time, however, other species of wildlife became adversaries,
impeding the frontiersman in his farming and ranching activities
and in some cases threatening his very existence.

CHAPTER 4

Nuisances, Hazards,
and Dangers

As immigrants moved into western Kansas, there were many opportunities for contact with the native wildlife. Although this contact was often to the settlers' advantage, in that they quickly discovered a rich source of food, income, recreation, and natural beauty in the animals, it also presented problems. These ranged from mild inconveniences to possible injury or death.

Minor problems included such sundry nuisances as untoward encounters with skunks, birds in homes and public buildings, incessant noise generated by the woodpecker's hammering, animals burrowing through dikes, buffalo breaking telegraph poles, and the odor of bone piles awaiting shipment at the local rail station. The prairie dog, too, proved to be a hazard at times, when a settler's horse would step into the opening of a burrow and break its leg.

The little English sparrow became a common inhabitant, and a nuisance, around most homesteads. Although some farmers had great hopes that these sparrows would control insects (see chapter 3), a few less boisterous voices argued that the sparrow would not eat many insects at all, as it was primarily a seed-eating species and would eventually become a greater nuisance than the insects. The settlers should have listened to these quieter, more astute, voices.

A major hazard, however, was the depredation of crops and livestock by many of the native animals. Most settlers who staked claims on the prairie did so in the hope of becoming prosperous farmers. These homesteaders usually had a small flock of chickens, and small herds of one or more kinds of larger livestock, such as cattle, sheep, and hogs. Often there was a garden in which vegetables were raised, and perhaps a fruit tree or two. The farmer hoped to produce enough to feed his family with ample amounts remaining to sell on the market. However, the livestock, croplands, and gardens so carefully tended by the settler attracted a variety of native animals, both herbivorous and carnivorous, that caused considerable depredation. To understand the underlying reasons for these unforeseen damages, it is necessary to examine the energy budget of an animal.

Herbivores do not eat every kind of plant encountered—some they find distasteful, others have natural protection, such as thorns. Herbivores thus prefer some species of plants and avoid others. Likewise, carnivores will not eat all species of prey they might encounter—although they do tend to be somewhat opportunistic and usually consume what is readily available.

No food item comes "free of charge" to any animal. To obtain food, animals have to expend energy. An efficient animal will limit its expenditure of energy as much as possible. For example, if potential food items of sufficient nutritional value are scarce and therefore relatively unavailable, an animal will have to spend considerable energy searching for the food of choice. No herbivore or carnivore, if it expects to survive, can expend an exhaustive amount of energy detecting, capturing, and consuming food.

In typical predator/prey interactions, prey species have evolved various mechanisms to avoid being captured and eaten. Two examples are the swift locomotion of jackrabbits and antelope, and the cryptic behavior and coloration of deer and antelope fawn. These and other methods of avoiding detection and capture, however, require a predator to "work harder," thereby expending more energy.

When settlers planted gardens and monocultural crops— wheat, oats, barley, corn—they created an absolute heaven for any herbivore that found these species palatable. After all, the plant adjacent to the one just consumed is just as palatable and nutritional, and the herbivore need expend little energy to locate it. The inevitable result was the depredation of gardens, crops, and fruit trees by a variety of native wildlife including mice, gophers, prairie dogs, rabbits, antelope, geese, cranes, and, of course, grasshoppers.

Native species of predators including the swift fox, skunk, gray wolf, mountain lion, raccoon, opossum, and coyote turned to the immigrant's livestock as a source of food. This development, too, was inevitable, as habitat degradation, and excessive hunting of these carnivores' natural prey, resulted in the reduction, or even elimination, of the predators' food source. Secondly, domestic livestock often were sequestered in corrals or shelters, allowing predators to expend minimum energy to capture them.

Reactions to this depredation of crops and livestock were varied. Poisoning, hunting, trapping, and paying bounties were all used to control destructive animals. Bounty acts were passed to encourage the hunting and trapping of wolves, coyotes, wildcats, foxes, rabbits, and gophers whereby the scalps of these animals could be turned in for cash. Because this practice was up to the discretion of each county, not all counties were involved; often one implemented a bounty-act law while adjacent ones did not.

In general these laws were ineffective in removing undesirable animals for two reasons: First, by removing undesirable species from a participating county a vacuum was created. If surrounding counties did not participate in removing the same pests, members of that species would immigrate to fill the void. Second, the law was abused in that animals taken in a county that did not invoke the option were transported to a county that did. There is little doubt that many of the scalps submitted for payment were from nonparticipating counties.

Damage done to trees and shrubs by rodents and rabbits was ameliorated by applying repellents of various kinds on or near the food items, or by using a physical barrier such as tar paper. Hawks were always viewed as undesirable species, as they were often observed killing poultry and other livestock. These birds were never protected by the early laws (chapter 5). Settlers failed to recognize their value in controlling more damaging pests such as rats, mice, and rabbits.

Some immigrants believed their lives were in danger from mountain lions and gray wolves. Mountain lions were probably more curious than intent upon attack. However, a number of reports indicated that people were pursued and occasionally attacked by both mountain lions and wolves. Probably most reports were more myth than truth; however, an exceedingly hungry gray wolf might be bold enough to attack a person. If these attacks indeed took place, they were most likely conducted by the gray wolf rather than the prairie wolf, or coyote, whose demeanor is much less ferocious. These incidents seldom resulted in death.

In hunting big-game animals there was always a chance that injured game might charge and harm the hunter. This did indeed happen, though infrequently. In one instance danger did exist when a settler decided to keep some native animals restrained within a zoological park. Failing to take proper precautions with the "pet" elk resulted in the deaths of three men. Occasionally even the introduced barn rats proved harmful. These rodents were not only a nuisance in fouling dry goods around the home, but in one case, at least, attacked and killed a young child.

Snakes presented another problem. All snakes are ectothermic (cold-blooded) and seek areas of relative warmth during the winter. As temperatures decline during autumn, the denning urge begins, and snakes migrate toward locations where they can find their way below the frost line and hibernate. In rocky locations this is often in deep crevasses; in open prairies snakes seek shelter in the burrows of mammals such as the badger and prairie dog. Klauber (1982) reports a correspondent's observation on the denning of prairie rattlesnakes thusly:

FULLY NINETY PERCENT OF THE MATURE RATTLERS CONGRE-gate annually in groups of from fifty to several hundred to hibernate in the same den. I think about 250 is the average number hibernating together, though I know of several times this number using some dens. The first frost starts them toward their winter refuge. Slowly but surely they find their way back. The old snakes seem to lead the way and the young ones, that is, the one- and two-year-olds, follow their trails. I have watched them coming to their dens for hours. It is my opinion that the majority of the young-of-the-year do not go to the dens, except where the older snakes hibernate in prairie-dog towns. I think these little ones seek ground holes and similar places of refuge. In fact, I occasionally find that even adult stragglers survive the winter in small burrows, such as are dug by the striped gopher.

There are two requirements essential for a den, depth and dryness. Snakes hibernate only in places that are not subject to floods, and in dens penetrating to a depth below the frost line. They must find such holes or cavities as nature provides. Prairie dogs and badgers are the only burrowing animals that dig deep enough holes; consequently on the open prairie many groups hibernate in dog towns. (P. 115)

In some cases a single den may contain from fifty to a thousand rattlesnakes. Other snakes will also congregate in these hibernacula with rattlesnakes, and all benefit from heat and moisture conservation (Klauber, 1982). On warm days in the late fall and early spring, the snakes will often lie about on the surface of the prairie-dog town. The activity just described, as snakes move to and from den sites, heralds both winter and spring. These were also the times, the early settlers found, when they could make easy kills.

Sometimes poisonous snakes would occupy dugouts and outbuildings, thus bringing them into close proximity to the settlers and their livestock. This resulted in many domestic animals— and, of course, the settlers themselves—being bitten. In most cases victims survived; often they did not. In the newspapers I have consulted, sixty-five cases of poisonous snakebite were reported. Of this total thirty-nine were children and twenty-six adults. Of the children bitten twenty-one (54 percent) survived and eighteen (46 percent) died, whereas twenty-three (88 percent) of the adults survived and only three (12 percent) died. Most of the fatalities on the frontier due to snakebite were children, who, because of their small body size, could not absorb the effects of the venom as could an adult. Those who survived did so either because the snake had a dry bite or did not get enough venom injected, or because the children were large enough to disseminate the poison without death occurring.

Current thinking on poisonous snakebites suggests that most adults, if bitten, would survive even if they received no treatment whatsoever. Such, however, is not true of a child. Today both child and adult are usually treated with antivenin shots; this type of remedy was not available, though, to the frontiersman. Newspapers reported the available treatments: In nine of thirty-seven cases of rattlesnake bite the only treatment given was whiskey. In another nine cases aid was given to the victim by sucking on the bite to remove the venom. In three cases soda and ammonia were applied to the bite, and whiskey was given internally. In many instances some sort of poultice was applied to draw out the poison. The primary ingredient in these poultices varied: Wet soda and kerosene, milk, iodine and iodine potassium, olive oil, hartshorn and sweet oil, coal oil, tobacco, indigo, salt, gunpowder, salt and egg yolk, bromide of potassium, corn snakeroot, indigo, and camphor were all used.

Hydrophobia (rabies) was also a danger to the settler. Skunks and canids—dogs, coyotes, gray wolves—are particularly susceptible to the rabies virus. During the course of the disease the animal may become uncontrollable and bite another animal or human, perhaps then passing the virus to the bitten individual.

The standard "cure" was to purchase the use of a madstone. According to Coffin (1976) the madstone was formed in the heart of a buck deer once every generation; therefore, these stones were quite rare. When applied to the bite, the stone adhered to the body until all of the virus had been drawn out. The madstone was found in the Midwest and was light in weight, porous, and green in color. Although we know today that the madstone had no healing power, the owner of such a stone could always claim that the patient, if he or she died, had not procured the use of the stone quickly enough. If the person lived, then obviously the stone was effective. Of course, the reason the madstone "worked" at all was that the victim had not contracted the disease.

Hunting and fishing involved still other dangers. Tragic hunting accidents in which individuals were either injured or killed were common. In some cases guns malfunctioned, and in others the hunter was careless. Occasionally fishing accidents resulted in drownings. Early in the settlement period hunting parties sometimes encountered bands of Indians who were often openly hostile to the encroachment of settlers onto their hunting grounds. Death of the settler was often the result.

Adverse weather conditions also took their toll. Hunting animals for pelts, from which coats and robes were made, usually took place in the winter, when the fur was of prime quality, and when meat could be shipped east without being dried and jerked. These hunts were often extended and required the hunter to be on the range for days, or even weeks, at a time. The abruptness and intensity of winter storms frequently caught hunters without protective cover, resulting in frozen feet and sometimes death.

Of all the various nuisances and hazards involved in sharing the environment with vertebrates, though, smaller animals were everyday pests, and skunks were among the most common. They developed a quasi-commensal relationship with the settlers and seemed to be particularly attracted to houses and outbuildings, often providing comedic encounters with the settlers, as the following accounts indicate:

> A WEDDING IN CLOUD COUNTY WAS POSTPONED LAST WEEK, because the bridegroom accidentally tread on the tail of a cat while walking to the domicile of his intended, the night the wedding was to take place. The cat was one of those dark-complexioned fellows that flourish a bushy tail when tread upon, and take the cologne out of a fellow's clothers [sic] in about one-eighteenth of a second. (*Hays City Sentinel*, 27 April 1878)

> A SKUNK WAS KILLED THE OTHER DAY. THE ELLUVIA [*SIC*] arising from the fetid liquor had become extremely offensive to the deniszens [sic] on Military Avenue. The nasty cross between a weasel and an otter was disspatched [sic] to eternity with broomsticks—and the chivalrous ladies on the avenue did it. (*Dodge City Times*, 31 August 1878)

Bird nests proved to be another nuisance, particularly those of pigeons, swallows, martins, and house or English sparrows. The nests, built in houses, barns, and public buildings, were not only unsightly but harbored lice and offensive fecal droppings:

THE MUD SWALLOWS HAVE TAKEN POSSESSION OF THE EXTE-
rior of the court house and are building their nests under
the eaves. Having been ordered from Ft. Harker by the
Government they thus seek to become citizens of our city.
(*Ellsworth Reporter*, 11 June 1874)

AN ARMY OF SWALLOWS SETTLED UNDER THE EAVES OF THE
court house at Great Bend suddenly migrated in a body to
the Catholic church. The noise of the lawyers was too
much for them. (*Dodge City Times*, 31 May 1879)

Dr. Coues, medical doctor and noted ornithologist, forecast
that the sparrows themselves would become almost as great a
problem as the grasshoppers that they were imported to control.
He wrote the following letter to a local paper:

TO THE EDITOR OF THE COMMONWEALTH.
I notice in your locals this morning, that the governor
has received a letter from Mr. Austin Corbin, of New York,
who is in London, suggesting that English swallows be imported into every county in Kansas, to devour the grasshoppers and other insects. I presume sparrows are meant. This
would be a needless expense, as there are enough English
sparrows in Topeka to populate every county in five years if
they were distributed. But this distribution throughout the
state would have little effect upon the grasshoppers. The
English sparrow is eminently a city gentleman, and doesn't
care to associate with the rustics of the rural districts. He
will clean out the worms from the trees of a large city and
its parks, but beyond that, his ravages on the insects of a
country, I do not believe are very extensive. A few years
ago, seventy-five English sparrows were turned loose in
Philadelphia. The city then was literally covered with
worms in the summer months. Now it is covered with sparrows, so to speak, and not a worm on the trees in its streets
and parks is ever seen. E. (*Commonwealth*, 3 July 1877)

DR. ELLIOTT COUES OF WASHINGTON, A DISTINGUISHED NAT-
uralist, declares that the English sparrow devours insects
only when it cannot get garbage, grain or young green herbs
to eat; that it is fast becoming a pest and nuisance in this
country: and that if these birds spread over the west, they
will become a "plague scarcely less formidable than the
grasshoppers." Dr. Coues will soon publish a pamphlet on
this subject. (*Ellis County Star*, 1 May 1879)

Birds such as woodpeckers require trees in which to nest and
to search for food. Once taller buildings such as churches and
courthouses were constructed, woodpeckers often "hammered"
away—a practice that was seldom appreciated:

THE *UNION*, OF JUNCTION CITY, SAYS THE WOOD PECKERS
have commenced their annual attack upon the steeple of a
certain church in that town. (*Ellsworth Reporter*, 3 June
1875)

At least one settler found the habits of ground squirrels to be
particularly costly:

A FARMER NEAR NEW BADEN, DICKINSON COUNTY, WHO DE-
posited his money in the walls of his dug-out, has been
robbed of his deposits by ground squirrels. (*Larned Optic*, 25
July 1879)

Bones that helped many a farmer survive financially were
viewed as a nuisance by others. Like the authors of the following
paragraphs, many settlers complained bones were unsightly, foul
smelling, and a potential source of fatal illnesses.

WITHIN TWENTY RODS OF THE GRAPHIC OFFICE, ALMOST IN
the center of town, one hundred and twenty tons of buffalo
bones and refuse lie piled and sweltering in the torrid heat
of the August sun, to the great annoyance of our citizens
who reside to the windward. We insist upon our dealers

Buffalo bones awaiting shipment. Kansas State Historical Society, Topeka.

having this nuisance abated. Pile your ossified nuisance at the stock yard switch. (*Kinsley Graphic*, 3 August 1878)

FIFTY-ONE CITIZENS OF SPEARVILLE HAVE SIGNED PETITIONS, asking that there be no more bones piled within one mile of the town, alleging the reason, that they are the cause of the fatal sickness that has visited the town. (*Larned Optic*, 19 December 1879)

One town even passed an ordinance against piling bones within the village limits:

AN ORDINANCE PROHIBITING THE UNLOADING AND PILING OF Bones of Dead Animals in the City of Kinsley, and to Provide for the Punishment of such Offenses. Be it Ordained by the Mayor and Councilmen of the City of Kinsley;

SECTION 1. The depositing, unloading from wagons, or storing of bones of dead animals in the corporate limits of the city of Kinsley, except at the stock yards, is hereby prohibited.

SEC. 2. Any person or persons violating section 1 of this ordinance shall be deemed guilty of a misdemeanor, and upon conviction shall be fined not less than five dollars nor more than ten dollars for each offense. (*Kinsley Graphic*, 31 May 1879)

Prairie dogs were common in the short-grass prairies grazed by buffalo. These colonial rodents lived in "towns" and constructed extensive burrow systems. Occasionally, however, mules and horses stepped into burrow entrances, resulting in the rider's taking a tumble and often being injured. One such instance is described in the following excerpt:

ON SUNDAY MORNING LAST, WHILE AN ESCORT OF THE 10TH Infantry, were about sixty miles southwest of here one of the number met with a serious accident. It seems that Private Anderson, of "A" Company, was riding a blind mule, and the animal stepping into a prairie dog hole, he was thrown over its head, breaking his fore arm. By the time the Fort was reached the arm had become so badly swollen that it was impossible to set it for some time. (*Ellis County Star*, 8 June 1876)

Sometimes even aquatic animals turned out to be pests and proved to be more than a minor nuisance to those people whose homes were flooded as a result:

A MUSK RAT BORED A HOLE THROUGH THE EMBANKMENT OF the mill race at Hutchinson, and a part of that city is again under water. (*Kinsley Graphic*, 11 January 1879)

Buffalo often found the telegraph poles set alongside railroad track to be ideal for rubbing against and scratching themselves. This practice resulted in the breakage of many poles.

THE BUFFALOES FOUND IN THE TELEGRAPH POLES OF THE overland line a new source of delight on the treeless prairie—the novelty of having something to scratch against, but it was expensive scratching for the telegraph company; and there, indeed, was the rub, for the bisons shook down miles of wire daily. A bright idea struck somebody to send to Saint Louis and Chicago for all the brad awls that could be purchased, and these were driven into the poles with a view to wound the animals and check their rubbing propensity. Never was there a greater mistake. The buffaloes were delighted. For the first time they came to scratch sure of a sensation in their thick hides that thrilled them from horn to tail. They would go fifteen miles to find a brad awl. They fought huge battles around the poles containing them, and the victor would proudly climb the mountainous heap of the fallen and scratch himself into bliss until the brad awl broke or the pole came down. There has been no demand for brad awls from the Kansas region since the first invoice. (*Junction City Weekly Union*, 25 April 1869)

Settlers planted gardens, crops, and trees that became food items for various species of native wild animals. The gopher, with its fossorial behavior of living underground, tended to attack corn, squash, and trees from below ground. As the following excerpts indicate, some settlers resorted to trapping, and to poisoning with strychnine:

MR. EDITOR.—I HAVE BEFORE ME A NEW STYLE OF TRAP called Walker's Mirror rat trap, which is a sure thing on gophers. If every person who has any trees or hedges, or ever expects to have any, would get this trap—which is for sale at 50 cts each by E. Wilcox & Co., and set it in the hole or underground roadway wherever a gopher shows his work, thousands of trees, and miles of hedge and a vast amount of disappointment might be saved every year. I have tried a great many ways to destroy gophers, but never found anything before so effectual as this trap. I won't attempt to describe the trap, but advise everyone having gophers to dispose of to call at Wilcox's hardware store, examine and make a purchase. S. T. Kelsey. (*Hutchinson News*, 24 July 1873)

E. F. VAUGHAN'S BIG SQUASH, OF WHICH MENTION WAS MADE some time ago, was raided by a gopher. It had grown to the enormous weight of one hundred and ninety pounds. The gopher bored into it on the lower side and stopped its growth. (*Hutchinson News*, 28 October 1875)

THE BEST WAY TO POISON GOPHERS IS TO USE STRYCHNIA IN crystals. Powdered will do, but it is not as convenient. Take a potato or piece of one not larger than a walnut, make an incision in it and insert the poison about double the size of the head of a pin; open the hole where the gopher is working, and put in the prepared potato, then close up the place where the hole was opened. The potato should be put far enough in the hole, so it will not get covered when filling up the opening. In the morning and evening, particularly in the spring and fall, a good many holes can be found open and the poison can be placed in them with but little trouble, but the opening must be closed in every instance as the gopher when he sees a window takes a load of dirt and proceeds to stop it up and would usually cover up the intended morsel. I have tried boys, dogs, traps, etc., for several years and have now to say that the above is the only effectual remedy I have struck; and I set it down as a conclusive fact that with strychnine and a little diligence, trees, hedges, etc., can be successfully cultivated even though gophers abound. (*Hutchinson News*, 7 June 1877)

Trees were not only a valuable commodity to the settlers but also to the native beaver. Beaver were controlled easily by trapping:

A NUMBER OF BEAVERS CARRY ON THE "TIMBER CHAWING trade" on the river, just above the Park. The boys think of trapping them. (*Saline County Journal*, 24 August 1876)

Rabbits were a problem too. Most of their damage was done in the winter, when food became scarce. They would even turn to eating the bark from young trees, and if girdled, the tree would often die. Control methods included trapping, hunting, and wrapping the tree trunks to protect against gnawing.

EVERY PERSON WHO HAS YOUNG ORCHARD TREES, SHOULD SEE to it immediately that they are protected against the depredations of rabbits. The prairie grass and almost everything is now killed by the frost, and the rabbits have little to feed upon except the tender bark of young trees, and they may girdle and destroy every tree in an orchard in a single night. There are many remedies recommended to protect the trees, such as rubbing with dead rabbit, or any other fresh meat, liver, bacon, or lard, whitewashing etc., nearly all of which I have tried, but while they will protect the trees for awhile and sometimes all winter, yet if the rabbits get really hungry, they will gnaw through and kill the trees. And the application of grease sometimes kills them—I mean the trees, not the rabbits.

The best and only certain remedy that I have yet found is to wrap the trees, so that the rabbits can't get at them. For this purpose anything will do that is cheap and handy, only put on enough to cover the tree as high up as a rabbit can reach, and tie on with good strong twine. I have used strong paper, cloth, corn stalks, and straw, and prairie hay, and while all of them answer the purpose, I prefer the prairie hay, for convenience and cheapness.

A man will tie up from three to four hundred in a day making an expense of not over one cent per tree. The rabbits have already commenced girdling trees, and those who wish to save their orchards, should lose no time in protecting them. (*Hutchinson News,* 13 November 1873)

TO PREVENT RABBITS FROM INJURING YOUR TREES, WASH them as high up as there is danger, with a dilution of fresh cow manure. Mr. A. S. Dimock, of Valley, informs us that he has tried this prescription for the last four years, and it has never failed. It is a preventive that is in the reach of every one. Try it.

Another remedy is said to be this. Kill a rabbit, cut it open and rub the tree with the fresh bloody parts of it. This is said to be very effectual. (*Hutchinson News,* 14 December 1876)

Mice of certain species also gnawed on trees. Wrapping the tree in tar paper was the following writer's suggested mode of protection:

WITH THE RETURN OF EACH SUCCEEDING SPRING THE PRAIRIE farmer is asked for a method or specific to save young trees that have been girdled by mice during the preceding winter. The various methods which are employed in repairing such injuries have been given, but, of course, they cannot always be effectual. Prevention, in this case as in others, is better than cure, and now is the time to prepare for and guard against this threatened injury.

It is only after snow falls that the depredations of the vermin occur, and it is not very difficult to head them off. The mice work under the snow and near the ground. To circumvent them it is only necessary to effectually exclude them from the foot of the tree. Various modes of doing this are employed, but the simplest and best, because the cheapest and most effective, is tarred paper, or, as it is commonly called, roofing felt. It can be had at almost any village, and is always found in towns of considerable population. It may be cut in strips of proper size, and these should be long enough to reach from the collar of the tree to a point up the bole beyond which the depth of snow will not probably reach. It should be tied tightly with twine.

A small outlay of money and time now may save valuable trees, which have cost far more in cash, besides the labor of preparing the ground, setting them out, and attending to them thus far.

Other materials may be used for the same purpose, but nothing is as good as roofing felt. (*Kirwin Chief,* 17 December 1879)

Wild geese, white cranes (egrets), blackbirds, and rabbits used the growing crops for food. Wild geese and cranes created depressions in the soil as they dusted themselves, and by so doing destroyed the wheat. Control methods focused on shooting the pests.

WILD GEESE ARE PLAYING HAVOC WITH THE WHEAT FIELDS along the Arkansas river—says the Arkansas *Traveler.* (*Ellsworth Reporter,* 15 April 1875)

THIS HAS BEEN A PROLIFIC SEASON FOR BLACKBIRDS, ESPEcially around the numerous lakes in Valley township. I am in favor of the preservation of birds. Most of them are the farmers friend, but the blackbirds are his worst enemy. They are not insectivorous birds, but go for grain of all kinds. In the spring they pull up our corn, during harvest they go for our wheat and oats, and then for the corn fields. They have eaten up acres of my corn. While the corn is green they strip down the husk and eats off the corn perhaps half the length of the ear, and then go to next. They so utterly destroyed a portion of my corn, that I was obligated to cut it for fodder. Some are in favor of the blackbirds. They say they only open the ends of the ear of corn, to get the worm usually found there, but I have got the dead-wood on them, I have watched them, in one instance after they had been getting out worms for some time, I shot three of them, found no worms in their crops, but plenty of corn. They had pulled the worms out on to the ground with their beaks. But their best friend was rather down on them last spring, for they pulled up his corn, so he advised the farmers to mix coal oil with water and soak the corn in it before planting. This was the first time that I ever heard oil and water would mix, and this gentleman is really entitled to great credit for the discovery. His farmer friends here think if he keeps on, he will soon find the philosopher's stone. But as I could not get my oil to mix with the water, I soaked my corn in the oil alone, but it had no effect upon the blackbirds. They liked the corn just as well. I suppose the chemical action of the soil had extracted the offensive oil flavor, on the principle that our grandmother used to advise us boys to bury our clothes after we had been skunk hunting.

Now my remedy for these pests, is a double barreled shot gun, in the hands of an enthusiastic boy. (*Hutchinson News*, 7 October 1875)

WINTER WHEAT IS LOOKING EXCELLENT IN THIS SECTION. THE jack-rabbits, however, are reported to be destroying small fields in some parts of the county. More grey-hounds are needed. (*Smith County Pioneer*, 2 November 1876)

WILD GEESE AND WHITE CRANES [EGRETS] ARE DOING THEIR best to acquire their share of the growing wheat crop, and some of our folks are doing *their* best to secure their share of said geese and cranes. (*Pawnee County Herald*, 14 April 1877)

THERE ARE A GREAT MANY YELLOW-HEADED BLACK BIRDS IN Langdon township, which have done much damage by pulling up the young corn and scratching up the millet seeds that were recently sown. But they are supposed to have aided the cold wet weather in killing the young 'hoppers, as none are left. B. P. HANAN (Langdon). (*Hutchinson News*, 17 May 1877)

PRAIRIE CHICKENS ARE VERY NUMEROUS—HELPING THEM-selves to the unhusked corn. (Bridge). (*Saline County Journal*, 26 December 1878)

Prairie dogs are primarily herbivores, living on the grasses and forbs of the prairie. As grasslands were broken for crops, prairie dogs became pests after the corn and wheat. Attempted control measures included shooting and spreading poisons in the burrows:

THE PRAIRIE DOGS ARE MAKING TERRIBLE HAVOC ON CORN and wheat fields in our immediate neighborhood. The farm-ers have waged war on them and say they intend to drive them away. (Smolan). (*Saline County Journal*, 12 June 1879)

And during the late 1860s and early 1870s, antelope and buf-falo not only ate but trampled the crops in the field:

IN 1870, THE AMOUNT OF CROPS PLANTED, CONSISTED OF about three acres of sod corn, a few beans and vines. But, the buffalo which were about the only inhabitants that could be utilized by man, and which roamed these hills in vast herds, completely demolished that small planting and nothing came to maturity. (*Smith County Pioneer*, 27 July 1876)

DROVES OF ANTELOPE FEED ON THE WHEAT FIELDS OF OUR county daily. (*Ellis County Star*, 4 January 1877)

Both the gray wolf and prairie wolf, or coyote, turned to domestic livestock and fowl for prey when available. Many edi-tors reporting the depredations simply referred to "wolves," and which species was actually involved remains unclear, though the gray wolf was probably to blame for killing larger animals than the coyote killed.

> OUR FRIEND DODGE FROM COAL CREEK CALLED ON US THE other day and says the wolves are numerous in his section; that they are killing calves and the other night succeeded in killing a cow. (*Ellsworth Reporter,* 29 February 1872)

> ELLIS COUNTY POSSESSES THOUSANDS OF THE GENUS COYOTE, and while their depredations never extend to the slaughter of humans they are inflicting incalculable damage upon herds, flocks, and poultry yards. Speaking on this subject, Mr. Tom Hamilton says . . . that a short time ago he and one or two others put out some poison and the next day found between forty and fifty dead wolves lying about, while the number of live animals seemed in no wise decreased. (*Hays City Sentinel,* 9 July 1880)

The smallest fox on the open prairie was the swift fox. This species was deemed to be a pest, eating chiefly chickens. A popular method of capture, at least in the Hays City area, was to "drown" them out of their burrows.

> IN COMPANY WITH TRACEY, LOWRY, BAZIN AND GUNTHER, WE went out on Monday afternoon to capture some young swifts. After emptying 27 buckets of water in the hole, we induced two to surrender. A mere mention of the fun we experienced would infringe upon our space. (*Ellis County Star,* 20 July 1876)

As with canids, there were two species of felids that also, from time to time, turned to domestic livestock as a source of food. These were the catamount, or mountain lion, and the wildcat, which we now refer to as the bobcat. Generally, the mountain lion took larger species of prey than did the smaller bobcat, as the following excerpt suggests:

"Prairie wolves" baying at the moon. *Harper's New Monthly Magazine.*

AN ANIMAL SUPPOSED TO BE A MOUNTAIN LION HAS KILLED
nine head of cattle and a number of sheep in Trego County.
(*Hays City Sentinel,* 13 June 1879)

Smaller animals such as the raccoon, opossum, and skunks
also preyed on livestock. The preferred prey was the domestic
chicken:

A SKUNK KILLED ONE-HUNDRED AND TWENTY-FIVE SPRING
chickens for a farmer near Ellis last week. (*Hays City Sentinel,* 19 July 1876)

TWO YOUNG MEN FROM OSBORNE COUNTY KILLED A LARGE
raccoon on Mr. Warner's lot last Tuesday evening. His
coonship was after Mr. Evans' chickens.—(Kirwin Progress) (*Russell County Record,* 13 September 1877)

FOURTEEN OPOSSUMS WERE KILLED IN ONE HEN-HOUSE, BY
one man, in one night recently, at Chanute—and it wasn't
a very good night for possums, neither. (*Hays City Sentinel,*
25 May 1878)

Sometimes hawks attacked and killed domestic fowl. One
farmer reversed the roles of predator and prey with the result
that the chickens killed the hawk:

GILBERT WHITE TELLS A MOST DRAMATIC STORY OF A NEIGH-
bor who had lost most of his chickens by a sparrow hawk
that came gliding down between a faggot pile and the end
of his house, to the place where his coops stood. The owner,
vexed to see his flock diminishing, hung a net between the
pile and the house, into which the bird dashed and was en-
tangled. The gentleman's resentment suggested a fit retalia-
tion; he therefore clipped the hawk's wings, cut off his talons, and, fixing a cork on his bill, threw him down among
the brood-hens. "Imagination," says Mr. White, "cannot
paint the scene that ensued; the expressions that fear, rage

and revenge inspired were new, or at least such as had been unoticed [sic] before; the exasperated matrons upbraided, they excerated [sic], they insulted, they triumphed. In a word, they never desisted, from buffeting their adversary till they had torn him in a hundred pieces." (*Hutchinson News*, 3 May 1877)

Continued depredation often resulted in the hunting and poisoning of animals. To encourage the extermination of pests, various "bounty" acts were passed by the state legislature that permitted counties, at their discretion, to pay for the presentation of scalps of the designated animals. The first such act was passed in 1864 and singled out the wolf for destruction:

SECTION I. THAT WHENEVER ONE-HALF OF THE LEGAL VOTers of any county shall, by petition, ask the board of County Commissioners of such county to make an order allowing a bounty for wolf scalps, it shall be their duty to make such order: *Provided,* such bounty shall not exceed two dollars for each scalp.

SEC. 2. That whoever applies for the payment of said bounty, shall present to the board of County Commissioners, or to the County Clerk in vacation, the wolf's scalp including the ears of the wolf, and make affidavit that he killed the said wolf or wolves within the bounds of said county wherein the application is made.

SEC. 3. That whenever application is made, as set forth in section 2 of this act, it shall be the duty of the board of County Commissioners to cause an order to issue to the person thus applying, on the County Treasurer of said county, for the amount thus appropriated; and when such claim for bounty shall be allowed, it shall be the duty of the board of Commissioners to cause such scalps to be destroyed.

Approved, February 27, 1864.
(Session Laws of Kansas, 1864)

In 1877 the bounty law on wolves was broadened to include coyotes, wildcats, foxes, and rabbits:

> SECTION I. THAT THE COUNTY COMMISSIONERS OF THE SEVeral counties within the state shall issue county warrants to the person killing to the amount of one dollar for every wolf, coyote, wild-cat or fox, and five cents for each rabbit, that shall be killed within said county.
>
> SEC. 2. No person shall be entitled to receive any bounty as set forth in section one, without first making it appear by positive proof by affidavit in writing filed with the county clerk that the wolf, coyote, wild-cat, rabbit or fox was killed within the limits of the county in which application is made.
>
> SEC. 3. Whenever bounty for any of the animals as set forth in section one is awarded, the person to whom it is awarded shall deliver the scalp of the animal, containing both ears, to the county clerk of the county, who shall cause the same to be destroyed. This act shall not apply to counties having a total property valuation of less than five hundred thousand dollars.
>
> Approved March 6, 1877.
>
> (Session Laws of Kansas, 1877a)

Large numbers of scalps were submitted for payment. As previously mentioned, this law probably was heavily abused. Not every incident violated the law, of course, but probably many did.

> CHASE CO. LEADER: FROM THE 1ST OF NOVEMBER, 1878 TO the 1st of [M]arch, there were delivered to the county clerk, and destroyed by him, the following number of scalps: 17 wild cat, 49 wolf, and 5,163 rabbit, at a cost to the county of $324.15. A good investment. (Ford County Globe, 26 March 1878)
>
> WHEN MASTER GEORGE KELLER, ON LAST SATURDAY AFTERnoon, marched into the office of County Clerk Hanon,

with upwards of thirty rabbit scalps dangling at his side, so far as the method of verifying his claim for bounty was concerned, he belonged to the class of uninitiated innocents. After signing the affidavit prepared for him, he was told to hold up his hand and swear to it. "Must I swear?" quickly interposed George, thinking, perhaps, of that certain commandment against profanity. "Yes:" said the Clerk, "it must be sworn to." Lured on by the prospective silver, George quickly elevated his right hand, and almost shouted, "By_____, I killed every one of them 'ere rabbits!" It is needless to add that he was enabled to pocket his hard-earned lucre. (*Hays City Sentinel*, 13 July 1878)

In an "act to protect fruit trees, hedge plants, and fences," the legislature in 1871 authorized counties to institute bounty payments for gopher scalps:

SECTION I. THAT THE COUNTY COMMISSIONERS OF ANY county of this state be and are hereby authorized to pay such premiums for gopher scalps taken in their county, as they may determine upon, not to exceed twenty cents for each scalp.

SEC. 2. When any person shall present to the county clerk of any county, any gopher scalp or scalps, and shall make proof by affidavit or otherwise, to the clerk of the county, that such scalp was taken from a gopher killed within the county, the county clerk shall issue to such a person a certificate showing where, when and by whom such scalp was taken, and the amount of premium to which such person is entitled therefor, which certificate, on presentation to the board of county commissioners of said county, shall be paid as other bills against the county.

SEC. 3. That this act shall take effect and be in force from and after its publication in the *Kansas Weekly Commonwealth*, February 23, 1871.

Approved February 16, 1871.

(Session Laws of Kansas, 1871a)

THE COUNTY COMMISSIONERS LAST WEEK ORDERED A BOUNTY
to be paid of three cents on each gopher (stripped [sic]
squirrel) scalp, and ten cents for each pocket-gopher scalp
delivered at the County Clerk's office any time between
this date and the first of July. The Commissioners deserve
especial credit for this order, and we hope it will have a
tendency to rid the county of a much dreaded pest. Boys,
now is your time to make some money. See Clerk's order
published elsewhere. (*Smith County Pioneer,* 18 April 1878)

Although proof was required that the scalps came from animals trapped within the county, the sheer numbers of scalps
submitted suggest that this injunction was often circumvented.
It is improbable that all of the scalps mentioned in the following
report, for example, came from within the designated county:

SINCE APRIL 1, 1871, JACKSON COUNTY HAS PAID $2,770 FOR
gopher scalps, the bounty being twenty cents each. This
calls for 13,850 scalps. (*Ellsworth Reporter,* 25 April 1872)

Poisoning with strychnine was the commonly used method of
controlling predatory animals such as gray wolves and coyotes,
and household pests such as rats. However, when the substance
was used carelessly, the results could be less than desirable, if not
tragic:

IN THE SOUTHWESTERN PORTIONS OF THE COUNTY SEVERAL
valuable dogs have been poisoned by baits put out for coyotes. People cannot be too careful in the use of Strychnine.
(*Hutchinson News,* 5 March 1874)

A LITTLE DAUGHTER OF H. O'NEAL, OF LYON COUNTY, WAS
killed with rat poison, a few days ago. (*Russell County Record,* 6 December 1877)

Most settlers considered large predaceous birds, such as hawks
and eagles, major nuisances. They believed these birds were
primary predators on livestock such as domestic chickens, young

sheep, and calves. Such birds never came under the protection of the law during the time period in question, and many were killed:

> CRICK SHOT. MRS. D. HOMER JENNINGS, HAVING LATELY LOST several fine chickens by hawks, determined to try her skill as a shootist, and while at dinner, yesterday, an opportunity presented itself. The old rooster gave warning that the enemy was approaching, and Mrs. J. took down the gun and walked to the door. There was fire in her eye as she stepped out and beheld his hawkship hovering over a group of her choice houdans. She quickly brought the gun to her shoulder and fired, and down came the hawk, as dead as a mackerel; and now his carcass hangs at the top of a high pole as a warning to any of his tribe which may chance this way. (*Russell County Record,* 14 October 1875)

> MR. SMOUSE OF LARNED, KNOWS HOW TO CATCH HAWKS. HE says this is the way: Drive a stake into the ground and set upon top of it a small steel trap without bait. The hawks will instinctively alight on top of the post and just as certainly "get their foot in it." (*Pawnee County Herald,* 30 July 1878)

A number of times carnivores such as wolves and mountain lions were reported to have jeopardized the very lives of the settlers. In most of the instances regarding wolves, the animals were probably simply following the person, whether from mere curiosity or with the intent to attack is not known. However, a few reports stated unequivocally that people were attacked:

> A FEW DAYS AGO, AS WE LEARN FROM THE LEAVENWORTH Times, two large grey wolves were seen on the Kansas Pacific road near Cayote, chasing a man, who was following a wagon, and running like the very old harry. The last seen of the party, he was in the wagon, firing at his audacious assailants. The section hands of the road do not venture out

after dark, owing to the ferocity of the wolves, who are rendered bold by hunger, the ground being covered with snow
and ice. (*Junction City Weekly Union*, 9 December 1871)

MR. MALSBARY IS JUST BACK FROM MEDICINE LODGE. WHILE
there W. E. Hutchinson, himself and others concluded to
visit the Salt Plains in the Indian Territory. After traveling
several days they turned back on account of supplies running short. One night they encamped near a small stream
to which Mr. Malsbary went for the purpose of getting water. He carried an axe to chop the ice. While engaging in
this job a huge gray wolf attacked him. After circling around
several times he came up so close that friend Malsbary hit
him a powerful stroke with his axe, killing Mr. Wolf instantly. Malsbary says "It takes more than one wolf to get
away with him." (*Hutchinson News*, 19 December 1872)

MR. WIGGIN, (LAND AGENT FOR THE K. P.) WITH HIS WIFE,
and Mr. Clark—grain merchant—while out riding last Friday about two miles south of the river was followed for some
distance by a large gray wolf. (*Ellsworth Reporter*, 25 May
1876)

Several incidents were reported in which catamounts and wild
cats stalked and sometimes attacked people. These animals were
probably attempting to satisfy their normal curiosity, but in cases
of extreme hunger, or if provoked by being cornered or wounded,
a mountain lion or bobcat might well have attacked.

ON SEVERAL OCCASIONS RECENTLY MR. EDWIN TAFT, A FARMER
on "F. Creek," four miles north of Brookville, has seen a
large and ferocious looking wild cat lurking about his corn
field. Keeping a sharp lookout, on the evening of Friday the
11th inst. he contrived to get within range of this unwel-
come intruder with a double-barreled shot gun. Discharging
one barrel, he merely lamed instead of killing the animal.
On pulling the trigger of the second barrel the cap missed

fire, and having no other ammunition at hand he instantly removed the useless cap and ran forward to despatch the brute with the butt end of his gun. The wounded and enraged beast with horrible growls turned upon him for a fight. When within ten feet of his assailant the cat exhibiting a formidable array of teeth and frightfully glaring eyes, prepared for a desperate spring upon Mr. T., who, anticipating this movement with the rapidity of lightning dealt him a terrific blow on the head disabling his infuriated enemy, which after a determined resistance accompanied with the most hideous yells, finally yielded under the repeated blows of Mr. F.'s gunstock. The "game" was carried home in triumph and found to weigh over thirty-five pounds. It was presented by Mr. F. to a friend of his in Brookville, who expressed his intention to have the skin stuffed, so as to preserve this monster specimen of the feline race. (*Saline County Journal*, 17 August 1871)

COURT HIGGINS KILLED A SEVENTEEN POUND WILD CAT ON the Saline river, last Tuesday. The brute was about to spring upon him from a ledge of rock, when he brougth [*sic*] his shot gun into action. (*Hays Sentinel*, 27 April 1878)

Sometimes the hunter became the hunted. This was particularly true with large game animals such as buffalo or elk. If a buffalo was wounded and the hunter unwary in his approach, the wounded beast often charged, resulting in many a hunter's being disabled and sometimes killed:

A NEGRO SOLDIER AT FORT HAYS, ONE DAY LAST WEEK WAS gored to death by a buffalo. There is vast amount of amusement in hunting buffalo, but when a wounded one turns on a fellow it is not so fine. (*Junction City Weekly Union*, 5 October 1867)

MR. MANNING OF KINGMAN WAS IN OUR CITY ON FRIDAY AND related to us a rather thrilling adventure of James Ball two

The hunter becomes the hunted. *Harper's New Monthly Magazine.*

miles north of Kingman on the 2nd inst. Ball and a comrade saw a buffalo about dark on a ridge bordering a valley through which they were riding. Dismounting they fired with a spencer rifle. The animal was wounded and charged down upon them. They could not get the gun to fire again and so they ran for their horses, and mounted with the buffalo in hot pursuit. They fled in opposite directions. The buffalo selected Ball and pursued, notwithstanding several revolver shots, so rapidly as to overhaul and kill his horse. The furious brute's horns struck astride of Ball's right leg. One of the horns was stopped by the saddle but the other plowed a mortal wound. Ball was thrown about ten feet and on regaining his feet is said to have done the fastest running ever seen on the Ninnescah. Fortunately the buffalo passed off in another direction, which, however, Ball did not notice until he was several hundred yards away. Ball says it was a d___d shame that a cow buffalo should "get away" with two men mounted and armed, but under the circumstances it could not be helped. (*Hutchinson News*, 16 July 1874)

SOME PARTIES THE OTHER DAY FOUND THE SKELETON OF A man about four miles west of town. From the shape of the skull it is supposed to be that of a white man. Near this skeleton lie the bones of a large buffalo, and a few feet away the barrel of a very large rifle was found, and a little to one side was found the broken gunstock. From the position of things generally, it is very evident that there has here taken place a life and death struggle between a wounded buffalo and a hunter. The broken gun would indicate that the struggle was a bitter one, and that away from camp and friends the hunter had fought the enraged animal until death, and, that they had then died together. (*Hays City Sentinel*, 11 April 1879)

Some settlers appreciated the wildlife so much that they enclosed them in a zoological park or zoo (chapter 3). At Bull City (present-day Alton), Kansas, the namesake of the town was killed along with two of his helpers when one of the captured elk attacked:

OUR CITY WAS THROWN INTO A STATE OF THE MOST INTENSE excitement, on Sunday about noon, by the arrival of a messenger from Bull's City conveying the sad and startling intelligence that General Bull, one of our county's most honored and worthy citizens, had met with a terrible and tragic death, having been attacked and gored by the large elk in his park, and that three other brave men in attempting to rescue a fellow being had been frightfully mangled and torn, two of them doubtless fatally.

The news seemed incredible at first, but as the conviction of its dread reality gradually settled down upon the community and the intelligence sped from house to house, a feeling of the deepest sorrow overspread the town. At no time in the history of our county has an event occurred which caused such a general shock, and throughout the entire northwestern portion of Kansas, in fact throughout the whole state, the news will be received with more than ordinary regret, as he was a man widely known and as universally esteemed.

Immediately on learning of the affair a large number of our citizens, intimate friends of the General, as many as could find conveyance, repaired to the scene of the disaster. We were kindly given a seat in a buggy with Treasurer Mohler and Esq. Walrond, but did not arrive until quite late. We were therefore much gratified to find that Hon. A. Saxey and R. R. Hays, who had preceded us some hours, had noted all the facts and circumstances in the minutest and most careful manner for our benefit, and to them we are indebted for the full and complete details we are able to lay before the readers of the FARMER. The following is a concise and correct account of the sad affair:

It is well known to the people of this section that Gen. Bull has a park which he has fitted up at great expense, and in it has enclosed a number of wild animals including three elk, one a powerful, huge-antlered male, a magnificent specimen of the moose family. The General was accustomed to walk through this enclosure daily and hundreds of visitors have, at different times been shown through the place, and petted the very animal which caused the sad loss of life.

At about half past 8 or 9 o'clock Sunday morning Gen. Bull's hired man, Robert Bricknell, entered the park for the purpose of caring for the elk. He immediately discovered that there was something unusual about the appearance of the animal, which showed hostile signs, compelling him to retire from the park. Bricknell hastened to inform the General of the fact, and arming themselves with heavy clubs both again went to the park, the General remarking that he could subdue the animal. Without a sign of warning the now infuriated beast made a charge at the men, striking Gen. Bull and knocking him down with great force. The elk then drew back and made a second attack on Gen. Bull, this time with increased force, using his antlers with terrible effect, piercing the prostrate body of the General through the breast until the prong protruded, then tossing his form high into the air and throwing him over its head. The elk then resumed his attack on Bricknell, inflicting terrible injuries, whilst doing which George Nicholas, who had witnessed the occurrence, ran to the rescue with a heavy club of hard wood 4½ feet long and about two inches in diameter, with which he expected to so disable the enraged animal as to compel it to desist. With redoubled fury and madness, however, the elk caught the club in its antlers, making indentures in it and rolling it upon the ground with great force. At this time there were two bodies lying prostrate, and with equal heroism and courage William Sherman hastened to the combat. The elk served Sherman the same as the other men, catching him in his immense antlers and throwing him over the fence. George Nicholas was tossed upon the fence.

Mrs. Bull was meanwhile a horrified spectator of the terrible tragedy and wild with grief and terror ran to the village crying for help. A number of men made haste to reach the scene of the disaster, but arrived too late to be of any service. They found Gen. Bull in a terribly disfigured condition and life quite extinct. His body, with the other injured men, was conveyed to the family residence and surgical aid at once summoned. Dr. Martin of Bull's City, and Dr. Dulin of Osborne, did all in their power to alleviate the sufferings of the injured men.

The scene at the house was heartrending. Women wept aloud and strong men could not restrain tears of sorrow. The dead General had a warm place in the affections of his friends and neighbors.

A surgical examination of the body of Gen. Bull developed 44 wounds of greater or less severity. The General was killed by a wound from the antler which entered the chest at the right nipple, passing diagonally through the body and coming out on the left side about the fifth rib. The prong passed through both lungs and probably the heart, thereby causing instant death.

Robert Bricknell received 32 wounds, one under the right arm, penetrating the cavity of the chest, and one in the groin injuring the bladder very seriously.

George Nicholas has 64 wounds, one over the stomach, penetrating the abdominal cavity, and one in the right side opening into the chest.

George Nicholas has since died and Robert Bricknell continues in a precarious condition. The elk has been shot. (*Osborne County Farmer*, 16 October 1879)

As settlers moved westward across the country, they brought with them two species of rodents that had immigrated with them from Europe (chapter 3). These two species, the Norway rat and the house mouse, both excel at cohabitation with humans. The lack of public sanitation systems and proper garbage disposal in the early frontier towns provided ideal habitat for rats and mice. In this environment the rats reproduced and occasionally were reported to attack humans:

A LADY WHO ATTENDED CHURCH SUNDAY EVENING WAS TROUbled with something crawling on her person, and on examination she caught a fine large rat, which had been previously making the cloak sleeve his ratship's domicile home. (*Larned Optic*, 19 February 1879)

MR. JOSEPH SIMMONS, MERCHANT TAILOR, WAS AWAKENED between the hours of 3 and four o'clock on Monday morning, June 23d, by the crying of his child, aged two months. On turning up the light, [he] found several wounds on the child's face and pool of blood on the pillow, but did not know the cause, no rat being in the house. On calling Dr. Seiber the following morning, he immediately stated that the child must have lost a large amount of blood, caused by the bite of some animal, after which he was informed of the circumstances connected with the case, and the doctor said the animal would return, and that they were to keep a strict watch, and gave directions to raise the bedstead about a foot from the floor, and to place a basin of water under each leg of the bedstead, and shake singly every article of clothing on and near the bed. Every order was attended to. On the morning of the 24th, about the same time as above stated, a loud noise was heard in front of the store room, and forward came an extraordinarily large rat, right in the direction of the child, causing Mrs. Simmons to scream. Mr. Simmons came to her rescue and drove it back, but the rat taking another route came again direct for the child, and it was after five or six attempts, and being driven back with a broom, did it desist, but Mr. Simmons did not succeed in killing the rat. The child died from the effects of the bite. (*Hays City Sentinel*, 4 July 1879)

Snakes, it seems, were always despised and killed whenever and wherever possible. Many times large numbers were dispatched in a single day:

ON THE 2ND, INST., JOHN R. PUTMAN AND SEVERAL OTHERS visited a prairie dog city three miles from town. . . . The day was warm and sunny, and about the holes were basking hundreds of snakes. "Put" and his comrades armed themselves with sticks and made terrible slaughter. They killed about two hundreds of which one hundred and seventy-five

Killing snakes in a military encampment. *Harper's New Monthly Magazine.*

were rattlesnakes. "Put" come back to town exultant, and with his pockets [f]ull of rattles plucked from the tails of his victims.

In spring and fall the "boys" all over the country have great sport visiting these towns and carrying out the scriptural injunction of bruising serpents heads. They carry on the business in a wholesale manner so effectively, that it is thought, after next spring, a snake will be a curiosity in the settled portions of Reno county. (*Hutchinson News,* 6 November 1873)

THIS IS NO "SNAKE STORY," IF IT IS ABOUT SNAKES. IT'S GENUine. L. F. Kench, who lives five miles north east of town, had a regular field day with rattlesnakes last Saturday. He killed 26 at one killing at a prairie dog town adjoining his farm; it was only a breakfast job at that. Mr. G. M[.] Stager killed seven more at the same place on Tuesday following. It wouldn't surprise us, to hear at any moment, that these gentlemen have snakes in their boots after their wholesale massacre. We shall dream of snakes every night for a week and see them coiled around the bed posts, frightening us to death; we wish now that we hadn't heard about this item, for already our flesh begins to crawl and bones rattle. (*Inland Tribune*, 28 October 1876)

Snakes, especially poisonous species (e.g., massasauga and prairie rattlesnake), posed a serious problem for the pioneer. Most snakes are subterranean or fossorial to one degree or another; therefore, dugouts on the prairie for human habitation were ready-made for invasion by various species of snake (Miner, 1986). However, when the weather became cold, snakes would seek any environment that was warm, including homes:

MISS NETTIE C. CARPENTER, A YOUNG LADY FROM MICHIGAN, had quite an adventure recently. She has taken herself a claim, built thereon a very neat stone dug-out, roofed with poles and dirt. To keep the dirt from falling down she put heavy paper on the under side of the poles, and, hearing a rattling noise on the paper, she thought that the mice were at work. She got the broomstick and gave the paper a gentle tap, when instead of mice as the young lady thought, she brought down a hissing viper. His vipership immediately took possession of the bed and coiled himself for a fight, but he got more of it than he could stand and had to succumb to the courage of Miss Nettie. He measured four feet in length. How many of your eastern ladies would have fought and killed it with a broomstick? (*Larned Optic*, 30 May 1879)

MONDAY LAST A YOUNG SON OF MR. BEACH WAS BITTEN BY A rattlesnake; the snake had gotten into the house by crawling through the sod wall, and bit him while in search of a marble under the bed. His sister immediately sucked the poison from the bite, and this with prompt medical attendance saved his life. (Spearville). (*Dodge City Times*, 16 August 1879)

In addition to biting humans, poisonous snakes also bit domesticated animals, including chickens, cows, calves, horses, colts, mules, and dogs. In general, the larger the animal, the less effective the poison. A larger body can often dissipate or assimilate venom without death occurring.

A REMARKABLE INCIDENT OCCURRED LATELY ON "F" CREEK IN this county at Mr. Ed. Taft's farm. Mr. Taft had occasion to place his hand in the nest of one of his setting hens; but he withdrew that member in double quick time, as the head of a large rattle-snake instantly protuded [*sic*] from underneath the hen. The latter (without leaving her nest) immediately made a vigorous attack on the head of the intruding offender. The snake made a desperate resistance and the two fought in most determined manner for about twenty minutes, when Mr. Taft put an end to the struggle by killing the snake with his pitchfork. The fierce combat ended, the hen quietly settled down upon her eggs apparently none the worse for the fight. Her feathers must have saved her from the venom of the reptile, as she completed the process of incubation and brought forth a fine brood of chickens. (*Saline County Journal*, 6 June 1872)

WE REPORT THAT THE MORTALITY AMONG HORSE-FLESH IS alarming of late. Madison Coleman, of Graham county who has been harvesting on the creek, lost a valuable mule from snake bite, all human efforts to save proving of no avail. (Twin Creek). (*Osborne County Farmer*, 3 August 1877)

A FEW DAYS SINCE, SOME GENTLEMEN WERE DRIVING OVER the prairie on the south side, one of them had a horse bitten by a rattlesnake. He was equal to the emergency. Being a tobacco chewer, he chewed his quid vigorously and then with his mouth thus protected, applied his lips to the wound and sucked the poison out. He did this two or three times, and then proceded on his way, his horse experiencing no difficulty whatever, from the bite. (*Hays City Sentinel*, 28 September 1877)

A VALUABLE SHEPHERD DOG, BELONGING TO MR. FRED HOhenstein, was bitten by a rattlesnake, the other day, but was saved by a good dose of whiskey, immediately applied. (Spearcville). (*Dodge City Times*, 10 May 1879)

REV. E. D. CARR HAD THE MISFORTUNE TO LOSE HIS ONLY COW by the bite of a rattlesnake, on Monday of last week. The cow had just been watered and picketed out, and died in about forty minutes after she was bitten. She was a very valuable animal and is a great loss to Mr. Carr's family. (*Larned Optic*, 12 September 1879)

The habit that many settlers had of going without shoes during the warm summer months resulted in many rattlesnake bites:

MRS. L. P. HADLEY, LIVING NORTH-WEST OF THE CITY A SHORT distance, was bitten by a rattlesnake, on last Thursday evening. She was out barefooted and was struck on the ankle. The wound was not fatal and we are glad to know that she is recovering. (*Hutchinson News*, 12 July 1877)

FRANK BAXTER, WORKING FOR I. M. YOST ABOUT TWO MILES north of town, so narrowly escaped death last Saturday that in years to come his blood will run cold as he thinks of it. He was plowing and turned up a bumble bees' nest, and while endeavoring to fight off the bees stepped out from the furrow and onto a rattlesnake and was bitten upon his bare foot. He felt the bite, but thinking a bee had stung him proceeded with his work until queer pains began to shoot through his body and limbs and a swollen and discolored leg and foot admonished him to act. He mounted one of his mules and succeeded in reaching town and relief only just in time. Two or three times he came near falling off, and when he arrived on Fort street was blind as a bat and almost unconscious. His leg was frightfully swollen, and, strangest of all, his body and arms were covered with blotches precisely the shape and color of those on a rattlesnake. Antidotes brought him around. (*Hays City Sentinel*, 21 September 1878)

MR. BRUMMIT GAVE THE ACCOUNT OF A BOY WHO DIED FROM a rattlesnake bite. It seems that the boy was barefooted, and that the snake reached his head out of a hole and struck him twice. He thought he had stepped on a sharp stick until alarming symptoms began to appear. He died in four hours after being bitten. (*Stockton News*, 22 August 1878)

Of the many recorded instances of people being bitten by poisonous snakes, most adults survived. Many children did not.

ON LAST THURSDAY EVENING, A LITTLE DAUGHTER OF A. J. Crawford's, living one-half mile north of town was bitten by a rattlesnake. The child is about four years old and was playing near a grain stack. She went into the house and said she had ran against a stick and hurt her knee. The mother immediately examined and found a small puncture just above the knee[;] realizing that the child was bitten by a rattlesnake, she applied her mouth to the wound and sucked quite a quantity of blood from it, (which courageous act, as the physician afterward declared, saved her life). Dr. Lillie was summoned, but notwithstanding he exerted his utmost skill, the limb and body swelled to an enormous size and assumed a dark green color. The case was a desperate one, but finally yielded to the excellent treatment, and to-day the child is out of danger. During the months of July and August, (dog days) the bite of the rattlesnake is more dangerous than at any other season, and great care should be taken to avoid them. (Wilson). (*Ellsworth Reporter,* 17 July 1879)

WE WERE PAINED TO LEARN THAT WEDNESDAY LAST A SON 12 years old of Mr. Schultz in Haven township, died from the effects of a rattlesnake bite. He had been bitten a week before. He was a mile and a half from home. He attacked the snake and supposing that he had killed it proceeded to cut the rattles off when the still animate reptile buried its fangs deep into his finger. It was so long before antidotes could be secured that the poison obtained fatal headway. The boy was buried on Thursday. (*Hutchinson News,* 25 June 1874)

A BRIGHT LITTLE FOUR-YEAR-OLD SON OF HENRY POSEY, LIVing twelve miles south of Larned, was bitten by a rattlesnake about two o'clock P. M., Monday, and died Tuesday morning about four o'clock. A physician was called, but reached the little sufferer too late to help him. The bereaved parents have the heartfelt sympathy of the entire neighborhood in their deep and sore affliction. But,

> The eye that shuts in a dying hour
> Will open the next in bliss;
> The welcome will sound in the heavenly world
> Ere farewell is hushed in this,
> We pass from the clasp of mourning friends
> To the arms of the loved ones lost;
> And their smiling faces will greet us there
> Which on earth we've valued most.
> (*Larned Optic,* 1 August 1879)

Many different kinds of home or folk remedies were used.

DR. CORNELL'S REMEDY IS INFALLIBLE. ONE TABLE SPOONFUL of gunpowder, and salt, and the yellow of an egg, and mix so as to make a plaster; place on a cloth and apply to the wound, letting it extend an inch on all sides of the wound. As the poison is drawn the plaster will lose its sticking qualities, and when full will fall off. Apply a new plaster until it sticks, which is sure evidence that the poison is all out. This will cure a snake bite on either human or beast. Cut this out and paste it on the window jam. (*Hutchinson News*, 16 July 1874)

LAWRENCE JOURNAL, 10: MR. GEORGE RISLEY WAS BITTEN BY A rattlesnake, yesterday morning, on the farm of Mr. Forest Savage. Up to four o'clock yesterday afternoon he had drank two quarts of whiskey without any particularly visible results of the usual nature. He will doubtless recover from the effects of both the bite and the whiskey. (*Ford County Globe*, 18 June 1878)

PROF. FRANK SNOW, ONE OF THE MOST ENTHUSIASTIC ENtomologists in America and at present at the head of the Natural History department of our State University, has been bug catching, geologizing and botanizing in the wilds of Western Kansas, during the past month, and will take many specimens to the University as the results of his labors. Last week while delving in the virgin soil of Lane county, about thirty miles south of Buffalo Station, the Professor was bitten on the hand by a rattlesnake. He applied his lips to the wound, sucked out deadly virus, and then coolly set him down to make a scientific examination of his case. His description of the various sensations which permeated his nervous system, the rise and fall of his pulse, and the rapidity with which the different conditions of the disease made themselves manifest, is highly interesting. Fortunately the plucky naturalist was not a victim to his science. He is still prosecuting his investigations in Western Kansas. (*Hays City Sentinel*, 13 July 1878)

Another threat to the life of the early settler was the danger of being bitten by a "mad," or hydrophobic, animal and thereby contracting hydrophobia—or, as we know it today, rabies. Dogs, cats, wolves, and skunks (or polecats) were all known to harbor rabies.

ON THE 5TH OF AUGUST (1868) AT 10 O'CLOCK PM A RABID wolf of the large grey species came into the post and charged round most furiously; he entered the hospital and attacked Corp. McGillicoddy C, C-3rd Inf. who was lying sick in the bed, biting him severely in the left hand & right arm. The left little finger was nearly taken off[;] the wolf next dashed into a party of ladies and gentlemen sitting in the moonlight on Col. Wynkoop's porch and bit 1st Lieu. T. T. Thompson 3rd Inf. severely in both legs[;] leaving there he soon after attacked and bit Priv. Thom. Mason C, of 10th Cav. member of the scaber guard, lacerating his right foot severely and penetrating it in two places. This all occurred in an incredibly short period of time and although those above mentioned were the only persons bitten, the animal left the marks of his prescence [sic] in every quarter of the garrison. He moved with great rapidity, snapping at everything within his reach, tearing tents, window curtains, bed clothing etc. in every direction. The sentinel of the guardhouse fired over the animals' [sic] back while he ran between the man's legs. Finally he charged upon a sentinel at the haystacks and was killed by a well directed and most fortunate shot. He was a very large wolf and his long jaws and teeth presented a most formidable appearance. The wounds were thoroughly cauterized with nitrate of silver on the place.

Sept. 1868. Corporal McGillicoddy C,C 3rd Inf. one of the men that were bitten by the rabid wolf on the 5th of August showed signs of commencing hydrophobia on the evening of the 6th inst. The symptoms were as usually described, were well marked and very characteristic[;] he died on the morning of the 9th. No treatment was attempted after the symptoms commenced, his wounds had been well

cauterized with lunar caustic from time to time & washed
with alkaline washes, and had he allowed the finger to be
removed at first there would have been a greater probability
of his recovery. . . . The wounds have healed in the other
two persons that were bitten and they appear to be in perfect health. (Report, Assistant Surgeon, Fort Larned, 1868)

ABOUT TWO WEEKS AGO A YOUNG MAN — WHOSE NAME IS NOT
learned—was out on the plains beyond Wallace, with a
party engaged in hunting buffalo. During the night the
young man to whom we refer was bitten by a skunk. He was
sleeping on the ground at the time, and the animal, through
some means, made the attack, inflicting an ugly wound.
The victim bandaged the cut as best he could, and troubled
himself very little about it at the time, as it gave him pain
only occasionally. Last Saturday he made his way to Wallace,—the wound having swollen and become extremely
painful,—in hope of having it dressed and inflammation
subdued. Shortly after his arrival at Wallace, the unfortunate
young man was seized with a sudden fit of drowsiness. To this
he succumbed, and within two hours after dropping to sleep
he breathed his last. Deceased was buried on Sunday last,
and when placed in his coffin his body threw off in a great
degree the odor of the much-detested animal that caused his
death. (*Daily Rocky Mountain News*, 17 January 1873)

THE OWNER OF A MADSTONE WHO LIVES ON TURKEY CREEK, IN
Cowley County, applied the same to a child of Mr. T. E.
White, who had been bitten by a mad cat, with most satis-
factory results. (*Hays City Sentinel*, 3 August 1878)

The cure for a bite from a rabid animal was the application of
a madstone to the bite. The only other remedy mentioned in the
sources I read was nitrate of silver.

WE BELIEVE IT IS DENIED BY THE FACULTY THAT A PECULIAR
substance known as the "mad stone," contains within itself

a specific cure for hydrophobia. If the mad stone does not cure, it is safe to say, after the sad experiences of last summer in New York, that there is no other cure for the frightful disease known to the professors of medicine. We occasionally find in our country papers an account of a stone possessing these curative powers, which remind us somewhat of the glassware, which in the mad times of Barges served as detectives to the poisoned wine, shattering it to pieces as the wine touched it. This, like the story of the mad stone, may be fallacious, but, in turn, also, both may be true. In Lincoln and Macoupin counties, Illinois, there are said to be two of the peculiar stones, which, according to local tradition are frequently called into requisition to remove the virus resulting from a mad dog's bite. A recent instance of cure is furnished by a Mr. J. G. Crouch, of Rochester, who was bitten and applied the stone with beneficial effect. The stone hung tenaciously to the wound until it extracted from the lacerated hand as much green matter as it could hold. It then fell off and was soaked in hot water until purified of the virus, and was then reapplied until it became filled again, and again fell off. Singularly enough, when not filled it could not be detached except by force, and would adhere tenaciously to the wound as it were sympathetically. Whether the cure is radical or not, Mr. Crouch is free from pain and his hand bears only the mark of a scratch. Perhaps doctors will say there was nothing in it, the dog was not mad and there was no hydrophobia. Perhaps so, but for all that it reads like a veritable case. (*Ellsworth Reporter*, 13 May 1875)

ON MONDAY OF LAST WEEK MR. LEWIS DALTON, OF LANGDON, this county, was severely bitten by a dog supposed to be rabid. The dog showing unmistakable signs of madness was killed by the owner, Gus Smith. Mr. Dalton having learned through Rodney Ferguson of a mad-stone in Kansas City, went to that city on Wednesday night, and found the stone as represented, and had it applied to the wound with the most favorable result. It adhered to the wound for ten hours and fifteen minutes; completely extracting the virus. The stone was in the possession of Wm. O. Shouse, northeast corner of Main and 13th streets, and has been in the same family for over two hundred years, and has effected a great number of cures. Such is the value attached to this stone that Mr. Dalton had to give a bond for $1,000 for its return before he was permitted to take it away. We are informed that a similar stone is in the possession of Mrs. Dr. Lizzie Dolan, Paola, Kansas. Mr. Dalton brought the stone to the *Interior* office; and we have had the privilege of examining it. It is about two inches square by one inch in thickness. It presents the appearance of a piece of honey-comb with closed cells, petrified, with an even surface and porous throughout. (*Hays City Sentinel*, 16 May 1879)

ALL PERSONS AND ANIMALS BITTEN BY DOGS SUPPOSED TO BE mad should as quickly as possible receive those attentions which are recognized as most effectual in destroying the rabific virus, or preventing its absorption. Mr. Youatt, the most distinguished authority on this subject, relied exclusively upon a thorough cauterization of the wound with nitrate of silver. By this simple treatment he was successful in over 400 instances in the human subject, and in innumerable cases of dogs; in his own person, moreover, as he was repeatedly bitten by rapid dogs [*sic*], and on one occasion severely by a mad cat. (*Dodge City Times*, 7 June 1879)

During hunting expeditions there were often accidents, most of them caused by the careless use of firearms, some caused by the weapon's malfunctioning. Sometimes, too, firearms were discharged near the dwellings of others:

WE HEAR COMPLAINT OF THE SHOOTING OF GUNS ALONG THE river near the slaughter house. A bullet was distinctly heard by Mr. Geo. Krueger as it passed near his house on Wednesday morning. There is great danger from this wild shooting and it is the duty of any one having knowledge of the persons doing the shooting to make complaint. It is only a few months since a ball passed through Mr. Graf's house and fell at the feet of Mrs. Graf. Stop that shooting. (*Saline County Journal,* 1 August 1878)

JUST AS WE TOOK OUR PEN IN HAND TO PEN THESE LINES A sad affair occurred in the shape of an explosion of a shot gun in the hands of Jeff Sweeney. From what we could learn of the affair, Jeff saw some plover while gunning and made an attempt to shoot the same, and the gun burst near the breach, and carried the thumb of the left hand away with it, and will cripple his left hand for life; as the doctor amputated the thumb at the lower joint. The young man has our sympathy. (*Hays City Sentinel,* 19 July 1876)

MR. EVAN LACEY, WHO BOARDS AT MR. PENNINGTON'S NORTH-west of the city, took a double barreled shot-gun and went out to shoot some game. He had been out only a half hour when he saw a duck and raised his gun to fire but instead of going off all right the barrel bursted [*sic*], tearing and lacerating his hand seriously. (*Hutchinson News,* 5 December 1878)

Aspiring nimrods often succeeded in fecklessly injuring their hunting partner or themselves and others. In far too many cases, the hunting accidents resulted in death to one of those involved. It is notable that in many of these instances the gun was being pulled muzzle first toward the person who was injured or killed. Such deaths were tragic indeed, due to nothing more than outright stupidity in those handling firearms.

THE MARION COUNTY RECORD SAYS THAT HENRY ONROH IS A genius, in his way. Blackbirds are bad on the farm; and Henry conceived the idea of strapping his shot-gun to his plow, and thus be prepared in the field to "go for" the feathery pesty. Unfortunately for the young inventor, the muzzle of the gun pointed toward the plow handles, and in drawing the gun from its place, one day last week, the fowling-piece was discharged, lodging a load of shot in Henry's shoulder, badly mangling it. (*Hays City Sentinel,* 27 April 1878)

MR. REEDER MONTGOMERY, WHO LIVES ABOUT FOUR MILES southwest of this place, met with a very serious accident yesterday. While out hunting antelope, in drawing his gun from the wagon it was discharged; the contents lodging in his left shoulder, mangling it dreadfully. We are unable to learn the exact extent of his injuries at the present writing; but he will probably lose his left arm. (*Hays City Sentinel,* 14 November 1879)

A BOY IN DAVIS COUNTY KILLED HIMSELF RECENTLY, TRYING to punch a rabbitt [*sic*] out of a brush pile with the butt end of his loaded gun. (*Ellsworth Reporter,* 27 January 1876)

A TERRIBLE ACCIDENT IS REPORTED TO US FROM RUSH COUNTY. Two of D. Cyrs' sons were allowed to go out rabbit hunting last Thursday, and armed with an old army musket proceeded to the creek. On their return and when within a short distance of the house, David, the youngest of the two, dropped the butt of his gun to the ground trailing it along. He had gone but a short distance when the gun was discharged and the entire load entered his right side, inflicting a mortal wound. He lingered until Friday morning and peacefully passed away. (*Hays City Sentinel,* 23 November 1877)

LAST SUNDAY EVENING A TERRIBLE ACCIDENT HAPPENED down in the Russian settlement on the Smoky, by which Wilhelm Beiger a Russian about forty-eight years old, was hurried into eternity. Beiger was out hunting rabbits with a single-barrelled shot-gun, and was passing through his corn-field, on his return to the house, when he carelessly placed the stock of the gun on the ground, leaned the muzzle against his body and commenced to gather a few ears of corn. In some unexplainable manner the gun was discharged; the entire load passing through his body and heart. He made a few steps toward the house, and fell. A little daughter, who witnessed the accident, hastened to him; but his form was already rigid in death when she reached him. He was taken to the house and cared for by kind neighbors; the simple funeral taking place the next day.

It is another added to the long list of those who have gone to their death through carelessness. (*Hays City Sentinel*, 12 September 1879)

Poisonous snakes were almost always killed when encountered, often shot. These incidents, sometimes resulted in self-inflicted wounds, whether due to the ineptness of the shooter or to the shooter's anxiety and nervousness caused by the snake is not known; I suspect the latter was largely responsible.

ONE OF THE AUSTRIAN SETTLERS, IN ATTEMPTING TO SHOOT A snake with a six-shooter, sent a bullet through the palm of his hand, last Wednesday. He is offering the shooter for sale. (*Hays City Sentinel*, 11 May 1878)

ON LAST MONDAY EVENING, A MR. D. BEAL, WHO LIVES IN THE north-east part of the county near Garfield, took out his shot gun to kill a rattlesnake, and after he had discharged one barrel at the reptile, he proceeded to reload, when from some cause unknown to Mr. Beal, the other barrel was discharged, and as he was in the act of reloading he received a very severe wound in the right hand. He came to town Tuesday and had his thumb and little finger amputated by Dr. McKinney. (*Pawnee County Herald*, 14 May 1878)

Of course, perils other than hunting accidents also existed. In the early years there was always the danger of Indian attacks, and not a few of these resulted in death, as the following accounts imply:

> ON THE 10TH OF MAY FIVE [SIC] MEN, LEWIS CASTLE, WALTER Haynes, ———— Tolman, ———— Roberts, and two brothers named Collins, left Clifton, on the Republican, to go on a Buffalo hunt, to be gone five days. Not returning at that time, their neighbors became uneasy, and they started in search of them. Near the Forks of the Solomon, they came upon an abandoned Cheyenne camp, where they found clothing that the party wore . . . , portions of their boots, and their pocket books. To render the circumstances more positive a pre-emption filing to a piece of land was found on the ground near by belonging to one of the men. No trace could be found of their wagons or teams. The above facts induced the party to return to Riley and seek Military aid. (*Junction City Union*, 2 June 1866)

> ON MONDAY, THE 8TH INST., ON LIMESTONE CREEK, A TRIBUtary to the Solomon, six buffalo hunters were pounced upon by thirty Indians. Three of the men were in camp, and three a short distance off, skinning buffalo. One of the men at work on the buffalo, named Keller, cut the harness off a horse and succeeded in making his escape, together with two of the men who were in camp. The remaining three are missing. Their names are Gates, Hardy and Smith. Twenty citizens started in search of them, but had not returned when our informant left. (*Junction City Union*, 13 July 1867)

Because winter was one of the best times to hunt buffalo, many hunters caught on the open plains in a Kansas blizzard faced frostbite, amputation of frozen toes and fingers, and even death. Sometimes the remains of bodies were not found until years later:

> THE SEVERE STORM WHICH PASSED OVER THE WESTERN PORtion of the State, on the 17th and 18th instants, has perhaps

never been equaled in severity and suffering for years past. This evening a party of Buffalo hunters, returned from a three week's [sic] hunt after the "bison of the plains," and report authentically the hardships endured by the many who had gone through this growing town during the past few weeks, some for the pleasure derived from the excitement attendant upon the chase, others mingling pleasure with that of seeking homes on the frontier, and then again, some who follow frontier life—bringing wild meat to market—for a livelihood. The party of hunters I speak of, consisted of J. Sallinger, Ed. Slaught, Henry Decker, of Clyde; the well known Max. Alwens, of Atchison, and Sol. Walling of Wagonda, men well known throughout the western portion of Kansas. They had ended the hunt and were preparing to return, having traveled into Graham county, where the great buffalo grounds lie. On the morning of the 17th instant, a fall of snow commenced, mingled with sleet, and continued to increase in fury until mid day, when the party besought themselves to seek shelter in brush wood growing on the ravines so numerous in that section. With the increasing storm the wind became more boisterous and the air intensely cold. Camping for the night, and sheltering themselves as best they could, Saturday morning the 18th instant, found the party in snow four feet in depth—the fall during the night—the cold still more intense, and the wind not quieted. The camping place not being properly defended from the chilling blasts, a new start for better security was made. Falling in with another party, consisting of Richard Lake and brother, Frank Smith, George Steele, and _____ Carnes, of Atchison county, Missouri, who were also on the road for the same motive, they all united and soon succeeded in selecting a place, where a "dug out" six feet square was made, and into which the entire party gathered, half frozen, with barely life enough in any of them to start the fire ablaze. Three armfuls of wood was the quantity at hand, with which to keep the blood in a state of warmth.

In this "dug out," until the storm abated, did they remain, each one endeavoring to enliven the spirits of the
other, that sleep, arising from the cold, might not so possess
them, that the final sleep of death should be made in the
rude hut. Sunday morning the 19th inst., the storm began
to cease, and the sun, cheerfully dissolving the clouds, gave
hope and such cheer, that with vigor, they began their home-
ward march. Not one of the entire party but what had served
in the army for three years and endured the har[d]ships and
fatigues of campaigns incident thereto; but, as they state,
the severest of them all bears no comparison with the sufferings of those two days on the plains of the great west.
During the time spent in the "dug out," frequent firings
were heard in different directions, indicating that there
were others who were in condition equal to their own. Approaching the settlements and returning, they learned that
a party of seven who had previously gone out, had five of
their number frozen to death, the two remaining having
hands and feet frozen. A party of Texas herders had found
one man in a "dug out" frozen to death, and his comrade
over a smoldering blaze with a portion of his hands burned
off in his effort to keep up life. Another party, three in
number, two men and a boy sixteen years of age, were found
in a wagon, dead. This latter party were from somewhere in
Nebraska, and the wagon they had was of the "Excelsior"
make. Names unknown. The number, to this date known to
have perished is twelve. Two of the returning party were
badly frozen, but will recover. Many will wonder why, at this
season of the year, parties go in search of buffalo, but old
hunters following the habits of the Indians, look upon the
November month of the year as the best in the year for
securing good robes.

More have gone out to the buffalo grounds this year
than ever known before, and how many were caught in the
storm it is unable to determine. Certain it is that many
have gone to a long home, and who they are, or where

they came from, will perhaps never be satisfactorily an-
swered.

There are parties out now, your correspondent under-
stands, endeavoring to discover the remains of others. Further news as developed, will be communicated. (*Junction
City Weekly Union*, 2 December 1871)

R. R. SMITH AND SAM'L. R. BOYD, TWO OF THE PARTIES WHO
had their feet badly frozen down on the Canadian river,
about Christmas, while buffalo hunting, arrived in town last
Saturday evening and were operated upon Monday afternoon. Mr. Boyd had one foot amputated at the ankle his
other foot being unharmed. One of Smith's feet was taken
off through the ankle joint, and the other one was taken off
about the middle of the foot leaving him two very good
heels, upon which it is hoped he will be able to walk toler-
able well. Drs. McKinney, Sidlinger, McKee, and Neal participated equally in the operations. Mr. Smith has a family
and is very poor. Mr. Boyd we believe is a single man. They
are both doing very well at present. They are stopping in a
building on Sherman, opposite the livery stable. (*Hutchinson News*, 22 February 1877)

Even fishing accidents could sometimes be fatal:

ONE OF THE SADDEST ACCIDENTS THAT EVER OCCURRED IN
this country happened at the junction of the Smoky Hill
and Saline rivers, five miles east of Salina, last Saturday. A
company of gentlemen, viz: Ransom Calkins, Esq., R. D.
Calkins, James Muir, Geo. Garvin, Thomas Conway, George
Burtch, Valentine Goodall, Alexander Goodall and Joshua
Cruthers, started for the above named point to catch fish.
After their arrival at the place, Mr. Cruthers entered the
stream with the rope of the seine and commenced swimming across for the purpose of fastening it on the other side.
When a little way out, it is supposed that he cramped, as he
let go of the rope and commenced sinking. As soon as the

danger was discovered, Royal Calkins hastily undressed, and, followed by Alexander Goodall and George Garvin, pushed out into the river to rescue the drowning man. In the confusion that ensued, Cruthers pressed Calkins down, who narrowly escaped; and locked with young Goodall, and both were drowned. Valentine Goodall, the father of young Alexander, while attempting to save his son, was also drowned. On Sunday, the three men were buried; the funeral procession to the cemetery exceeding in size any other ever witnessed before in our county. The funeral sermon was preached by the Rev. Mr. Boynton. We had never formed the acquaintance of the deceased, but have heard them highly spoken of. Each leave widows and large families of children. (*Saline County Journal*, 1 June 1871)

A MINER BY THE NAME OF HUNT, WHO LIVES AT BONAZI, HAD one of his hands blown off by the explosion of a charge of giant powder, with which he intended to kill fish in Spring River. The Galena Miner says: "While we do not wish any body any ill luck, we don't find our heart overflowing with sympathy for a person who meets with misfortune while engaged in so pernicious an undertaking as killing fish in the manner above mentioned." (*Hays City Sentinel*, 25 January 1879)

Prairie fires were a hazard in autumn and early spring. Often these fires were purposely set to burn off the dead grasses so plows could more easily turn the sod. In other cases they were set accidentally. If adequate preparation had not been made, settlers could lose all of their possessions. The following excerpt indicates the general concern over the consequences of accidental prairie fires:

THE PRAIRIE CHICKEN SHOOTING WILL COMMENCE NEXT WEEK. Several farmers have requested us to state that it is their desire that hunters will take pains not to shoot into stubble, as damaging fires may arise from using their firearms too carelessly. If the stubble should take fire it might be impossible for some of the farmers to save their wheat stacks. We hope our town people, while in search of amusement, will properly regard and respect the wishes of the farmers with reference to their property. (*Saline County Journal,* 29 July 1875)

Wood rats, which were evidently fairly common, caused some problems that we might consider humorous now, but couldn't have been so at the time:

A MAN NAMED PARKS, MET WITH A SERIOUS ACCIDENT A FEW days ago, while chopping in Elm Grove. He and a brother were endeavoring to kill a wood rat that they had found, one trying to step on the rat and the other striking at it with an ax—when the former received a full force of the blow on the instep of his right foot, cutting it nearly half off. Dr. E. J. Donnell dressed the wound, which is doing well. (*Stockton News,* 16 January 1879)

A YOUNG CHAP DOWN AT THE RIVER ACCIDENTLY SAT DOWN on a wood rat Christmas Eve. He will probably be able to sit down again in about six weeks. (Cawker City Free Press) (*Kirwin Chief,* 31 December 1879)

Clearly, the advantages of interacting with the native wildlife were somewhat offset by hazards great and small.

CHAPTER 5

Concerns for Wildlife

Although many early Kansas settlers appreciated and enjoyed the animals of the prairie, this appreciation was not pervasive enough to prevent populations of some species from suffering. Not surprisingly, greed was one major reason for the decrease in numbers. The early market hunter (chapter 2) found an abundant supply of game on the prairies of Kansas and a ready market in the east, linked by the Kansas Pacific and Atchison, Topeka, and Santa Fe railroads. Hunters thus found a quick and relatively easy way to make a great deal of money in a brief period. Thousands availed themselves of that opportunity.

Secondly, populations of game animals were so bountiful as to appear inexhaustible to many immigrants. It seemed, to most, impossible that any amount of hunting, fishing, and trapping would have a deleterious effect on the populations of these native animals. Records of the incredible numbers of wildlife taken, and the virtual absence of documented criticism thereof, seem to substantiate that this was so.

Thirdly, and perhaps most significantly, the early settler did not comprehend the impact that agricultural activities would have on the native fauna. In the eastern United States, whence most Kansas immigrants came, environmental conditions were, in general, more benevolent. Precipitation was not only more abundant but was more evenly distributed throughout the year. Wind was not a significant environmental factor, and annual temperature extremes were less severe. Therefore, the environment in the eastern United States was more forgiving and resilient to the perturbations imposed by the settlers. On the prairies of Kansas the immigrants found a harsher, more extreme environment that was much less forgiving in nature. Habitat degradation occurred quickly with devastating results to the native wildlife.

As trees were cut along the rivers, habitat for riparian creatures such as turkey, grouse, quail, beaver, elk, and deer was totally destroyed. As prairies were broken to provide fields for corn, wheat, and millet, soil was exposed to wind and water erosion. The water runoff, heavily laden with topsoil, was carried to the streams and rivers, where the increased turbidity degraded the aquatic habitat. As a result, some populations of fish, mink, otter, beaver, and muskrat suffered. Land broken for crops destroyed available habitat for such grassland creatures as buffalo, antelope, prairie dog, and jackrabbit.

The combination of overharvesting for market and recreation with habitat degradation and destruction resulted in dwindling numbers of many species of native animals. On balance, the activities of the early settlers during 1865 to 1879 were clearly detrimental to several species of native wildlife.

Some Kansans, however, did become concerned for the welfare of wildlife species within the state. Out of this concern was born a variety of game laws that protected specific kinds of wildlife. Protection was provided for two reasons: first and foremost to assure Kansans that populations of game animals would be available to hunt; and second, to protect the beneficial birds of the region against predators. After the devastating plague of grasshoppers in 1874, many believed that protection for nongame yet beneficial species of birds was necessary. The smaller nongame birds (i.e., songbirds) frequently were hunted for food and sport. The bounty laws mentioned in chapter 4 were enacted partially to put an end to this practice.

Game laws and amendments thereto were passed in 1861, 1865, 1871, 1876, and 1877. These laws established the length of the hunting seasons for certain species of game animals and proscribed the killing of others. The problem of trespass was also addressed by the state legislature. Some property owners desired to prohibit the hunting of all birds—game and nongame alike—on their land. They were convinced that the avifauna were more beneficial in controlling insects than they were as meat for the table. Property owners were also concerned about errant bullets or unscrupulous hunters who might shoot pets or livestock. Trespass laws were passed in 1868 and 1872.

Hunters were urged by the local press to adopt a self-imposed limit on the number of animals killed on any given hunt. Some local hunting clubs also suggested that setting bag limits would be beneficial, but no such bag limits or possession limits, either daily or seasonally, were ever legislated.

Although penalties were prescribed for violating the letter of the law, there was little effort at enforcement. No officials were designated with the specific duty of upholding the game laws and protecting wildlife. The principal law-enforcement officer was the local sheriff, and perhaps a deputy—and some small villages had none. The local constabulary, if it existed, had little or no incentive to enforce the game laws of the state. Consequently, enforcement of the bird law was lax or totally absent, and much poaching undoubtedly occurred.

Primarily it was left to the individual hunter to observe the laws. Some hunters, no doubt, did so, but it is safe to assume that others took game when and wherever they chose. The illegal taking of game was reported by some of the papers, but other than personal embarrassment, this method had little effect. Some local newspapers strongly articulated the belief that there should be no hunting on the Sabbath, a tenet held by many of the early settlers who had a fundamentalist orientation. There is little evidence, though, that this approach was effective either. Game birds apparently did not receive their "day of rest."

A public policy without enforcement, of course, is no policy at all. A game department with enforcement responsibility did not exist in Kansas until early in the 1900s, when unpaid "game wardens" were appointed. Large game animals—antelope and buffalo—were never protected. Legislation was introduced at the state level in 1872 and at the federal level in 1876 to provide protection to the buffalo, but at neither level was the legislation enacted into law. In Kansas the buffalo herds were gone by 1873.

The rivers harbored abundant fish. Capture of fish was not initially regulated by law. Fish could be taken by any means, including the use of nets and seines. This nonpolicy, according to local observations, led to a decline in populations of fish. The suggested remedy was twofold: first, regulate the manner in which fish could be caught, and second, establish fishing seasons, which would allow the fish population to reproduce and thereby reestablish their numbers. However, some interested observers argued that an even greater increase in numbers could be realized if new stocks, representative of exotic species of game fish, were introduced into the waters of the state, and that additional habitat could be created through the construction of small ponds. Finally, in 1877 a state law was enacted that not only included all of these ideas but created the office of fish commissioner to see that the objectives were met.

The fish commissioner pursued his duties with considerable vigor. Citizens were particularly interested in the stocking of game fish as a way of increasing populations rapidly and also providing new species. However, knowledge of fish and their habitats and behavior was poor in 1877, and much effort and not a little money went for naught. To understand this, one need look no further than the efforts to stock salmon in Kansas with the expectation that they would emigrate to the Gulf of Mexico, then return large enough to be caught for food.

Almost from the inception of statehood there was a game law that protected some kinds of the native wildlife, as most settlers who immigrated to Kansas came from states where there had been game laws in effect. It is not so surprising, then, that Kansas enacted its first game law in 1861, the year it acquired statehood. But this initial law established season limits for only five species of game animals:

> Be it enacted by the Legislature of the State of Kansas:
> SECTION 1. That it shall be unlawful for any person or persons to shoot, kill or trap, within this State, any prairie chickens, quails, partridges, wild turkeys and deer, between the first days of April and September, of each year.
> SEC. 2. That any person convicted of violating this act, shall be fined in a sum not exceeding five dollars, and shall be liable for costs of prosecution.
> SEC. 3. That justices of the peace shall have jurisdiction of the offenses under this act, and all proceedings shall be in the

name of the State, and shall be regulated as other criminal proceedings of a minor character, before justices of the peace.

SEC. 4. That all fines imposed under this act shall be paid to the justice before whom the proceedings are had, who shall, within thirty days, pay the same into the county treasury, for the use of the common school fund of the county in which the offense shall have been committed.

SEC. 5. That, whenever the county board of commissioners shall have received a petition from at least twenty freeholders of such county, praying that this act be inoperative in such county, they may, in their discretion, so proclaim; and, after the date of such proclamation, no provision of this act shall be in force for twelve months.

SEC. 6. This act to be in force from and after its publication. Approved May 10, 1861.

(Session Laws of Kansas, 1861)

This law gave no protection to waterfowl, songbirds, hawks, owls, and other birds. These species could be, and often were, hunted throughout the year whenever the opportunity arose. For the animals listed the season was an ample seven months in length. In 1865 the legislature amended the 1861 law. It left the length of the hunting season the same but removed prairie chicken from the list, thereby permitting them to be hunted throughout the year:

Be it enacted by the Legislature of the State of Kansas:

SECTION 1. That section one of the act to which this is amendatory be and the same is hereby amended, so as to read as follows: Section 1. That it shall be unlawful for any person or persons to shoot, kill or trap within this State any quails, partridges, wild turkeys or deer, between the first days of April and September of each year.

SEC. 2. That section 1 of said act be and the same is hereby repealed.

Approved February 13, 1865.

(Session Laws of Kansas, 1865)

The removal of prairie chickens from the list of protected birds resulted in an increased number being killed and sold cheaply in the eastern markets. Concern over this development led a few people to urge that they be included once again on the protected list:

> THE PRAIRIE HEN, OR PINNATED GROUSE (*CUPIDONIA CU-pido*), will soon become extinct unless steps are taken for its protection, where alone it is now common, upon the prairies of the West. Ten years more of indiscriminate slaughter will make these beautiful birds almost as rare upon the prairies of Illinois as they are upon Long Island, where they were once equally plenty, but are now nearly extinct.
>
> The wholesale manner of their destruction may be understood from the fact that they are often received in such quantities in New-York as to only be worth from 20 to 40 cents apiece, and we have known tuns [sic] of them to spoil upon the hands of dealers. We remember when the price for them in Indiana and Illinois was six to twelve cents each and we have seen them sold ready dressed for the table, within thirty years past, less than forty miles from Chicago at 37½ cents per dozen.
>
> So much for description. Now for the object of writing this article. It is to urge the legislators of all the States where the prairie hens now abound to make stringent laws for their protection—to make it the duty of somebody to enforce these laws—to make the penalty fine and imprisonment for killing these birds at any time between Feb[r]uary and November, or making a wholesale destruction of them at any season with such traps and snares as are now used at the West for the purpose of supplying the people of New-York with this delicious game at the price of ordinary scalawag beef. (*Junction City Union*, 29 July 1865)

In 1868 a revised game law, which follows, restored prairie chicken to the protected list and added elk, snipe, and woodcock, with a seven-month season from 1 August to 1 March.

Quail and pheasant (ruffed grouse) remained on the protected list but with reduced seasons of five months from 1 October to 1 March. Additionally, for the first time fifteen species of songbird were protected throughout the year, but birds such as waterfowl, hawks, and owls remained unprotected. The early settlers viewed hawks and owls as undesirable species because of the supposed depredations against the farmer's domestic fowl. Consequently, on the prairies of western Kansas these large, predaceous birds were avidly hunted (see chapter 4).

Be it enacted by the Legislature of the State of Kansas:

SECTION 1. It shall be unlawful for any person to kill, destroy or take, or pursue with intent to kill, destroy or take, by any device, contrivance or means whatsoever, any grouse, prairie hen or chicken, woodcock, snipe, wild turkey, deer, elk or fawn, between the first day of March and the first day of August, or any quail or pheasant between the first day of March and the first day of October, in each and every year. Thrushes, robins, bluebirds, woodpeckers, mocking birds, yellowhammers, peewees [peewits], swallows, martins, bluejays, kildees [*sic*], snowbirds, wrens, meadow larks and doves shall not be killed at any time.

SEC. 2. It shall be unlawful for any person to buy or sell any of the above mentioned birds or animals which shall have been killed or taken during the time when the killing or taking of the same is prohibited by the last section; and the having in possession any of the above birds or animals, recently killed or taken by any person or persons, shall be deemed and held as *prima facie* evidence that the same were killed or taken by the person or persons having possession of the same, in violation of the provisions of this act.

SEC. 3. Every person offending against the provisions of either of the two preceding sections of this act, shall be subject to a fine of fifteen dollars for each deer, elk or fawn, and three dollars for each bird of the classes above described, which he shall be convicted of having taken, killed or destroyed, or having bought, sold or had in his possession.

SEC. 4. It shall be unlawful for any person, at any time, to take, catch or kill, within this state, by means of any trap, net or snare of any kind, any of the birds, of game of the kinds above described, except upon his own premises; and any person offending against the provisions of this section shall be subject to the same penalty as is prescribed for offenses against the first two sections of this act.

SEC. 5. Any person who shall go upon the premises of another, or of any corporation, whether inclosed or not, and shall be found hunting, trapping or ensnaring any of the above named birds or animals, in violation of the provisions of this act, shall be deemed guilty of trespass, and may be prosecuted by any person in possession of said premises, before any justice of the peace of the county, or other court of competent jurisdiction, and subjected to a penalty in any sum not less than five nor more than fifty dollars, to be paid, one moiety to the complainant, and one moiety into the county treasury for the benefit of the common school fund of the county: *Provided, however,* That a judgment against a person for a violation of this act under either of the first four sections thereof, shall be a bar to any prosecution under this section for the same offense.

SEC. 6. All fines imposed under the first four sections of this act shall be paid into the county treasury, for the use of the school fund of the county in which the offense was committed.

SEC. 7. This act shall be in force from and after its publication in the statute book.

Approved, March 2, 1868.

(Kansas, State Statute, 1868)

In 1871 the legislature passed the following law providing protection for the California quail from March 1871 to November 1876. This law is rather curious in that California quail were not known to inhabit Kansas, occurring far to the west, in California and Arizona. I could find no explanation for the introduction and passage of this statute. It's possible that some important individual or sportsmen's club introduced the California quail into Kansas and desired protection for it until it became established as a game species.

Be it enacted by the Legislature of the State of Kansas:

SECTION 1. On and after the first day of March, 1871, and until the first day of November, 1876, it shall be unlawful for any person or persons to net, entrap, shoot, or in any manner capture or kill a bird known as the California quail.

SEC. 2. Any person who shall violate this act shall, upon conviction thereof, be fined not more than fifty dollars, nor less than thirty dollars for each offense; and the possession of any such bird so killed or captured shall be *prima facie* evidence of a violation of this act; and that such persons stand committed until said fine is paid, or released by due process of law.

SEC. 3. This act shall take effect and be in force from and after its publication in the *Kansas Weekly Commonwealth.*

Approved February 6, 1871.

I hereby certify that the foregoing is a true and correct copy of the original enrolled bill now on file in my office, and that the same was published in the *Kansas Weekly Commonwealth,* February 23, 1871.

W. H. SMALLWOOD,
Secretary of State
(Session Laws of Kansas, 1871b)

Although section 5 of the 1868 game law addresses trespass, a separate trespass law was introduced and passed during the 1872 legislative session. Permission of the land owner was required prior to hunting:

Be it enacted by the Legislature of the State of Kansas:

SECTION 1. That any person who shall hunt with gun, dog, net, or other hunting apparatus, upon the enclosed grounds or lands of another, without first obtaining leave of the owner so to do, shall be deemed guilty of a misdemeanor, and shall, on conviction thereof before a justice of the peace, be punished by a fine of not less than five dollars, nor more than twenty dollars for each offense.

SEC. 2. This act shall take effect and be in force from and after its publication in the *Kansas Weekly Commonwealth.*

Approved March 1, 1872.

(Session Laws of Kansas, 1872)

There was little in the way of enforcement for any of these laws. From time to time hunters were apprised of the trespass law and admonished to adhere to it by editors:

IT MAY BE INTERESTING TO SOME OF YOUR READERS TO KNOW that farmers northeast of the city, (and elsewhere I believe,) are not unmindful of the hard lesson they learned last year, nor heedless of the many well-intended hints which accompanied contributions for their relief; and the time has now come when they seem unanimously resolved to discharge a well-known, though hitherto neglected duty, in protecting themselves against the wanton slaughter of chickens, which a Providence has bountifully bestowed upon western farmers to check the ravages of grasshoppers, and mitigate locust scourges. Farmers are practical if not theoretical, and though they trouble themselves little with abstruse calculations, they are expert at the four first rules, especially the first and third. By these they find that a chicken which eats about 100 grasshoppers daily, destroys about 12,000 of them before they begin to deposit their eggs in the fall; and if, as "bugologists" tell us, each hopper lays an average of about 5,000 eggs, then each chicken would this year destroy 60,000,000 of next year[']s grasshoppers, and consequently the vast numbers of chickens annually slaughtered by professional gunners and sportsmen, who ought to be in better business, would be sufficient to destroy such numbers as Prof. Tice himself could not calculate—such numbers as no repetition of our limited number of figures is capable of expressing; but, as we can easily guess, quite all the grasshoppers and locusts from here to the Rocky Mountains and as far beyond, together with myriads of other voracious tribes which every year mock the patient farmer's toil. In this determination to protect their protectors, farmers are considerably influenced by being continually overrun by hunters who have no respect for game laws and little sense of propriety in them, some even possessed of effrontery enough to ride over hedges and hedge rows, and around people's gardens shooting barn-yard fowls, chickens, ducks and turkeys, alike. This, of course, is done only when there happens to be nobody around. It may seem incredible, but is nevertheless strictly true and the perpetrators or suspected ones, are watched for. (*Wichita City Eagle*, 5 August 1875)

NEXT WEEK TUESDAY THE HUNTERS WILL MARCH TO THE prairie chicken grounds. We hope they will obey the law in every respect, and hunt on grounds only after the owner's consent. One man may not care whether a hunter kills all the chickens within fifty miles of him, while another man may have a special interest in preserving all the birds upon his place. There are more chickens this year than there has been for many years before. There is a great plenty for all, without violating in any way the spirit and provisions of the law. Ask the farmer's consent first, and then enjoy yourself. (*Saline County Journal*, 10 August 1876)

Many hunters did not observe the trespass law and, in addition, occasionally shot farm animals. This practice irritated farmers, who published the names of the guilty parties and proclaimed their property to be off-limits to hunters:

THE VOICE OF THE QUAIL IS HEARD IN THE LAND; ALSO THE voice of the farmer whose dog has been shot by mistake for quails. It is "voicy" enough in either case. (*Saline County Journal*, 19 November 1874)

ALL PERSONS ARE HEREBY FORBIDDEN TO SHOOT OR OTHERWISE capture quails on my premises, under penalty of the law.—
W. Rader. (*Osborne County Farmer,* 9 November 1877)

IN ADDITION TO THE NAMES FOUND ON THE OUTSIDE OF THIS weeks [sic] paper, the following persons have the same proclamation in regard to the shooting of prairie chickens: "We the undersigned, farmers of Empire township, give notice to hunters, that are in the habit of shooting chickens and quails upon our farms, that we will not allow such wholesale slaughter as has been practiced in the past few weeks. Persons found violating this notice will be dealt with as tresspassers [sic]: Robert Hudson, David Essick, B. A. Wood, C. M. Clifton, J. S. Essick, T. Sternberg, W. B. Essick, D. B. Long, M. Schivsagan, A. Horney, J. Potter, G. P. Stiner, F. Sternberg." (*Ellsworth Reporter,* 28 August 1879)

Excessive hunting and fishing, coupled with habitat degradation, destruction, and natural calamities reduced the populations of some species of wildlife dramatically. When those species were of obvious benefit to the majority of settlers, many expressed concern, which usually resulted in the passage of new laws, or amendments to existing laws, to protect the species in question. Voices were often raised to protect birds. These animals not only were affected by hunting, plowing, and the cutting of timber, but were also victims of their natural predators. Some, like the farmer who wrote the following letter, argued that crows and skunks should be controlled, thereby permitting the survival of beneficial birds. Not everyone, however, agreed with this strategy:

THE MOST EFFECTUAL WAY TO SPARE USEFUL BIRDS IS TO DEstroy their worst enemies, viz: the crow and the skunk. Thirty years ago the meadow larks in flocks of a dozen or twenty were often seen. But now two or three pairs are all I see during the season. The nest mowed over yesterday is found empty this morning. Nothing is left but two wings of the mother bird, while the skunk tracks are visible on every square rod of newly-mown grass.—Thirty years ago the place to find robins' nests was the corners of rail fences. But now robins build their nests in the shade trees nearest the house, under piazzas in old barns and under sheds. The crow is an omnivorous feeder. During the winter he will live on carrion, in the fall on grasshoppers, but in June nothing delights his palate more than young birds' [sic] and eggs. During the early morning hours I have known crows to alight in a tree, containing a robin's nest, not ten feet from my front door. Later in the morning they have been seen in the orchard pursuing birds on the wing. A crow is seen to start from the hilltop, sail majestically down into the meadow, and alight by the side of a stump or clump of willows. Instantly two small birds are seen fluttering about, and filling the air with their piteous cries. Or, he directs his flight to a solitary maple by the road side, when two red-winged black birds fly out uttering cries of alarm. The crow leaves in a few minutes, and the black birds disappear the next day. Their nests have been destroyed. It may be that crows destroy a few grubs. It is quite certain he destroys a great many birds in the eggs or embryo. Grubs in a potato field are a nuisance. But a skunk is a greater nuisance, for he will destroy more potatoes than the grubs. One season I was obliged to go around daily and pick up the potatoes unearthed during the night. I set a trap and caught a skunk, which put an end to the evil. That one skunk did more mischief than a bushel of grubs could do. This crow and skunk question has two sides. Careful observation has satisfied one that if birds are the friends of man, the crow and skunk are among his worst enemies, and when I read in the *Times,* of a man in Pennsylvania killing nine hundred and forty-four crows last winter, I say good! That man is a benefactor to his race.—J. H. P. in *New York Times.* (*Ellsworth Reporter,* 5 August 1875)

A GENTLEMAN WHO KNOWS, SAYS THAT THE POLE-CAT OR skunk will do more than thirty cents worth of good any sea-

son, destroying vermin, insects and small animals. This being true it is bad economy to kill them and sell their hides
for that price. They do no harm and much good. They
should be cultivated. (*Hutchinson News*, 13 January 1876)

Natural calamities, such as early hard freezes and hailstorms,
took their toll on birds. These periodic weather phenomena
must have accounted for the deaths of many.

AN ITEM IN THE BELOIT *GAZETTE* SAYS THE QUAILS OF THAT
section are all frozen to death, and it will be years before
these beautiful birds will be so plentiful in Mitchell county
as during the past year. (*Ellsworth Reporter*, 18 February
1875)

THE LATE FLOOD HAS BEEN DEATH TO GOPHERS, GROUND
squirrels[,] rabbits, snakes, etc. Scores of them can be seen
lying dead along the streams and on the prairie. (*Stockton
News*, 31 May 1877)

KIRWIN WAS VISITED WITH ONE OF THE MOST SEVERE AND DE-
structive hail and rain storms on the 21st ult., that ever
passed over this section of the country, some of the hail
stones measured 5 3-4 inches in circumference, and weighed
over 3 ounces[.] The ground was covered with hail in some
places to the depth of 2 inches. Prairie chickenes [*sic*] and
birds were killed on the prairie by the hundreds. 438 window lights were broken in [K]irwin. (*Stockton News*, 7 May
1879)

Quail especially were appreciated by both farmers and hunters,
and their killing stridently condemned by some editors. Any
reduction in their population was noticed, and many suggested
that hunters should limit themselves to taking no quail, relegat-
ing instead their hunting to other species.

THE *UNION* SAYS THE RAILWAY AGENT AT ST. GEORGE, FROM
Oct. 25th to Dec. 23rd, 1874, killed 934 quails, 84 grouse,

59 rabbits, 8 geese, 4 ducks and 1 deer. We think for each quail, and grouse, he ought to receive twenty lashes well laid on with a raw-hide. (*Ellsworth Reporter*, 22 July 1875)

A MR. REESE OF BOURBON COUNTY, TRAPPED 920 PRAIRIE chickens in five days. He ought to be caught in the jaws of a powerful steel trap, and kept the remainder of his life. (*Ellsworth Reporter*, 11 February 1875)

IT IS A DEPLORABLE FACT THAT A GREAT MANY QUAILS WERE killed by the severe winter and that something must be done to prevent their entire extermination. Several of the prominent hunters of this place propose that a written agreement be entered into by all the sportsmen of Saline county in which they shall agree to refrain from shooting quail until another year. Most of the quail killed each season are shot by town hunters, and this agreement if carried out as intended, will serve to populate the now almost depopulated quail districts. (*Saline County Journal*, 27 May 1875)

In 1876 the game law was amended. It removed elk from the protected list. At the same time the hunting season was reduced to 4½ months for deer, turkey, prairie chicken, and ruffed grouse and to only 2 months (November and December) for quail, due in large part to the reduced numbers. Not all hunters approved (the *Saline County Journal* of 3 February reported that "the prairie chicken and quail hunters begin to mourn over the 'anti-hunting' disposition of the present Legislature"). The law, which follows, also listed twenty-eight species of birds that were totally protected; however, it made no changes in the 1868 law that excluded waterfowl, owls, and hawks.

Be it enacted by the Legislature of the State of Kansas:
    SECTION I. It shall be unlawful for any person or persons to hunt or pursue, kill or trap, net or ensnare, destroy or attempt to kill, trap, net, ensnare or otherwise destroy any wild buck, doe or fawn, wild turkey, prairie hen or chicken,

ruffled grouse (commonly called partridge or pheasant), between the first day of January and the fifteenth day of
August in each and every year, or any quail between the
first day of January and the first day of November, or any
woodcock between January first and July first: *Provided,
however,* That it shall not be lawful for any person at any
time to kill any quail other than upon the party's own
premises, unless permission first be had.

SEC. 2. Any person or corporation violating any of the
provisions of the preceding section shall forfeit and pay a
fine of fifteen dollars for each wild buck, doe or fawn thus
killed, trapped, netted, ensnared or otherwise destroyed,
bought, sold or had in possession; and a fine of ten dollars
for each wild turkey, prairie hen or chicken, ruffled grouse,
pheasant or woodcock thus killed, trapped, netted, ensnared
or otherwise destroyed, bought, sold or had in possession as
aforesaid.

SEC. 3. No person shall at any time within this state kill or
attempt to kill, trap, net, ensnare or destroy any California
quail, turkey buzzard, robin, blue bird, swallow, martin, mus-
quito [*sic*] hawk, whippoorwill, cuckoo, woodpecker, cat
bird, brown thrasher, red bird, hanging bird, blue jay, finch,
thrush, lark, cherry bird, yellow bird, oriole, bobolink, English sparrow, wren, phebpeewee, indigo bird, swallow, king
bird, or other upland insectivorous birds, or rob or destroy
the nests of such birds or any of them; and every person so
offending, on conviction thereof, shall be fined in a sum not
exceeding five dollars for each and every offense proven:
Provided, That it shall not be necessary on the trial of any
action or prosecution to prove that the bird killed, trapped,
netted or ensnared was an upland insectivorous bird: *And
provided further,* That it shall not be necessary on the trial of
any prosecution under the provisions of this act to prove the
true name of the bird caught, killed, trapped, netted or
ensnared, it being sufficient to show that a bird was caught,
killed, trapped, netted or ensnared.

SEC. 4. No person shall at any time within this state, with a trap or snare or net, take or attempt to trap, snare or take any wild turkey, prairie chicken, Virginia partridge, pheasant, grouse or quail, except on his or her premises and for his or her family use; and any person so offending, on conviction thereof, shall be fined in a sum not less than five nor more than ten dollars for each and every offense.

SEC. 5. It shall be unlawful for any person to intentionally destroy or remove from the nest of any prairie chicken, grouse, quail or wild turkey any eggs of such fowl or birds, or for any person to buy, sell or have in possession or traffic in such eggs, or willfully destroy the nest of any such birds or fowls; and any person so offending, on conviction thereof, shall be fined in the sum of five dollars for each and every offense.

SEC. 6. It shall be unlawful for any person, railroad corporation or express company, or any common carrier, knowingly to transport or to ship, or to receive for the purpose of transporting or shipping, any of the animals, wild fowls or birds mentioned in this act in or out of the state of Kansas; and any common carrier so offending shall forfeit and pay to the state of Kansas, for each and every offense, the sum of one hundred dollars, the same to be recovered in an action brought in the name of the state of Kansas by any person against any such person, corporation or company before any court of competent jurisdiction in any county into or through which said game may be taken; and any agent of any such person, corporation or company who shall knowingly violate the provisions of this section by receiving or shipping any such game as the agent of such person, corporation or company, shall, on conviction thereof, be fined in a sum not less than ten nor more than fifty dollars; and the having in possession any of the above birds or animals recently killed or taken by any person or persons, shall be deemed and held as *prima facie* evidence that the same were killed or taken by the company, corporation or person having possession of the same in violation of the provisions of this act: *Provided,* That such penalty shall not apply to the transportation of such birds and animals in transit through this state from other states and territories.

SEC. 7. The provisions of this act shall not apply to any person who shall kill any of the birds or animals protected by this act for the sole purpose of preserving them as specimens for scientific purposes, nor to any person who shall collect the eggs or nests of any birds for such scientific purposes: *Provided,* That in a prosecution for the violation of any of the provisions of this act, it shall not be necessary for the prosecution to prove that the killing of the birds or animals, or the taking of the nest or eggs, as the case may be, was not done for scientific purposes.

SEC. 8. All prosecutions or suits under this act shall be commenced within three months after the offense is alleged to have been committed; and the court before whom any action is prosecuted under the provision of this act shall tax, as part of the costs of the case, against the defendant, on conviction, the sum of ten dollars, to be paid when collected to the attorney prosecuting such action.

SEC. 9. Chapter forty-five of the general statutes of eighteen hundred and sixty-eight is hereby repealed.

SEC. 10. This act shall take effect and be in force from and after its publication in the *Commonwealth.*

Approved February 23, 1876.

(Session Laws of Kansas, 1876)

In 1877 the game law was again amended. Instead of listing the species that were protected, it listed those species that were not. The law protected all species (including turkey) except waterfowl, hawks, owls, and snipe. The hunting season for prairie chicken was increased to six months, and quail to three months.

Be it enacted by the Legislature of the State of Kansas:

SECTION 1. That it shall be unlawful for any person or

persons at any time to catch, kill or trap, net or ensnare, or to pursue with such intent, any wild bird, except the wild goose, duck, hawk, owl and snipe; and any person or persons violating the provisions of this act shall be fined in any sum not more than fifteen dollars nor less than five dollars, for each and every offense, to be recovered in any court of competent jurisdiction in the proper county: *Provided,* That it shall not be unlawful to kill the prairie chicken between the first day of August and the first day of February; and it shall not be unlawful to kill quail from the first day of October to the first day of January of each year: *And provided further,* It shall not be necessary on the trial of any action or prosecution to prove the true name of the bird caught, killed, trapped, netted or ensnared—it being sufficient to show that a wild bird other than those excepted in this act was caught, killed, trapped, netted or ensnared by the defendant or defendants.

SEC. 2. It shall be unlawful for any person intentionally to destroy or remove from the nest of any wild bird any eggs or the young of such bird; or for any purpose to buy, sell or have in possession, or traffic in such eggs, or willfully destroy the nest of any wild bird; and any person so offending, on conviction thereof, shall be fined in the sum of five dollars for each and every offense. . . .

SEC. 7. This act shall take effect and be in force from and after its publication in the *Commonwealth.*

Approved March 5, 1877.

(Session Laws of Kansas, 1877c)

There was little effort to enforce the game laws. In a few cases grangers or farming groups and gun clubs took the initiative to prosecute those hunters who operated outside the law, an action that some editors publicly lauded:

WE ARE GLAD TO SEE THAT SOME OF THE GRANGES ARE TAK-ing up the bird question in the proper spirit, and propose to prosecute offenders under the law. Keep the ball moving. (*Ellsworth Reporter*, 20 May 1875)

THE SMOKY HILL GUN CLUB WILL PROSECUTE ANY PERSON found [g]uilty of violating the law, as above stated, in this county. It is to be hoped that the law will not be violated. (*Ellsworth Reporter*, 9 January 1879)

With limited law enforcement, however, there was little respect for opening day of hunting season, and many hunters chose not to honor it. Editors had a rather unique way of suggesting that some nimrods had opened the season early:

PRAIRIE CHICKENS WILL BE RIPE NEXT SATURDAY. SOME THAT were accidently killed last Saturday are reported good. (*Ellsworth Reporter*, 30 July 1874)

IN SPITE OF THE LAW THE SHOOTING OF PRAIRIE CHICKENS has been going on over a fortnight, some parties bringing in 30 or 40 birds. These same parties are the first to squeal about horse stealing, but they violate the law as much as a horse thief. (*Ellsworth Reporter*, 1 August 1878)

All of the gaming laws enacted from 1861 to 1877 listed the protected animals and set the season during which the game animal could be hunted. None, however, addressed the number of animals that could be taken in a day's hunt. A local hunting group in the Saline valley suggested that such a measure would help protect the birds:

THERE SEEMS TO BE A DISPOSITION AMONG SOME OF THE sportsmen to form a regular association for the government of hunters in this section of the country. They regard it as necessary to establish certain rules, and that they should be rigidly enforced. One of them would be the limiting [of] the number of birds to be killed by one hunter during one hunt or for the season. The usual wholesale slaughter of birds repeated each season, will soon deprive the country of

game, and it is only through the medium of a sporting association that this can be checked. What do the hunters say?
Shall such an association be formed? (*Saline County Journal,*
26 July 1877)

Prairie-chicken populations especially were reduced. This
fact, along with the chicken's value in consuming insects, led
some to suggest that prairie chicken should be removed from the
list of game birds:

> WE BELIEVE THE KILLING OF PRAIRIE CHICKENS OUGHT TO BE
> wholly prohibited at all seasons of the year, and hope the
> farmers all over Kansas will work this matter up so as to
> secure the necessary enactments at the next term of our
> State legislature. (*Pawnee County Herald,* 11 August 1877)

In a few cases hunters reached a mutual understanding that
they would limit themselves and not hunt certain species. This
was especially true for quail. Concern for quail was widespread,
and many state newspapers, as indicated by the following excerpts, implored hunters not to shoot them and to stay within
the law. Evidently some hunters did indeed impose a self-limi-
tation on quail hunting.

> SALINA'S SPORTSMEN HAVE ENTERED INTO A SOLEMN COM-
> pact not to shoot any quail until another year. The severity
> of last winter very nearly exterminated this beautiful bird,
> and we hope our hunter's [*sic*] will follow the example of
> Salina. (*Ellsworth Reporter,* 3 June 1875)

> WE ARE GLAD TO NOTICE THAT OUR HUNTERS RETURN FROM
> the fields with no quails. It seems to be a general under-
> standing among them that they will not shoot these beauti-
> ful little birds, for at least a year or so. (*Saline County Jour-
> nal,* 6 December 1877)

It wasn't long, however, before the portion of the game law
prohibiting the shipping of birds across the state line was found

to be unconstitutional, as the *Saline County Journal* reported on 10 January 1878. This development allowed even more market hunting to occur. Nearly two years later, according to an article in the *Ellsworth Reporter*, a law was enacted by the state legislature that prevented quail from being hunted for one year from 1 November 1879 to 1 November 1880:

A SPECIAL LAW, ENACTED AT THE LAST SESSION OF THE LEGISlature, provides that no quail shall be shot within the limits of the State for one year from November 1, 1879. This law was enacted in response to an urgent call from sportsmen, because of the growing scarcity of this species of game, chased by the ravages of persons who have no regard for the game law. A heavy penalty is inflicted for its violation, and we should like to see it enforced. (*Ellsworth Reporter*, 4 December 1879)

The article in the *Ellsworth Reporter* is interesting in that no game law was passed in the 1879 state legislative session. Upon reading the *Journal of the House* for March 5, 1879, I found the following notation concerning House Bill 202:

HOUSE BILL NO. 202, AN ACT TO AMEND SECTION I, CHAPTER 118, of the Session Laws of 1877, entitled "An act for the protection of birds," was read a third time, and the question being, Shall the bill pass? the roll was called, with the following result: Whole number of votes cast, 90; constitutional majority, 65. Yeas, 84; nays, 6; absent or not voting, 39.

And so, a constitutional majority having voted in favor of the passage of the bill, the bill passed, and the title, being again read, was agreed to. (Kansas, *House Journal*, 1879, p. 973–74)

However, in the *Journal of the Senate* on March 10, 1879, House Bill 202 was considered but not passed:

ON MOTION OF SENATOR TAYLOR, THE FURTHER CONSIDERAtion of House bill No. 202, An act to amend section 1, chapter 118, of the Session Laws of 1877, entitled "An act for the protection of birds," was indefinitely postponed. (Kansas, *Senate Journal*, 1879, p. 737)

Evidently the *Ellsworth Reporter* was in error when it reported that such a law existed, because the bill passed the House but not the Senate. The precise wording of House Bill 202 is no longer extant, but one might assume that it was the Quail Protection Bill referred to by the *Ellsworth Reporter*.

An entirely different approach to animal conservation could be found in the strict religious orientation of many early settlers who believed that no activity save worshiping the Lord should take place on Sunday. This included hunting. Some settlers believed that this higher law should protect the birds, at least on the Sabbath:

IN MOST SECTIONS OF THE WEST SUNDAY IS BUT LITTLE OB-served. In fact we know of no city of any importance, in the Arkansas Valley, outside of Hutchinson, where the day is observed with eastern decorum and exactness. In most border towns Sunday is the big day for dissipation, and such a thing as divine service is a rarity. But that is not the case here. When the sacred day rolls around the song of praise and the voice of prayer is heard, and our streets are quiet. Almost the only thing in connection with the Sabbatical Institution we can complain of is the practice some of our young men have of hunting. Since the chicken season has come in, nearly every Sunday certain parties hasten off to the prairies for the purpose of amusing themselves. At most of the western towns this would not be regarded as derelict. However, here it is different. It is looked upon, and very properly, as a bad habit, and one not in keeping with the spirit and character of our city. It is an express violation of the Fourth Commandment and he who indulges in it has no excuse if he regards religion as the basis of society, and sees any virtue whatever in Sabbatical Institutions—institutions which were directly originated by God. Such parties cannot get off by exclaiming like Shylock, "my sins upon my own head," because they owe something to society as well as other people. The influence of their example is contagious. If that example is not of the right kind its tendencies are bad, and this increases the labor of the good people of the city to keep matters "straight." As a further consideration for those who engage in hunting on Sunday, we would suggest that they are observed by their fellow citizens, and such conduct is sure to be set down as details of their character, and as such, it may at some time or other enter into an estimate of them, in such a manner as to hurt. We hope we may not have our attention drawn to this matter any more. (*Hutchinson News*, 5 September 1872)

A NUMBER OF OUR CITIZENS WERE OUT CHICKEN SHOOTING on Sunday; every one of their wives would have been better pleased if they had chosen some other day. Even if men disregard the laws of the land and of God, I think they will agree that it is wisest to abstain from all that shocks the moral sense of a good woman. E. PARSON (Brookville) (*Ellsworth Reporter*, 7 August 1879)

In a scathing editorial condemning those individuals who killed large numbers of prairie chicken, the remarks of the *Ellsworth Reporter* were particularly vitriolic toward those who hunted on Sunday:

IT IS WELL KNOWN BY THE SPORTING AND GAMING GENTRY OF the country that they are now licensed by law to make a business of killing the prairie chickens and grouse which a kind Providence has made it congenial for their growth among all civilized communities of this once barren wilderness of hills and plains. As civilization and habitations for man are spreading over this vast country, it is with gratifying delight we welcome the approach of this beautiful and luxurious bird, evidently designed for the sustanance [*sic*] of man. These birds, at a certain season of the year are protected from the ravages of the shot-gun in the hands of a certain class of gentry, who seem to live for nothing else but to ramble the earth and kill and destroy, unwontonly [sic], everything which comes in their course. These birds make their nests around and about the fields of the farmers who take almost as much pride in the fine display of the wild chicken that hovers over and about his place and feeds upon the sweat of his brow, as he would over his domestic fowls. It is with a feeling of sadness for one to witness the wholesale destruction of his companions of the field. In the past few days there have been hundreds of these birds slaughtered and hauled away. Only two guns killed over one hundred in an afternoon; it cannot certainly be that such a number could be consumed in an equitable manner. This *kill* gentry is not only content to play their foul game on the working days of the week, but will openly and above board violate the laws of both God and man, and all honor of decency and respect, to the quietness of a peaceful and reli-gious community, will march deliberately out before the as-tonished and worshiping people on the holy Sabbath day and engage in their murderous destruction of the fowls of the field, that even our domestic fowls will start up and hunt a place of safety. This community is aroused with in-dignation at such outrageous proceedings against respect-ability and moral principals. The time has now come to as-sert our rights by interfering, and protect, as far as the law will assist, in arresting this wicked conduct.

Hereafter be it known that if there be any more shooting or hunting on the Sabbath day in the community known as the Buck-Eye or Crown Hill lands, if such is the case, the law will be consulted, irrespective of parties.

Yours, WM. FARIS (*Ellsworth Reporter,* 21 August 1879)

The buffalo, which along with the antelope was never provided protection under the law, was the most common large game mam-mal in Kansas. Interestingly, many of the hunters of the buffalo felt twinges of conscientious regret after killing large numbers. In most cases this resulted in the hunters taking a vow that in the future only the number that could be used would be shot, or that an effort would be made to be less wasteful: They would try to use all of the animal rather than a small part, such as the tongue and hide. Sometimes this concern took the form of a plea to the public to reduce the numbers that were killed. In extremis, legislation was introduced in an attempt to preserve the buffalo:

THE CITIZENS OF PEACE AND VICINITY INCLUDING SOME PARties living in this country, recently took a big buffalo hunt. They left Peace on Wednesday of last week, and did not get back until Monday the 28th. The party consisted of eight ladies and fifteen men and boys, conveyed in four wagons drawn by as many spans of spirited horses. About twenty miles south of the Arkansas they found thousands of buffalo, and had a glorious time shooting at them. They secured four very fine ones and wounded several others that got away. The ladies showed as much gallantry as the men and boys. Miss Ninde shot a very large animal, and her little brother 11 years old sent a bullet into another with such force as to knock him down although he afterwards escaped. Nothwithstanding [sic] the success of their expedition our moral friends at Peace express the intention to kill no more buffalo until cold weather. This is in consequence of all the meat secured in the above described expedition spoiling. We hope they will stick to their determination, and that their example will be followed by the rest of the people of the Arkansas Valley. The wanton and wholesale destruction of buffalo is outrageous and we would be glad if the U. S. Congress would pass a law restraining the abuse. (Hutchinson News, 1 August 1872)

THE SHIPMENT OF BUFFALO HIDES AND ROBES FROM THIS point is astonishing. Mr. Marsh informs us that an average of two car loads per day, or about one thousand hides per day, for the past two months, have been sent forward from Wichita. Some of these hides have been consigned to par-

The "monarch of the plains." *Harper's New Monthly Magazine.*

ties in Liverpool, and will be manufactured into leather. The destruction of these animals for the past winter has been fearful. Whole car loads of buffalo tongues have been shipped. A Congressional law should be enacted against the wanton destruction of these monarchs of the plains. (*Hutchinson News*, 27 March 1873)

More and more often, newspapers would openly express sympathy for the buffalo, and outrage against the manner in which they were taken:

THE PARTY OF ENGLISH CAPITALISTS WERE AT WALLACE AND killed thirty of the poor buffaloes. (*Ellsworth Reporter*, 10 October 1872)

BUFFALO HUNTING IN THIS NEIGHBORHOOD IS ALL THE RAGE just now. No less than a dozen parties have passed through Hutchinson within the past week on their way to the buffalo range, now about twenty-five miles southwest. At that distance generally plenty of buffalo are found. A few miles further on, and they appear in countless thousands, blackening the prairie with their shaggy forms. One man with his team brought in eighty hides a few days ago. Some of the hunters are in quest of meat, but a very large majority hunt to kill for the mere sport of the thing. Experiments to see how much "lead" a certain buffalo bull can get away with are of common occurrence. This sort of sport seems to us the very acme of human cruelty and should be discouraged everywhere and at all times. (*Hutchinson News*, 17 October 1872)

WE SAW NO BUFFALOES ALIVE, THOUGH ENDLESS SKELETONS lay on each side of the track, and we passed several dead bodies in various states of decomposition. A most cruel and foolish fashion prevails on these trains, of shooting the poor animals from the cars as they go along, for the mere pleasure of killing. Of course, many more are missed than hit: but when they are wounded there is no means of stopping to despatch them; so they die in misery along the line. (Kingsley, 1874, p. 39)

There was limited activity at the state level to protect the buffalo. In 1872 Mr. Edwards, representative to the state legislature from Ellis County, introduced House Bill 106 that would have provided some protection to the buffalo. The exact wording of that bill is evidently no longer extant, but the bill was passed from the house and ultimately vetoed by the governor. The *Kansas Daily Commonwealth* gave only a few brief notices to the bill:

> H.B.106. TO PREVENT THE WANTON DESTRUCTION OF BUF-falo—by Mr. Edwards. (*Kansas Daily Commonwealth*, 18 January 1872)

> MR EDWARDS MOVED THAT THE BILL 106 TO STOP THE WAN-ton destruction of buffalo, be referred to a special committee of three, composed of the members from Lincoln, Wallace, and Ellsworth. Adopted. (*Kansas Daily Commonwealth*, 2 February 1872)

> H.B.106, TO PREVENT THE WANTON DESTRUCTION OF BUF-faloes was read the third time and passed. (*Kansas Daily Commonwealth*, 1 March 1872)

This was the first and last attempt to provide legislative protection for the buffalo at the state level. As long as trade involving buffalo was profitable to the railroads, and therefore to the state, there was little incentive and even a lesser chance of passing laws to save the buffalo. In 1912 T. S. Palmer of the U.S. Department of Agriculture wrote the following assessment of the sorry fate of the buffalo:

> NEITHER KANSAS NOR TEXAS EVER ESTABLISHED ANY CLOSE season, the reason for which is apparent. With the building of the Kansas Pacific and the Atchison, Topeka, & Santa Fe Railroads in the early seventies, an important trade in buffalo hides and meat arose at several points in southern

Kansas, notably at Dodge City, Leavenworth, and Wichita. From these centers persistent and concerted attacks were made on the southern herd between 1871 and 1874; and so long as buffalo killing remained profitable it was impossible to secure any legislation which would interfere with the traffic. With the disappearance of the southern herd about 1874 the need for a close season vanished. Briefly stated, not the slightest protection was afforded in the way of legislation in the States in which buffalo were most abundant and in which, through its accessibility, the species was most quickly exterminated. (*Palmer*, 1912)

In 1865 it appeared as though the vast herds of buffalo would last forever. However, as early as 1869 the decline was noted. Hunters made deliberate reductions, but it was the demand for hides that finally spelled doom for the herds in western Kansas and elsewhere (chapter 2). By 1875 herds were noticeably smaller, and hunters were forced to go south into Oklahoma and Texas. Even there they were often disappointed:

THE BUFFALO IS CERTAINLY DECREASING SINCE 1858. THEY have been pressed more than a hundred miles west in Kansas and Nebraska. . . .

That the buffalo is fast disappearing there is certainly no reason to doubt. The Indians tell you that the herds are less numerous; the "rancher" vouches the same fact; the trader has raised the price of the robe; and many of the eastern trails are "mossed over" from disuse. The Indians and buffalo are moved about as far to the west as they can well go. (Davis, 1869, p. 153)

BUFFALO HUNTING ON THE PLAINS, THE PRESENT SEASON, IS not so profitable as heretofore. Indeed, between the Arkansas and Platte valleys but few are visible, and those few are confined to the head waters of the Republican and Smoky rivers. (*Denver Daily Tribune*, 24 November 1875)

THERE WAS A HERD OF BUFFALO STRAYED BACK TO THIS county to look at the progress we are making. Mr. McIlvain discovered that they were on his farm and they were traveling in an easterly direction. (*Kirwin Chief,* 17 April 1878)

By the close of 1873 newspapers were declaring the end of the large herds of buffalo:

THE BUFFALOES OF THE PLAINS HAVE MET THEIR FATE. EN-croaching civilization has sealed their doom; and the inordinate greed of man has swept them from the face of the earth. Where years ago the mammoth herds of bison roamed the plains and were hunted only by the Indians as necessity demanded, now lie the bleaching bones of millions of those noble animals sacrificed simply for their hides. For the past two years the work of destruction and annihilation has gone forward, and to-day there are not enough buffaloes to form what was at one time considered a moderate sized herd. Millions of these animals ranged the plains, their natural home, feeding upon the rich grasses. To-day there are not enough to graze on a quarter section of land and eat the feed bare. Hunting parties are to be met all over the plains in the vicinity of the Republican, and also in the southern portion of the territory, who slaughter indiscriminately every herd upon which they come. The traveler over the Kansas Pacific road may see cords of white bones piled up at various stations in the buffalo country, awaiting transportation east where they enter into a thousand and one articles of commerce and trade. Besides the bones are thousands of hides, rough dried, ready to be sent to the commercial marts of the east where they are tanned and placed upon the markets. These bones and hides are the fruits of the huntsman's labors, in killing the noble game of the plains. The meat from the carcases of the slain buffaloes is seldom used, although in a few instances it is cut up and shipped to eastern packers where it is disposed of as mess beef at largely enhanced prices.

We yesterday met Mr. John A. Lessig, brother to General Lessig, the surveyor general, who has been out on the plains several months, running correction lines and town-shipping the eastern portion of the territory. He informs us that the destruction of buffalo is almost incredible. During the perambulations of his party they had an opportunity of forming opinions as to the slaughter of the bison on the plains. On the south fork of the Republican they came upon one spot where were counted six thousand five hundred carcases of buffalo from which the hides only had been stripped. The meat was not touched and was left to rot on the plains. Only a short distance farther on hundreds more of carcases were discovered, and, in fact, the plains were literally dotted with putrefying buffalo carcases. On the Rickaree river, which lies between the two forks of the Republican, the camps of buffalo hunters were of frequent occurrence. Mr. Lessig estimates that there are at least two thousand hunters in camps along there, waiting for the buffalo. He came across one party of sixteen who stated that they killed twenty-eight thousand buffaloes during the past summer, the hides of which, only, were utilized. If sixteen hunters can kill this number of animals, how great must be the slaughter upon the broad extent of the bison range? Evidently millions of the animals must have been killed during the past summer alone. Mr. Lessig says there are no buffaloes to be seen on the plains, except dead ones, and that hunt as much as they may the sportsmen cannot at present find any game. (*Daily Rocky Mountain News,* 21 December 1873)

In 1876 an attempt to provide limited protection for the buffalo was initiated at the federal level. The proposed legislation would have provided protection only on United States territories but not within individual states. In 1876 Representative

Greenbury Lafayette Fort of Illinois introduced House Bill 1719, which was described as follows in the *Congressional Record:*

> IT PROVIDES IN THE FIRST SECTION THAT IT SHALL HEREAFTER be unlawful for any person who is not an Indian to kill, wound, or in any manner destroy any female buffalo of any age, found at large within the boundaries of any of the Territories of the United States.
>
> The second section provides that it shall be, in like manner, unlawful for any such person to kill, wound, or destroy in the Territories any greater number of male buffaloes than needed for food by such person, or than can be used, cured, or preserved for the food of other persons, or for the market. (*Congressional Record,* 1876, p. 1237)

Mr. Fort made the following remarks in introducing his bill:

> THE BUFFALOES WHICH ROAM OVER THE TERRITORIES OF THE United States are fast disappearing. The intention and object of this bill is to preserve them for the use of the Indians, whose home is upon the public domain, and to the frontiersmen, who may properly use them for food. Where once there were thousands of buffalo there are now but hundreds. They have been, and are now being, slaughtered in large numbers, and must soon disappear. Thousands of these noble brutes are annually slaughtered, not for food, but slain out of mere wantonness. Hundreds and thousands of them are shot down upon the plains, as I am informed, for sport. The Indians are disposed to look upon these creatures as their own herds, their own cattle, and they regard with jealousy the destruction of what they deem to be their property, and believe they should be preserved for them.
>
> Certainly no good can come from this continued slaughter. These animals are harmless; they injure no one. Civilization has no war with them. In the judgment of the committee, they should be as far as possible preserved for the use, not only of the Indians upon the plains, but for those

settlers who go to the frontier for legitimate purposes and settlement, and should only be killed for food and for their robes.

It is said by some that the bill is well enough, but that it relates only to the Territories, while in Kansas, where large numbers of these buffaloes are destroyed, it would have no force. Every gentleman, upon a moment's reflection, must see that this cannot be otherwise. The United States Government has no jurisdiction within the boundaries of any State for such purpose. It must be left for the different States to make such regulations as they choose for preserving the game within their limits. All we can do is to preserve these buffaloes where we can.

Every member of this House is aware that we are annually furnishing at heavy cost thousands and thousands of beef cattle to the Indians for food. It seems to me wrong that these vast herds of the plains, which have grown up in the course of nature without any cost to us, should be uselessly, cruelly, and wantonly destroyed, while at the same time we are called upon to expend so much money annually for the purpose of supplying the place of these animals with domestic cattle. I can see no reason why the bill should not pass now, as it passed before. (*Congressional Record*, 1876, p. 1238)

In support of the bill, Representative Mark Hill Dunnell asked the clerk to read into the record supporting statements from a paper in New Mexico, a letter from General William Babcock Hazen, and a letter from Lieutenant Colonel Albert Gallatin Brackett:

QUITE RECENTLY COL. W. B. HAZEN, STATIONED AT FORT Hays, Kansas, sent the following letter to Mr. Bergh, in respect to the destruction of buffaloes on the Western Plains.

DEAR SIR:—Hoping to interest you, and through you the people of the country and Congress, I would respectfully state that the extraordinary introduction of railroads into and across the wilds of our country has made the vast herds of buffalo accessible to all classes of people, and each year vast numbers are slaughtered for so-called sport, and a greater number by hunters for their hides, which net about $1. I have seen numbers of men this winter who have the past season killed one thousand each for the paltry sum of $1 apiece, the carcases being left to rot on the plains! The buffalo is a noble and harmless animal, timid, and as easily taken as a cow, and very valuable as food for man. It lives upon short grass, which grows luxuriantly upon the high, arid plains of this middle region, that is, from dryness, unfit for agriculture. The theory that the buffalo should be killed to deprive the Indians of food, is a fallacy, as these people are becoming harmless under a rule of justice. In view of these facts, I would most earnestly request that you use such proper influence as may be at your disposal to bring this subject before Congress with the intention of having such steps taken as will prevent this wicked and wanton waste, both of the lives of God's creatures and the valuable food, they furnish. I am, very respectfully, your obedient servant, w. b. hazen. (*Ellsworth Reporter,* 7 March 1872)

THE BUFFALO SLAUGHTER WHICH HAS BEEN GOING ON THE past few years on the plains, and which increases every year, is wantonly wicked and should be stopped by the most stringent enactments and most vigilant enforcement of the law. Killing these noble animals for their hides simply, or to gratify the pleasure of some Russian duke or English lord, is a species of vandalism which cannot too quickly be checked. United States surveying parties report that there are two thousand hunters on the plains killing these animals for their hides. One party of sixteen hunters report having killed twenty-eight thousand buffaloes during the past summer. It seems to us there is quite as much reason why the Government should protect the buffaloes as the Indians. (*Congressional Record,* 1876, p. 1238)

OMAHA BARRACKS, NEBRASKA,
January 30, 1872.

SIR: I have read with a great deal of interest the letter of General Hazen to you respecting the needless killing of buffaloes. What he says is strictly true; and there is as much honor and danger in killing a Texas steer as there is in killing a buffalo. All the reports about fine sport and good shooting are mere gammon. It would be equally as good sport and equally as dangerous to ride into a herd of tame cattle and commence shooting indiscriminately. The wholesale butchery of buffaloes upon the plains is as needless as it is cruel. Hundreds and hundreds of them have been killed in the most wanton manner, or for their tongues alone. It is time that something should be done for their protection; and I trust you will make an effort to have Congress interfere in their behalf. It is an abuse of language to call the killing of harmless and defenseless buffaloes sport.

I am, sir, very respectfully, your obedient servant,

A. G. BRACKETT
Lieutenant-Colonel Second United States Calvary. (*Congressional Record,* 1876, p. 1238)

Representative John Henninger Reagan added his support for the passage of the bill:

I HAVE NOT EXAMINED THE BILL AND DO NOT KNOW EXACTLY what are its provisions, but the object it has in view is altogether proper and right. I know this from some personal experience among the Indians and of the wanton and reckless destruction of buffaloes. It has been for many years a common practice for hunting parties and for men upon pleasure excursions to kill buffalo by the hundreds and thousands. It is a very large animal and useful to man, and should be protected from useless and wanton destruction.

They are not only killed out of mere sport, but it has been common to destroy them by hundreds and thousands merely for their hides and tongues. This certainly is a cruel waste, and when we remember that now, instead of having to travel on horseback a great distance in order to reach them, the country over which they roam is penetrated by railroads, and access is made more easy, we can readily see how this sport can be indulged in to a greater extent than formerly. It will be understood that, unlike domestic cattle, they roam over the plains from north to south and from south to north according to the season. In winter they go toward southern New Mexico and Texas, and in summer they pass up into our northern Territories. They gather together in vast herds, which makes their destruction comparatively easy to those who seek it. It is not like hunting other game scattered about, only a few in each place; but these buffalo, roaming from south to north or from north to south, as the weather and the grass invite, in large bodies, we find that, in addition to killing them for food and for useful purposes, persons out of mere sport indulge in their wanton destruction, while others engage in killing them merely for their hides and tongues. A law certainly should be made to prevent this. (*Congressional Record*, 1876, p. 1238)

Reasons for opposition to the bill within the house varied. One representative believed that the Indians were primarily responsible for reducing the numbers of buffalo, and that, furthermore, allowing Indians to hunt buffalo as they wished would cause Indians to leave their reservations. Other representatives believed buffalo to be harmful to domestic crops and livestock. Several House members were of the opinion the Indian problems were best solved by reducing the number of buffalo. (For a thorough discussion of this proposed legislation see B. D. Thomas, *The Near Extinction of the American Bison: A Case Study in Legislative Lethargy in Western American History in the Seventies*, J. D. Tyler, editor, 1973.)

Although the opposition to House Bill 1719 was vocal, the bill passed the House and was referred to the Senate Committee on Territories. Presumably it was tabled and thereby killed in that committee, as it was never considered by the full Senate. The following editorial, however, appeared in the *Hays City Sentinel* shortly after the bill's passage in the House:

MR. FORT, OF ILLINOIS, SHOULD RECEIVE THE COMMENDATION of the country at large for his success in securing the passage of a bill by the lower House of Congress, for the preservation of buffaloes, and to prevent the further useless slaughter of these animals. Several years ago since General Hazen wrote a very elaborate and comprehensive paper on the subject, which resulted in the Kansas Legislature taking action in the matter of their preservation, but the law was never executed, and the wanton slaughter of these animals was enormous in point of numbers. There were shipped from Hays City, Kansas in the month of May, 1872, no less than seventy-five thousand buffalo hides, procured for the most part within a radius of fifty miles from that point, and these animals killed solely for their hides. This number was, however, but an item in the aggregate number killed during that and previous years. During two years there were killed in the state of Kansas alone, over two and a half millions of buffaloes, and not one per cent of the number killed was used for meat.

We can distinctly remember at Hays City, Kansas of seeing in 1871, countless numbers of these animals grazing within two and three miles from town and in 1875, a wild buffalo north of the Arkansas River, within a hundred miles of Hays City, was as much a rarity as one would be east of the Mississippi today.—Columbus Ohio Gazette. (*Hays City Sentinel*, 8 March 1876)

A local editorial against the proposed federal legislation appeared in the *Ellis County Star*. The arguments were similar to those that took place within the halls of the U. S. Congress:

EDITORIAL: THE BILL RECENTLY INTRODUCED IN CONGRESS "to prevent the useless slaughter of buffaloes by any person not an Indian" is certainly humane in its intent, but utterly impracticable, of execution, even if it [was] made a law. How the buffaloes are to be protected from the whites is not as yet known, unless it be by a soldier detailed to watch each buffalo, and see that it is killed by no one but a duly accredited copper-colored savage. No more buffaloes are to be killed "than are needed for food or market," but this expression leaves a loop hole large enough to drive a whole herd of buffaloes through and renders ungatory [sic] the whole bill. (*Ellis County Star*, 6 April 1876)

Newspapers began reporting buffalo as oddities, stragglers, or strays. Shooting even one was viewed as newsworthy, whereas five to ten years earlier killing hundreds was so commonplace as not to be mentioned. In a matter of twelve years, from statehood in 1861 to 1873, the seemingly endless herds of buffalo had been destroyed.

PEOPLE LIVING IN THIS VICINITY, WHO HAVE NEVER SEEN ANY buffalo should ride out a few miles west and they will find small detachments of the former immense army of buffalos that used to roam over our prairies. (*Ellsworth Reporter*, 12 June 1873)

MESSERS. ORRILL AND MCCOY, RAN ACROSS A HERD OF SEVEN buffalo near the southwest corner of the county, last Monday, but did not succeed in killing even one. Probably these are the last buffalo that will cross the line of Ellis county in their native state of wildness. (*Hays City Sentinel*, 30 March 1878)

Along with the disappearing buffalo, other populations declined as well, namely the antelope, elk, and prairie dog:

ANTELOPE ARE NOT NEAR SO PLENTIFUL AS IN PREVIOUS years. (*Hays City Sentinel*, 10 August 1877)

ELK HAVE DISAPPEARED SINCE THE INFLUX OF SETTLERS DROVE them from the timbered valleys of the Saline River and its tributaries. (Guild, 1879)

THE PRAIRIE DOG RETIRES BEFORE CIVILIZATION EVEN AS EGG-
nogg [sic] before he who is athirst. A few years ago there
were many towns in the vicinity of Hays. (*Hays City Sentinel,* 14 December 1877)

As the years progressed, settlers believed even the numbers of
fish were declining. This development was blamed on overfish-
ing, primarily through seining, and on the construction of small
dams that prevented fish from swimming upstream:

THE FISH HAVE SUFFERED MORE THIS DRY WEATHER THIS YEAR
than usual. The reason is that more than the usual number
have been pulled out of the water. (*Ellsworth Reporter,* 30
July 1874)

The perceived decline in fish populations caused concerned
people to lobby the legislature for assistance in creating a position for a fish commissioner and passing laws that would reverse
the trend of decline. The following article on the subject appeared in the *Ellsworth Reporter:*

SOMEONE HAS SAID: "THAT THE FREEDOM OF FISHING IS THE
most ancient of man's rights, conferred upon him by his
Maker at the creation." The importance of fish for food
cannot be over estimated, and the causes of their decrease
in the waters of Central and Western Kansas, and the remedies necessary to arrest their yearly diminution, should
engage the earnest attention of the Legislature. Stringent
laws should be immediately imposed, comparable to the sig-
nificance of the subject in its relation to the welfare of a
large portion of the people. That the rapid disappearance of
fish from our streams is no idle fancy, we simply refer to the
fact that our supply has to be brought now by rail a distance
of eighty or a hundred miles, while only a few years ago, an
abundance could be caught in every little pond and creek in
our vicinity. The primal cause of this decrease is in the
erection of impassable dams, which preclude the possibility

of the fish returning to their spawning grounds, and unless legislative action is promptly taken in the premises, our rivers and ponds will soon be as destitute of fish as a buffalo wallow. Other States long ago attaching the importance to this subject it rigidly [sic] deserves appointed Commissioners whose duty it is to consider the question of supply of fish in all its bearings, and under the obligations of their office the streams are rapidly becoming stocked again, principally by artificial propagation. To know there can be no Constitutional objections, and that the Legislature has the power to compel the owners of dams to construct suitable fishways, we quote from the report of the United States Commission on fish and fisheries: "The most serious artificial obstruction in any of the American rivers to the upward movement of the salmon, as well as other fish, so far realized, has proved to be the Holyoke dam at South Hadley Falls; and a persistent effort has been made for many years, by the Commissioners of Massachusetts, aided by those of other States, to cause the powerful corporation owning the dam to introduce a proper fish-way. An act of the Massachusetts Legislature requiring this to be done was contested by the company, the suit being carried successively to the Supreme Court of the State, and then to that of the United States. Beaten at all points, the company has finally yielded gracefully to the necessity, and is now actually engaged in erecting a fish-way, devised by Mr. Brackett, one of the Fish Commissioners of Massachussetts [sic], in accordance with the unanimous recommendation of the Commissioners of all the States through which the Connecticut River flows." Only two or three years ago, literally, and the immense water power of Kansas was unknown. As soon as it was discovered it was rapidly utilized, and at intervals along our rivers impassable dams were erected, and then commenced the disappearance of our fish. Without the facilities of ascending to suitable spawning grounds, (an absolute necessity to the function of reproduction) this portion of the State received its first check in the supply of this excellent food, and unless soon remedied, will end in the practical extermination of all its fish. We should like to enlarge upon this subject, but our space forbids. We simply demand then, a legislative enactment to enforce the construction of suitable fishways around the dams, and the law should become operative at once. (*Ellsworth Reporter*, 23 December 1875)

Mr. H. B. Long from Ellsworth introduced a bill to establish a fish commissioner in Kansas during the legislative session of 1876. This bill, however, failed to receive the support required for passage. The *Reporter* continued to voice its editorial concern:

THE LEGISLATURE FAILED TO TAKE COGNIZANCE OF THE IMportance of protecting and increasing the fish in our streams by the appointment of commissioners as provided for in Mr. Long's bill, and upon the wiseacres of that body last winter rests the responsibility of postponing this really necessary measure. Only a few States are left, our own among the number, who have failed to appoint commissioners. We hope that our next Legislature will not fail to make proper provision in this direction. The matter is absolutely of great weight, and should not be ignored. (*Ellsworth Reporter*, 30 March 1876)

NEARLY A YEAR AGO WE WROTE AN ARTICLE ON THE "DEcrease of Fish in Central and Western Kansas"—the first agitation of the subject in the State we believe—which met with a cordial approval by the Press generally. Of course there were a few "old fogy" sheets whose editors (?) are up to their shoulders in the mud of antiquity, and have almost become fossils in their antediluvian ideas, who did not see the necessity for the protection we demanded at the hands of the State. Our Representative at our solicitation, whose views in the matter accorded perfectly with our one, presented a bill for the establishment of Commissioners, and also one compelling the construction of "Fishways" around all dams. But our *heaven-directed, cool-headed, and long-*

sighted, Legislature failed to attach that importance to the measures which they merited, and they became abortive.— Since then we have received several letters from prominent people—journalists and others—to commence bringing the matter before the public again, but should have declined, were it not that the most influential and brainy papers in the State are (since one hundred thousand shad have been placed in the Kaw under an act of Congress appropriating money for the cultivation of fish in Western waters) in a quiet way stirring up the subject. . . .

The last Legislature failed to take cognizance of the importance of protecting and increasing fish in our streams by the appointment of Commissioners as provided for in Mr. Long's bill, and upon the wiseacres of that body rests the responsibility of postponing this really necessary measure. Only a few States are left, our own among the number who have failed to pass a law creating a Commission.—We hope our next Legislature will not fail to make proper provision in this direction. The matter is really one of great weight with our people, and should not be ignored. (*Ellsworth Reporter,* 31 August 1876)

Finally, in March 1877, the law passed, thereby providing for a fish commissioner to implement activities that would protect and increase the size of fish populations in Kansas. The text of the law reads as follows:

Be it enacted by the Legislature of the State of Kansas:

SECTION. I. A commissioner of fisheries of the State of Kansas is hereby established, as hereafter provided for in section three of this act.

SEC. 2. It shall be the duty of the commissioner to examine the various rivers, lakes and streams of the State of Kansas, with a view of ascertaining whether they can be rendered more productive of fish, and what means are desirable to effect this object, either in restoring the production of fish in them, or in protecting or propagating the fish that at present frequent them, and to stock the same with fish as means for that purpose may be supplied by the United States fish commissioner, and by the societies and individuals interested in the propagation of fish or otherwise; and such commissioner shall report the result of his labors, and any recommendations he may offer, annually, to the governor of the state.

SEC. 3. The governor shall have power to appoint a commissioner, to hold office for two years, who shall receive three dollars per day and ten cents per mile for actual time and distance traveled: *Provided,* That the amount actually paid shall be charged as mileage on railroads, and that not more than fifty days in each year shall be devoted in carrying this act into effect.

SEC. 4. It shall be unlawful for any person or company to obstruct any of the streams in the State of Kansas, by building a dam, or otherwise, without constructing a "fishway."

SEC. 5. Any person or company owning or operating a dam on any of the streams of the State of Kansas shall, within one year after passage of this act, construct a fishway that will permit all kinds of fish to pass up the stream, except in cases where in the opinion of said commissioner such dam will permit the passage of fish.

SEC. 6. It shall be unlawful for any person to fish with a seine, net, or otherwise, within eighty rods of any fishway, or from any private fish preserve, pond or stream, owned and used for the propagation of fish, without the owner's consent.

SEC. 7. It shall be unlawful for any person to catch with a seine or net any of the fish in the waters of the State of Kansas, during the months of April, May and June in each year.

SEC. 8. Any person or company violating any of the sections of this act shall be deemed guilty of a misdemeanor, and upon conviction thereof, before any court of competent jurisdiction, shall be fined for violating section four or five of this act, not less than one hundred nor more than one thousand dollars; and for violating section seven or eight of this act, shall be fined not less than five nor more than fifty dollars, and shall stand committed until such fine is paid.

SEC. 9. It shall be the duty of the fish commissioner to see that the provisions of this act are enforced, and for this purpose shall have the power to call to his assistance the county attorney of any county in which the provisions of this act are violated, to manage and prosecute the case.

SEC. 10. Five hundred dollars for the year eighteen hundred and seventy-seven, and five hundred dollars for the year eighteen hundred and seventy-eight, or as much of it as is necessary, are hereby appropriated out of any funds not otherwise appropriated, to carry this act into effect.

SEC. 11. This act shall take effect and be in force from and after its publication in the *Daily Commonwealth*.

Approved March 5, 1877.

(Session Laws of Kansas, 1877b)

In accordance with section 3, the governor appointed the Honorable H. B. Long of Ellsworth as the first fish commissioner for the state of Kansas. The following excerpts soon appeared in local newspapers:

HON. D. B. LONG, OF ELLSWORTH, THE NEW FISH COMMIS-ssoner [*sic*] of Kansas, has written a letter to the Topeka *Commonwealth*, stating that his attention has been called to the fact that the fish law is being violated in different parts of the State. His closing remarks are as follows: "I do not wish to make any person trouble, but the fish in our State must be protected and allowed their liberty. I desire the assistance of every person interested in this important enterprise to use their influence for their protection, and if necessary prosecute parties violating the acts of the law above refered [*sic*] to.

In answer to numerous requests from different parts of the State asking to have private ponds stocked with fish, I will say that I can make no distributions for private purposes, but will do as much as I can with the limited means I have to stock the principal streams for the public good. Through our energetic Senator, Col. P. B. Plumb, arrangements are made with Prof. S. F. Baird, United States Fish Commissioner, to stock the Arkansas river at Larned, the Cottonwood at Florence, the Marais de Cygnes at Reading, Lyon county, the Smoky Hill at Ellsworth, the Blue at Marysville, and the Grasshopper at Grasshopper Falls, with shad and salmon, the only supply furnished at present by the United States Fish Commissioner. (*Ellsworth Reporter,* 10 May 1877)

WE HEAR SOME RUMORS OF A FISHING PARTY GOING OUT TO fish with a net. All parties should remember that seining is unlawful during the months of April, May and June. For violation of this law the fine is not less than $5, nor more than $50. (*Saline County Journal,* 11 April 1878)

Soon after the legislature created the office of fish commissioner, the practice of stocking fish was initiated to supplement the native populations. The construction of small ponds, which were then stocked with fish, provided the settlers with fish for both recreation and food. The following items indicate how welcome the new policy was to Kansas residents:

HON. D. B. LONG, FISH COMMISSIONER OF THE STATE OF KANsas, was in town the first of this week, attending to the duties of his office. He gave us some very interesting items on the fish question, and we are convinced that he is a very capable officer and has his whole mind absorbed in this work. He states that the "fish ways" for the dams, which are required by the statute, are very simple in construction and will not cost to exceed fifty dollars, and will in no way impair the force of the water power. So parties owning dams need not tremble at the expense and damage they expected to be put to. Mr. Long informs us that a few weeks ago some 80,000 shad were unloaded at Topeka. These fish were to have been used in stocking the rivers at various points. He did his best to be on hand and superintend the distribution of the fish, but was prevented by reason of irregular trains during the high water from so doing, and the fish had to be consigned to the Kaw. He will receive another lot of fish in September, when he will proceed to stock the Smoky Hill at Ellsworth and this place. He designs making extraordinary efforts to secure the California salmon, the bass and other varieties of fish with which to stock the Kansas rivers. (*Saline County Journal*, 21 June 1877)

OUR STATE HAS TAKEN PROPER INITIATORY STEPS TO STOCK our streams with fish, and we hope that she will continue to inaugurate necessary measures, and by practical legislation protect the work already done. Fresh supplies of fish should be placed in the streams each year, until they are sufficiently plentiful to supply at least the sanitary demands of the people. Fish make an important item of food for those who hope to be perfectly healthy. As near as we can learn that our present Fish Commissioner is doing his work well, and we hope the Legislature this winter will provide every means necessarry [sic] for him to carry on his good work. (*Saline County Journal*, 12 December 1878)

The new fish commissioner was besieged with requests for particular species of fish to be placed in streams and private ponds. Shad and salmon were both stocked within Kansas. In the following letter to the editor, Commissioner Long detailed the difficulty in obtaining salmon eggs from the coast and hatching them along the Smoky Hill River:

ELLSWORTH, November 21. TO THE EDITOR OF THE COMMON-wealth: Allow me to say through the columns of your paper, for the information of those that are interested in fish culture in our State, that I am not purchasing and cannot purchase the different kinds of fish requested by parties in different parts of the State anxious to have their pond or stream stocked with their favorite kinds. If inquirers would read the law upon the subject it would furnish much of [the] information asked for and relieve me of the task of answering numerous letters upon the subject. I will say that the small amount appropriated for the two years shall be judiciously expended as the law provides. The success of fish culture in Kansas to a great extent will be to protect for a few years the twenty-eight or thirty native varieties now in our waters, or at least a protection of the best varieties. I have procured for our State a donation of 100,000 shad, which were placed in the Kaw river, at Topeka, June 5, 1877. These shad were hatched at the Maryland fish hatchery, and brought through to Topeka in six large cans of ten gallons each, in charge of two men, as the water required changing very often. When they reached Topeka the fish were in a sickly condition, and would not, as the agent in charge of claimed, stand further delay in transportation, and to save them they were deposited in the Kaw. From reliable information these young shad have made a fair growth, and are doing well, some having been caught by the young sports of Topeka. (Thanks to the city marshal for promptly putting a stop to the catching of the young fry.)

I received from Hon. Livingston Stone, department of the fish commission, 100,000 salmon eggs (not 1,000,000 as reported by several papers in the State,) which were shipped from Redding, Cal., October 2d, in refrigerator cars to Chicago, from Chicago to Ellsworth by express, received by me October 10th, (just in time to prevent my attending the meeting of the grand lodge of the I. O. O. F.). The eggs were packed in two boxes, a layer of moss, and then a strip of netting, then moss, etc. The boxes containing the eggs were packed in leaves about three inches in thickness, and fastened in a crate having a nice chamber between the two boxes, in all making a package of about 400 pounds. On account of the length of time en route, or some other cause, I found many of the eggs were dead, which had to be separated from the good eggs, which was a tedious job, in which all . . . my help took part. The dead eggs are readily distinguished from the good eggs by turning a lighter color. It is a very important part of fish culture to separate the bad eggs from the good ones, as disease is rapidly communicated and death is sure to follow. The dead eggs will fasten their poisonous fibres to all that are near when allowed to remain any length of time. By picking out the dead eggs you will find these fibres stretching out and clinging to all near it with such strength that it will require the free use of a feather to relieve the good eggs from the dead ones.

The California salmon eggs are much larger than the eggs of most other kinds of fish, being as large as a pea. They require a much longer time to hatch than other fish, from four to six weeks, while the shad requires but five to ten days.

To successfully hatch these eggs without a fish hatchery, appeared to me the undertaking of a task more than I was able to accomplish, but I went to work with the determination to do the best I could under the unfavorable circumstances. It may be of interest to give a description of my "hatchery."

Instead of cool spring water conducted in pipes into a building supplied with tanks, where the temperature, force, etc., could be controlled, I used the water of the treacherous Smoky river, (which runs near my residence,) and for a regulator of the tempreature [sic], force, etc., I used Prof. Tice's almanac, and willow boughs, and the broad canopy of heaven for a shelter from the burning sun or fierce blast. Not having regular hatching boxes, supplied with wire trays, I used boxes 16 feet long, 12 inches deep, ends partly open, spreading sand on the bottom sufficient to weigh the boxes down so as to have the eggs covered with three or four inches of water. The eggs were evenly spread on the sand and the boxes anchored in the middle of the stream. The 10th, 11th, and 12th of October were very warm and the temperature of the water to my surprise reached 80 degrees. From the high tempreature [sic] or some other cause, many of the eggs turned white in the boxes most exposed which had to be separated, a back aching job, and then with the water knee deep, afforded an excellent opportuniny [sic] to take a cold, and the rheumatism, both of which, as Prentice would say, I gracefully received. The result of my labors is not flattering; not over 5,000 were hatched; yet I am not the least discouraged, and know from experience, that success in any undertaking must be met at every turn with difficulties that none but the brave can stand. I am very truly, D. B. Long. (*Ellsworth Reporter*, 21 November 1877)

The release of shad, mentioned in Long's letter, increased the expectations for greater populations of fish, as the following item indicates:

BY THE SOLICITATION OF D. B. LONG, OUR STATE FISH COMmissioner, Prof. Baird, the United States Fish Commissioner of the Smithsonian Institute, has just sent 80,000 little fish of the celebrated shad variety, in six tin cans to Topeka. The fish were turned into the raging Kaw, and are reported on their way up the Smoky. Another cargo of young Salmon will soon be sent to keep company with the shad, and are intended to seed the rivers of Kansas with the best fish in the world. Look out for fish soon in Big Creek. (*Hays Sentinel*, 8 June 1877)

Of the shad released in the summer of 1877, one was reported to have been caught in May 1878:

MR. FISH COMMISSIONER LONG, MAY NOTE DOWN IN HIS NOTE book, that the editor of this paper caught one of his shad in Spring Creek last Thursday. It was about six inches long, and seemed to take to worm bait just like the plebeian chub and sunfish, common to these waters. (*Ellsworth Reporter*, 23 May 1878)

Section 4 of the fish law made it unlawful to construct a dam across a stream without providing a "fishway" for fish to navigate upstream. This provision was based on criticism that dams, many built before 1877, prevented fish from swimming upstream to replenish populations depleted by overharvest and habitat degradation. The editor of the *Ellsworth Reporter* suggested that dams indeed hindered the movement of fish within the waterways of Kansas. The proof for this contention was a break in a dam at Lawrence, which presumably allowed fish to get to Ellsworth via the Smoky Hill River:

SINCE THE BREAK IN THE LAWRENCE DAM SOME VERY LARGE fish have been caught in the Smoky at this place. We hope the commissioner will compel that company to put up a fish-way at once. That dam has been the cause of the decrease in the fish supply all over the Central and Western portion of the State. (*Ellsworth Reporter*, 31 May 1877)

HON. D. B. LONG, FISH COMMISSIONER[,] IS AT LAWRENCE THIS week, to see that the water power company at that place put a fishway around their dam in accordance with the law. (*Ellsworth Reporter*, 14 June 1877)

As the fishing season of 1878 approached, the newspapers of Kansas alerted fishermen to the letter of the law:

D. B. LONG, STATE COMMISSIONER OF FISHERIES, WRITES TO the Topeka Commonwealth calling public attention to the fact that the laws of Kansas prohibit the catching of fish with nets, seines or otherwise, except with hook and line, during the months of April, May and June, and at no time whatever within eighty rods of any "fish way" or dam, as he construes the law. He has noticed that this law has been violated in different parts of the State, and he appeals to all parties guilty of this wholesale destruction and slaughter of the fish to fold up their nets and tackling, and allow the few remaining fish now in our streams to deposit their spawn unmolested. If they are allowed the freedom of going to their spawning ground without being caught or prevented by dams or other obstructions, our streams in a few years will afford an abundant supply of cheap, wholesome food sufficient for all. Mr. Long says that he does not wish to make trouble for any one, but the fish must be protected, and he will prosecute any one guilty of violating the law. (*Saline County Journal*, 10 May 1877)

Additional shad were scheduled to be released during the summer of 1878. However, this proved to be impossible, as the following correspondence from the fish commissioner explains:

FOR THE INFORMATION OF ALL CONCERNED, I BEG LEAVE TO report that I made applications to the U. S. Fish Commissioner, S. F. Baird, for a supply of shad to be delivered at six different places in Kansas, viz:—Marysville, on the Blue; Concordia, on the Republican; Ellsworth, on the Smoky; Bedding, on the Masha; Florence on the Cottonwood; and at Dodge or Larned, on the Arkansas.—My application was forwarded to Senator Ingalls, endorsed favorably and notice received by me from the Commissioner that the request would be granted. The following letter will explain why I failed to receive them.

I have made arrangements to have a large number of Salmon hatched this fall.

D. B. LONG.

Com. of Fisheries.

SMITHSONIAN INSTITUT'N
Washington D.C. June 26, '78.

DEAR SIR:

It is with very great regret that I find by the report of Mr. Milner that he was unable to make the shipment of shad for which you asked. He reports that he had deferred all the long trips until the close of operations, so that the messengers, when entering upon the same, would not need to come back to the Susquehanna river, most of them residing in Illinois, or Wisconsin. Unfortunately June 10th, is the day fixed by law for all shad fishing on the Susquehanna to cease; and for the five days previous to that date, the time when Mr. Milner expected to obtain the best and healthiest fish for the long trips, the weather was so stormy as to preclude entirely the possibility of taking any spawn. This has prevented shipments to Kansas, Arkansas, Texas, Minnesota, Iowa, and other remote points.

I greatly regret this failure which I trust however, to remedy another year, as the arrangements now being made will insure to us an ample supply of fish, and I hope better modes of distributing them.

In compensation for your disappointment, I shall be quite willing to supply to you an extra stock of California Salmon, if you will designate the number that you are willing to receive and care for.

Yours truly,

s. f. baird, Commissioner.

To D. B. Long, Commr. of Fisheries,

Ellsworth, Kansas. (*Ellsworth Reporter*, 11 July 1878)

Many residents of southwestern Kansas wanted assurances of a share of the fish stocked in that area. Senator Kelly wrote Commissioner Long and requested that stocking be so conducted. In his reply Long pleaded for the development of a fish hatchery in Kansas:

HON. D. B. LONG, THE KANSAS STATE FISH COMMISSIONER, IN answer to a letter from senator John Kelly, of Sedgwick county, writes from Ellsworth, under the date of May 30th: "I shall do all I can in the nature of stocking the streams of the southwest. I do not think I will be able to deposit in more than one or two places this summer owing to the fact that the great distance and the short life out of their natural element. What we now need and what the senate refused to allow is a fish hatcherie. Now we are compelled to depend on other hatcheries to do our hatching of the spawn. I have requested and will try to have the Arkansas stocked at Larned. In that case you at Wichita will receive the same benefits as if the fish were deposited there."

We would suggest to the commissioner that he is probably mistaken in his conclusions as to the best point. The Little Arkansas is a better fish stream than the big river, and were the fish deposited at its mouth the chances for both streams would be improved. The Little Arkansas river is about one hundred and fifty miles long and a beautiful clear stream and gravel bottom. (*Hutchinson News*, 20 June 1878)

By October 1878 Commissioner Long received 100,000 salmon that had been hatched in the Iowa State Fish Hatchery at Cedar Rapids, Iowa. These were stocked in streams throughout much of Kansas:

HON. D. B. LONG, COMMISSIONER OF STATE FISHERIES, LEFT for Cedar Rapids, Iowa[,] last Monday to get 100,000 fish which were hatched there according to an arrangement made with the Commissioner of Iowa. Mr. Long informs us that 20,000 of these fish will be distributed in the streams along the line of the railroads in the northern part of the State, 40,000 in the streams in the Central part of the State and 40,000 in the streams along the A. T. & S. F. R. R. (*Ellsworth Reporter*, 28 November 1878)

ACCORDING TO THE STANDARD, 5,000 SHAD WERE DEPOSITED in Big Creek west of the Ellis dam, last week. (*Hays City Sentinel*, 14 December 1878)

Evidently the 5,000 shad reported to have been stocked in Big Creek were in fact a portion of the 100,000 salmon released within the state boundaries. Stocking occurred during December

1878 in streams close to the major rail lines, as Commissioner Long explained in a report printed by the *Hays City Sentinel:*

IT WILL NO DOUBT BE OF INTEREST TO MANY OF YOUR READERS to know that I have made a success in the planting of 100,000 California salmon in our streams. The spawn from which they were hatched was collected from the salmon of the McCloud River, California, by Livingston Stone, Deputy United States Fish Commissioner. They were shipped in a refrigerator car to Chicago October 2d, and placed in hatching boxes October 12th, at the fish hatchery three miles northwest of Cedar Rapids. This is a private hatchery, owned by B. F. Shaw & Co., where parties wishing to stock their ponds can be supplied with lake trout, brook trout, salmon, and other kinds of fish at prices much lower than eastern establishments.

The fish were taken from the boxes December 2d, and placed in ten large cans, holding from fifteen to twenty gallons each, and making 2,000 pounds of freight. I had some trouble in securing transportation for so large a bulk in the express trains, but to have taken freight trains, would have been death to my fish and failure to the enterprise; but throu[g]h the courtesy of the officials of the B. C. & Northern road I received free transportation, with perm[i]ssion to occupy the baggage car from Cedar Rapids to Burlington. I left Cedar Rapids on the 2:25 p. m. train, reaching Barlington [sic] at 7:20 p. m. At this place I had ten minutes to transfer. To get a permit from the Superintendent of the C. B. & Q was the greatest difficulty, as their baggage car was packed full. Had it not been for the urgent plea made by Mr. Shaw, who accompanied me as far as Creston, I would have been compelled to take a slower train. Mr. Shaw's assistance and knowledge was very valuable to me. At Burlington we secured ice sufficient to last until I reached Atchison. It kept Mr. Shaw and myself busy to keep the water supplied with oxygen, which was done by changing the water when it could be done by use of ice—and agitating the water. The weather was cool, which was in our favor. The fish carried splendidly, only losing a few. I arrived in Atchison a few minutes after 10 a. m[.], December 3d, where I was met by Col. G. A. A. Dean and A. B. Bradish, to whose care I turned over 30,000 to be distributed as follows:—

Stranger creek	2,500
Independence creek	2,500
Delaware river, at Muscotah	1,000
Spring creek, at Wetmore	1,000
Red Vermillion, at Centralia	2,000
Black Vermillion, at Frankfort	2,000
Clear and South Forks, at Barret's	1,000
Blue, at Blue Rapids	5,000
Little Blue, at Waterville	2,000
Republican, at Concordia	5,000
Solomon, at Beloit	5,000
Mill creek, at Washington	1,000

I made the following deposits on the line of the Santa Fe:—

Delaware, at Valley Falls	2,000
Soldier, near North Topeka	1,000

On the line of the K. P.:—

In Silver Lake	500
Vermillion, near Wamego	2,500
Blue, at Manhattan	5,000
Republican, at Junction City	3,000
Chapman creek	2,000
Solomon, near Solomon City	2,000
Saline, near Salina	3,000
Spring creek, at Brookville	1,000

Smoky, at Ellsworth	5,000
Big creek, at Hays	5,000
Big creek, at Ellis	5,000

I also distributed in the county of Ellsworth, to be placed in ponds, springs, and creeks, for experimental purposes, about 1,000[.]

IN ADDITION TO THE DEPOSITS MENTIONED IN MR. LONG'S REport above he also deposited 28,000 salmon in the streams along the Santa Fe; commencing with 5,000 in the Pawnee at Larned, and thence east. It is to be hoped the experiment will prove a success. The fish now in our waters are of an inferior sort; and for this very reason people have too little interest in fish culture. Big Creek could and should yield tons of food for man annually; and it is to be hoped Mr. Long's efforts will have this result. (*Hays City Sentinel*, 21 December 1878)

THE DISTRIBUTION OF SALMON FOR THE KANSAS RIVERS DID not extend further west than Poineer [sic] Fork, at Larned. The fish instinct won't bring him this way. He will go to sea. (*Dodge City Times*, 21 December 1878)

The following article suggests that 100,000 young shad were to be released in Reno County. Whether this was true, or whether the editor confused the 100,000 salmon to be released, with Reno County getting some of them, is not known, although one might suspect the latter:

FROM DEPUTY FISH COMMISSIONER THOMPSON WE LEARN THAT one hundred thousand young shad are to be furnished him to be placed in the waters of Reno county. This is good news. The waters of Reno county ought to yield an abundance of food of this kind and can be made to do so with a little care. Mr. Thompson has taken quite an interest in fish culture and it is mainly through his efforts that the spawn above referred to is secured for Reno county. He deserves credit. (*Hutchinson News*, 28 November 1878)

As the 1879 legislative session neared, there was a general plea to retain the office of fish commissioner and to continue stocking the rivers and streams:

KANSAS SHOULD BY ALL MEANS CONTINUE THE WORK INAUguratrd [*sic*] by the last Legislature: that of stocking the streams with fish. It is the cheapest food that can be raised and if the work of raising and protecting the fish is properly managed, a sufficient supply can be obtained from our streams to feed the people of the State. The coming Legislature should make a suitable appropriation to carry on the work. (*Ellsworth Reporter*, 5 December 1878)

In January 1879 Commissioner Long reported to the legislature. The report, which follows, detailed his successes and failures of 1877 and 1878 and projected his activities through 1879. He also requested the construction of a fish hatchery and that the fish commission be increased to three people.

THE FOLLOWING IS THE CONCLUDING PORTION OF COMMISsioner Long's report to the Legislature:

Immediately after receiving the appointment of Commissioner, I made application to the United States Fish Commissioner, S. F. Baird, for such allowances as Kansas was entitled to receive in the general distribution by the Government. On the 5th of June, 1877, 100,000 young shad arrived in Topeka for distribution. They were shipped in charge of an agent, Mr. Quine, who neglected to give me notice in time to receive them on their arrival. He took the responsibility upon himself to deposit the entire shipment in the Kaw at Topeka, claiming that they were in an unhealthy condition, and would not bear further transporting. I was greatly disappointed, as I had made several promises in distributing them that I was unable to fulfill.

On the 10th of October, 1877, I received from Deputy U.S. Fish Commissioner Livingston Stone a crate containing 100,000 California salmon eggs, which were shipped from Redding, Cal., in a refrigerator car, to Chicago, Ill., and from Chicago to Ellsworth by express. It required nine days to reach me, after shipments. The eggs were in very good condition—not over five per cent were found dead. I had prepared hatching-boxes, using gravel instead of wire screens, and placed the eggs on the gravel beds, after picking out the dead eggs, which were readily discovered by their turning white. The water was permitted to flow through the boxes, covering the eggs to the depth of about three inches. The weather being very warm, the temperature of the water rose to 75°, causing large quantities of the eggs to turn white—making a very tedious job to separate them, which had to be done every day. After working patiently and watching carefully for two weeks, a sudden rise of the river washed the covering of the boxes away, and the eggs had also disappeared. Many no doubt made food for other fish, but I have a hope that others escaped, and will in time return full-grown salmon.

I failed to receive our share of the distribution of shad for 1878, as did Iowa, Missouri and Arkansas, on account of the failure on the part of the United States Commission to collect them. I have the promise of a double portion for 1879.

I have made arrangement with the Commissioner of Iowa, B. F. Shaw, to hatch 100,000 California salmon for distribution in November next. They are to be hatched at the State fish hatchery, at Anamosa, Iowa.

The duties of your Commissioner involves [sic] a vast amount of correspondence, especially with people who see some violation of the laws for the preservation of fish. I desire to call attention to the fact, that it is the duty of every law-abiding citizen to see that the law is observed, as well as the Commissioner. It is an impossibility for the Commissioner to act as a police, detective and witness. Many devices have been resorted to in order to evade the law. I would therefore recommend that for a period of five years, all fishing with every device whatever be made a violation of law—excepting with hook, line and rod, and with seine and net for the purpose of propagation only.

I would recommend that a plan be adopted, and the same be lithographed, and copies be furnished to all persons erecting dams, and to owners of dams. The plans furnished should [embrace] cheapness and durability, and should not [i]nterfere with the use of the water for power. Some of the dams require no fish-ways, where they are built on the "rip-ray" style, and have but little perpendicular fall.

I would recommend and urge that an appropriation of not less than $2,000 be made for the purpose of erecting a fish hatchery. The necessity of such a building is apparent to every person who will give the subject any notice.

I would recommend that the Commission be increased to three members, one of whom to be superintendent and to have a fixed salary, and that his whole time be devoted to the fish interest of the State.

I would further recommend an appropriation of $3,000 for the year 1880, and $3,000 for the year 1881, to be used by the Commission in paying the necessary expenses in collecting fish, spawn, etc., for our State. These appropriations are very small in comparison with other States. Michigan, in 1875, appropriated $14,000; Wisconsin appropriated, in 1876, $10,000 for that year.

D. B. LONG,
Commissioner of Fisheries for the State of Kansas. (*Ellsworth Reporter*, 9 January 1879)

Evidently some people wished to introduce other nonnative fish in addition to salmon into Big Creek. They believed that in order to have a successful introduction, no fishing should be allowed until 1882. A bill to this effect was introduced in the state legislature but failed to pass:

L. F. EGGERS WILL INTRODUCE A BILL IN THE HOUSE WHICH, IF passed, will prohibit fishing in Big Creek in any manner whatsoever until 1882. This has been suggested by several gentlemen who are desirous of propagating several varieties of fish unknown to our waters, and to do it must have absolute protection. Commissioner Long's experiment with salmon will be watched with interest. Under the ordinary course of events the ten thousand salmon placed in Big Creek last fall will find their way to the Gulf of Mexico in one year from next spring. Then, when the spawning age, they are expected to return through the sinuous course of the Mississippi, Missouri and Kansas rivers to their starting point—there to lay their eggs. It seems almost incredible. The young salmon are said to be doing finely. (*Hays City Sentinel*, 28 February 1879)

Fish numbers continued to decline, as the following item from the *Larned Optic* indicates. The law prevented catching fish with a seine or net during April, May, and June of each year. During this time fish could spawn without danger of being caught; the young produced would supplement the population. The expiration of the moratorium was usually reported in the papers each year.

THE FISH IN THE PAWNEE CREEK ARE FAST DISAPPEARING owing to the great quantities netted for our market. A few years ago the creek was swarming with them, and it was an easy matter to procure a fine "string" with the hook and line. There are no places on the creek near Larned which is practicable, that has not been "dragged." Fish Commissioner Long of this State, placed in the Pawnee Fork, a quantity of eggs of the California salmon, a few of these have been caught, and they should be allowed to multiply. All persons using this means of procuring fish should bear in mind that a law was passed at Topeka, in 1877; restraining the use of nets, seins, [*sic*] &c., in all streams during the months of April and June. This is a good law and should be enforced. (*Larned Optic*, 12 March 1879)

If apprehended, people catching shad were to be prosecuted as provided in the law:

> D. B. LONG, FISH COMMISSIONER, HAS INSTRUCTED THE COUNTY Attorney of Wyandotte county to prosecute all parties engaged in catching shad in the Kansas river. A considerable number of them have been taken. Mr. Long has just deposited some fine land locked salmon in several streams in the State. (*Hays City Sentinel*, 6 June 1879)

The first fish hatchery in Kansas was established in 1879 in Ellsworth County. Erroneously reported to be on the farm of Fish Commissioner Long, it was actually located on the adjacent farm of Mr. Sternberg:

> WE VISITED THE STATE FISH HATCHERY THIS WEEK ON THE farm of Hon. D. B. Long, Fish Commissioner. Mr. Long received 10,000 salmon spawn about three weeks ago from Maine, and placing them in a well arranged hatching box, managed through great care, to hatch out about 75 per cent, of healthy minnows. During the late heavy rain the river rose and tore out one of the boxes and as a consequence, about 2500 were lost in the river, leaving but 5,000. These will be placed in the small lakes and at the head of streams through the State in a week or so. Mr. Long has done extremely well, considering the many disadvantages he has labored under. The State should pay more attention to fish culture and make an appropriation so that a hatching house can be built and greater care taken in fish propagation. (*Ellsworth Reporter*, 8 May 1879)

> STATE FISH COMMISSIONER LONG INFORMS US THAT WE MADE a mistake in saying that the fish hatchery is on his farm as he uses the spring on the farm of Mr. Sternberg, adjoining his place. (*Ellsworth Reporter*, 15 May 1879)

In May it was reported that the fish commissioner would receive $1,000 to continue stocking efforts:

HON. D. B. LONG, WHO HAS BEEN CONFIRMED AS FISH COM-
missioner, gets $1,000 to carry on the work of stocking the
streams of Kansas with fish. (*Ellsworth Reporter,* 20 May
1879)

In June, Commissioner Long reported a salmon hatch, which
he used to stock Lake Inman in McPherson County:

ED REPORTER:

It may be of interest to some of your readers to know that
I have succeeded in hatching out a large percent of the fish
spawn of the schoodic or land locked salmon I received
from Maine in April last. Not having a suitable location,
Rev. L. Sternberg kindly offered me the use of one of the
large springs on his farm, where I placed my hatching boxes.
The water was of the right temperature, as the spawn rapidly hatched out and made a fine, healthy growth. Not
having the necessary convenience for protecting and keeping the young fry, many of them escaped into the river
while moving them from the hatching trays into the boxes
during the late freshet. The balance of the first fry I deposited in Lake Inman, McPherson county, Kansas. This lake
was named after our friend Col. H. Inman, who is a very
enthusiastic advocate of the fish interest of our State, and
who aided me more than any other editor in the State in
bringing this important enterprise before the people. Lake
Inman is a beautiful lake containing 192 acres of water. In
places it is quite deep—from 10 to 20 feet. The water is not
as clear as it ought to be for salmon, but I believe they will
live and grow. Black bass would do well in this lake. I was
informed that some very nice fish had been caught out of
the lake by fishing parties. The country between Ellsworth
and Lake Inman—distance about 60 miles—is the finest
country I ever traveled over. The old Harker and Wichita
trail, over which the supplies were transported to Fort Sill
in 1868, 1869 and '70, is almost obliterated by fields of

waving grain, but to the old settler the long train of covered wagons with five or six yoke of oxen to each wagon, the cracking of the long whips, the camp fires, and sometimes prairie fires, are still fresh in our memories, and will not be so easily obliterated as the Harker trail.

D. B. LONG. (*Ellsworth Reporter*, 5 June 1879)

The 100,000 shad that Kansas had been promised in 1878, along with an additional 60,000 shad, were received in June 1879 and immediately stocked:

LAST TUESDAY MR. J. F. ELLIS, ASSISTANT OF PROF. BAIRD, U. S. Commissioner of Fisheries, arrived from Washington, D. C., with 160,000 young shad for our Kansas rivers. State Fish Commissioner Long met Mr. Ellis at Topeka and took a portion of the fish and proceeded to distribute them in the rivers south of the A. T. & S. F. R. R. Mr. G. A. Atwood, who happened to be coming up on the K. P. train from Topeka, Tuesday, assisted Mr. Ellis in making the distribution along this line of the road. At Manhattan 20,000 fish were planted in the Blue river; 20,000 were turned loose in the Republican near Junction City; 20,000 in the Solomon and 20,000 in the Smoky at Ellsworth. Mr. Atwood learned some facts concerning these shad that may be new to some of our readers. The eggs from which these fish were hatched were obtained at Havre de Grace, Md. They were hatched in 48 hours, under the supervision of Mr. Ellis, who proceeded with them at once for Kansas. The water in the cans in which they were stored had to be changed once in two hours, and he felt much relieved when he had them safely disposed of. These shad will remain in the Kansas rivers until about September 1st when they will go for salt water— which will take them to the Gulf of Mexico. There they will remain for two years, when they will return to the very places they were planted in Kansas, where they will spawn and after a few weeks will again return to salt water. This journeying will be annually continued by the shad and their descendants. Prof. Baird is an enthusiast in the work of propagating fish, and annually distributes millions of the finny tribe in all the States of the Union.

If the good work now in charge of Commissioner Long is continued a few years the people of Kansas will soon find an abundance of fish in our rivers and creeks, and then the labors of our Commissioners and our members of Congress will be appreciated. (*Ellsworth Reporter,* 5 June 1879)

Some of the rivers in which fish were stocked turned out to be ephemeral, including even the Arkansas River, which went dry as early as the 1870s. One such incident had an obvious adverse effect on stocked fish:

THE ARKANSAS RIVER AT DODGE CITY IS PUZZLING SCIENTISTS, as the following taken from the Larned *Chronoscope,* will show:

The river has presented a series of unusually interesting phenomena during the past week. First it suddenly dried up, and remained so for some twenty-four hours, when lo! it as suddenly assumed its normal condition. Again it dried; and at the moment we pen this it is to be found in that condition. Thousands of fish were caught in nets improvised for the occasion, which had become land-locked in little pools on the bars; and thousands died from the intense heat engendered in their limited quarters. We cannot account for this phenomena at present upon scientific grounds. Capt. C. A. Morris, the booming Hoisington, and V. C. Jarboe, Esq., of Great Bend, visited it for investigation, but came away unsatisfied. (*Ellsworth Reporter,* 31 July 1879)

STRANGE TO SAY, AND CONTRARY TO THE PREDICTIONS OF the scientists of the Valley, the Arkansas River is dry; not a drop of water to be seen, and the fish deposited by Mr. Long, the Fish Commissioner of the state, are compelled to hunt their holes. (*Hays City Sentinel,* 26 September 1879)

The stocking of additional salmon, along with lake trout and black bass, was anticipated as the decade of the seventies closed:

> FISH COMMISSIONER LONG HAS JUST PURCHASED OF ED. Shaw, Cedar Rapids, Iowa, 100,000 lake trout and black bass which he will bring to this State within a few months. He also purchased of the same party 100,000 salmon which are now ready for delivery. (*Ellsworth Reporter*, 13 November 1879)

The establishment of a commissioner of fisheries in 1877 anticipated the founding of a department that would oversee both fish and other wildlife. In Kansas a department dealing with both game and fish was finally established in 1905.

Epilogue

The 1865–79 period witnessed changes that caused some populations of wildlife to decrease. However, none became extinct within the borders of Kansas during this time. At the close of this fifteen-year period at least some animals remained that were representative of all the species originally present. Time, however, would change this. In 1880 most of the western third of Kansas had yet to be settled, and environmental modifications necessary for an agriculturally based economy had just begun. Rapid population growth in western Kansas occurred primarily in the final two decades of the nineteenth century, and continued agricultural development simply served to augment those forces already acting to diminish populations of the native fauna.

One might think that the settlers could have foreseen the demise of these populations of wildlife and taken necessary steps to prevent it. A few were concerned and made efforts to implement conservation measures, but there were strong factors working against them.

Land was cheap; if abused, there was always more, and the immigrant could move on. This understanding prevented the development of a lasting attachment to the land and its wildlife. To most settlers it was inconceivable that the immense herds of buffalo, antelope, elk, and deer would disappear. It seemed not even remotely possible that the huge flocks of turkey and prairie chicken and the abundant stream life of beaver, otter, mink, muskrat, and fish could ever be decimated. These creatures were not numbered in hundreds or thousands, but in millions! Surely they could never be destroyed. The early pioneer probably did not understand that the animals depended upon the habitat that the immigrant was changing to sustain his needs. Most of the settlers, if they reflected upon this reality at all, probably did not expect economic factors to play such a major role. The demand for robes, leather, fur, and meat by an expanding economy in the east created a market that was willingly met by hunters and fur trappers. The impact of this trade was simply not anticipated, and by the time the few concerned individuals clearly understood what was taking place, it was too late.

Crop production and ranching activities placed these immigrant agriculturalists in direct competition with the herbivorous buffalo, antelope, elk, deer, prairie dog, and jackrabbit. The pioneers, through hunting and poisoning, directly reduced the number of these competitors and in some cases eliminated them entirely, at least locally. This reduction of herbivores, in turn, was responsible for a reduction in the numbers of carnivores. Finally, recreational and commercial hunting, fishing, and trapping had a direct effect on diminishing certain populations of the native fauna, as did the control measures against "pest" species.

However, the early settlers' attempts to establish a society based on agriculture had both a positive and negative effect on native fauna. It is certainly true that for the larger, more visible, grazers, for the carnivores that preyed upon them, and for aquatic furbearers, the consequences of human settlement were pernicious. It is not true for a variety of smaller species that actually increased their numbers.

Initially the riparian community was negatively affected. The immigrants arrived in an area largely devoid of trees. The few trees present were removed for fuel and construction, thereby destroying most of the riparian habitat in western Kansas. However, the woodland present today is much greater than it was in 1865, for several reasons:

Most immigrants came from timbered areas, so it was not surprising that they attempted limited plantings of trees around their homesteads and farms. The Timber Claim Act of 1862 encouraged tree planting, as did the Kansas "tree bounty act" of 1868. Newspaper editors constantly urged their readers to plant trees, not only for aesthetic reasons, but also to attract birds, which would help diminish the number of dreaded grasshoppers. Pioneers began to control prairie fires, which helped to preserve timber. Periodic flooding on the streams in western Kansas decreased, partly because of drought and partly because of the conservation measures implemented in the early twentieth century. This in turn reduced the scouring action of high water that had prevented the establishment of seedlings and subsequent mature trees along the streams. Thus there has been an increase of forested area in central and western Kansas.

Animals that utilized the grassland ecosystems were also affected both positively and negatively. The sod that was broken for croplands destroyed the grassland habitat, thereby decreasing the total amount available for the grazing herbivores. However, at the same time, these farming activities increased the diversity of available habitats. With the advent of agriculture arose several different types of croplands as well as remnant areas in roadside ditches, along field borders, and around farmsteads that supported various types of "weedy" vegetation. As a result, some populations of wildlife were reduced in numbers while others increased.

As the large herds of native grazing mammals were slaughtered, the short grasses in central Kansas began to be replaced by a habitat dominated by taller, midheight grasses. This habitat had more overhead cover and mulch than had existed previously. Another habitat was created as the settlers constructed homes for themselves and outbuildings for their livestock. These dwellings became preferred shelter for house mice, Norway rats, spotted skunks, pigeons, barn swallows, barn owls, house sparrows, and others.

Many species that were eventually extirpated from Kansas have been reestablished by an aggressive reintroduction program of the Kansas Department of Wildlife and Parks. The most obvious animal on the prairies was the buffalo, but the great herds were decimated and fragmented by 1875. A few small groups wandered about after that and were hunted, but by 1890 the buffalo was largely extirpated from Kansas (Choate, 1987). Buffalo will never be established again as free-roaming herds in Kansas. Such herds are incompatible with modern agriculture. However, the state established smaller herds near Garden City in 1927 (Coleman, 1961) and on the Maxwell State Game Refuge Preserve in McPherson County in 1951 (Wellborn, 1976). These herds were established for their aesthetic value.

By 1956 there were five separate buffalo ranges on state-owned land. The Finney County State Game Refuge had 150 head, and the Maxwell State Game Refuge 80 head; smaller herds occurred in state parks in Kingman, Meade, and Crawford counties (Valyer, 1956). Today Kansas has several small herds of bison. Many are kept on small ranches and in zoos. *The Buffalo Book* (Dary, 1974) lists twenty-eight zoos and ranches that harbor some buffalo in addition to those kept by the state. Kansas State University currently has a herd numbering 160 on the Konza Prairie near Manhattan.

Antelope fared a little better. Although not congregating in the large, continuous herds of the buffalo, they may have been equally abundant (Choate, 1987; Hlavachick, 1967). By 1877 records kept at Fort Hays indicated that numbers of pronghorn were declining (Choate and Fleharty, 1975). The fort's annual report for 1877 stated that "the antelope still linger on the hills hereabout, but in diminished numbers; whether his stay is due to the peculiarity of his habits or to the fact that he eludes his pursuers more easily than the Buffalo, I do not know."

The pronghorn received no protection in Kansas from 1861 to 1902 but was protected from 1903 to 1920. Antelope were not protected between 1921 and 1924 but were from 1925 to 1973 (Funk, 1988). Pronghorn numbers continued to decline. Small numbers were reported in 1921 northwest of Cimarron and southwest of Garden City (Nelson, 1925). By 1925 the pronghorn was nearly eliminated from Kansas (Nelson, 1925). There were a few stragglers in Hamilton County in 1931 (Brennan, 1932). The last pronghorns were seen in Morton, Wallace, and Clark counties before 1925, 1930, and 1935 respectively (Choate, 1987). Probably a few pronghorn always remained in the state or wandered back and forth from adjacent states (Sexson and Choate, 1981).

In 1964 aerial surveys indicated small scattered bands in Wallace and Sherman counties in extreme western Kansas. Other areas of the state in Logan, Gove, Barber, and Clark counties were thought to contain enough habitat to support small herds of antelope. With this in mind the Forestry, Fish, and Game Commission embarked upon a program of reintroduction whereby wild antelope from other states were released into Kansas (Hlavachick, 1964). Antelope from Montana were released into Kansas in 1964, from Colorado in 1966 (Hlavachick, 1967), from Nebraska in 1967 (Miller, 1967), and from Wyoming in 1978 (Baughman, 1980). An initial three-day hunting season for antelope was held in 1974 in Wallace and Sherman counties. Seasons have continued in these and other counties to the present date.

Although present in western Kansas, deer were probably never numerous. Fires, frequent flooding of streams and rivers, the removal of timber, and excessive hunting by the settlers resulted in deer being extirpated from Kansas by 1905 (Lantz, 1905). They were still not present in 1933 (Sexson, Hlavachick, and van Zwoll, 1985).

However, by the early 1950s deer frequently were seen in Kansas (Sexson, Hlavachick, and van Zwoll, 1985). The increase in populations of deer was due to a few introductions by private citizens and the state Game Commission plus some immigration from surrounding states (Modern day deer season, 1965). As strange as it might seem, deer habitat increased during the drought of the 1930s. The drought, coupled with conservation measures such as the construction of dams and terraces, reduced and stabilized the flow of water in the rivers and streams. This stabilization of flow reduced the scouring action of the periodic floods and permitted the establishment and growth of seedlings. Additionally, many shelterbelts were planted, which increased habitat available for deer (Todd, 1962; Mathews and Sexson, 1989). In 1965 Kansas had its first deer season, and these have continued yearly.

Elk were present in Kansas primarily along the wooded streams, but as with deer, they suffered from habitat destruction and overharvesting. By 1890 no elk were to be found in western Kansas (Choate, 1987). Currently Kansas has three herds of elk that have been reintroduced into the state. In 1951 elk were reintroduced onto the Maxwell Game Preserve in McPherson County, and in 1981 twelve elk were transplanted from the Maxwell Refuge to the Cimarron National Grasslands in Morton County (Montei, 1986). Additional elk were released there in 1982, 1984, 1988, and 1990. A third herd was established at the Fort Riley Military Reservation. Releases consisted of twelve animals in 1986, seven in 1987, five in 1988, eight in 1990, two in 1990, and two in 1992. Hunting seasons with severely limited permits were established in 1987 in the Cimarron National Grass-land and on the Fort Riley Military Reservation in 1990 (Keith Sexson, personal communication, 1993).

The loss of the large populations of grazing mammals, along with habitat destruction and hunting pressures, caused a decline in populations of mountain lion and gray wolf. Gray wolves almost exclusively used buffalo for food and were relatively com-mon into the late 1870s (Choate, 1987). Wolves were seen in only ten counties by 1895 but still occurred occasionally until 1939 (Choate, 1987). Bee et al. (1981) reported no gray wolves in Kansas after 1905.

The mountain lion was generally felt to be uncommon in western Kansas during settlement (Choate, 1987). The decline in numbers of mountain lion probably was tied closely to the decline of their primary prey species—deer. The last recorded specimen was taken near Catherine in Ellis County in 1905 (Dyche, 1905).

Evidently there were few grizzlies in western Kansas, and they became extirpated relatively early during the settlement period. Grizzly bears were seen in Kansas in Barber County prior to 1885 and in Osborne County during 1865–75 (Choate, 1987). Cock-rum (1952) reported specimens from Gove and Logan counties. Black bears were reported primarily in the rugged terrain of Barber, Clark, Comanche, and Harper counties from 1885 to 1894 and in Jewell County in 1875 (Choate, 1987); Cockrum (1952) listed no records of black bear after 1875.

The history of furbearers is less clear. It was mostly French trappers who carried on an active fur trade with the Indians in Kansas until 1875. After that date Americans of British descent also began to trade with the Plains Indians (Henderson, 1960). The steel trap was introduced in 1823; this increased the effi-ciency of the trappers (Henderson, 1960; Johnson, 1981). During the settlement period of Kansas (1850–1900) populations of fur-bearers continued to decline under trapping pressure and dwin-dling habitat.

Beaver in Kansas were extensively trapped through 1846, when demand for beaver hats was replaced by silk hats (Johnson, 1981). However, there was enough continued pressure to reduce the population further. The last beaver trapped in Kansas supposedly was one taken near Lawrence in 1907 (Johnson, 1981), but prob-ably isolated colonies existed in north-central and northwestern Kansas.

There was no protection for Kansas furbearers until 1911. At this time the trapping of raccoons, skunks, civet cats, opossums, muskrats, and minks was legal only from 16 November to 14 March. In 1911 the legislature prohibited the taking of any re-maining beaver for at least ten years. In 1921 the legislature pro-scribed trapping for another ten years; seasons remained closed until 1943. At that time the responsibility of establishing a trap-ping season for beaver was delegated to the Fish and Game Com-mission; a beaver season was not opened until 1951–52 (Johnson, 1981).

Otters were common in the major streams of Kansas. How-ever, fur trapping and habitat destruction evidently extirpated the otter shortly after the turn of the century. The last reported record was cited by Lantz (1905, p. 178) as being "captured near Manhattan in September, 1904." Subsequently, seventeen otters from Minnesota and one from Idaho were reintroduced onto the south fork of the Cottonwood River in Chase County in 1983, 1984, and 1985. Although young have occasionally been killed on nearby highways, the current status of otter in Kansas is unknown (Keith Sexson, personal communication).

Wild turkey were no longer found in Kansas by the early 1900s (Thompson and Ely; 1989, 1992). In 1941 wild turkey were rein-troduced onto two game farms for extensive study (Wild turkeys, 1941). By 1959 some wild turkeys were immigrating into south-eastern Kansas from Oklahoma (Hanzlick, 1960). Additional turkeys were released in 1966 and 1967 to fourteen sites in Kan-sas. These birds came from Texas and Oklahoma. The first spring hunting season was held in 1974, and the first fall season in 1979. Seasons have been held every year since (Keith Sexson, personal communication, 1993).

The effect of the early pioneers on prairie chicken (greater and lesser), sharp-tailed grouse, and ruffed grouse was a mixed bag. The easily hunted ruffed grouse was gone from Kansas by the turn of the century. Ruffed grouse from Wisconsin were reintroduced into Kansas from 1983 through 1989 and from Min-nesota in 1991. It appears that populations are established at some locales in northeastern Kansas (Randy Rodgers, personal communication, 1993).

The greater prairie chicken, in presettlement times, extended westward to about the middle of Kansas but was probably not abundant. Initially, with the removal of the buffalo and the change that was brought in the structure and complexity of the grassland, the populations declined. However, as small farms became established and grazing of domestic cattle occurred, the populations increased dramatically (Greater prairie chicken, 1978).

By 1900 with more intensive and extensive agriculture, the populations of the greater prairie chicken in the east began to dwindle, whereas those in appropriate areas in the northwestern Kansas expanded. These populations too essentially disappeared after the mid-1920s. Today we find greater prairie chickens where there is extensive cover of tall- and midgrass prairie, mostly in the Flint Hills and north-central Kansas (Greater prairie chicken, 1978).

The lesser prairie chicken was found throughout southwestern Kansas before the arrival of the immigrants. Although these birds were hunted for market as well as for local consumption, populations survived the frontier period in relatively good condition. However, in the 1930s populations were damaged because prolonged drought reduced water supplies, cover, and food (Greater prairie chicken, 1978). Prior to the drought the lesser prairie chicken expanded its range into most of western Kansas, southwestern Nebraska, and northeastern Colorado (Harrison, 1974).

Populations of both species of prairie chicken increased because early agriculture broke relatively little land in the vast prairie expanse and the crops provided food for the chickens. However, as farming technology increased to allow greater acreage to come under the plow, populations of both greater and lesser prairie chicken again declined (Harrison, 1974).

Since the 1950s populations of both the greater and lesser prairie chicken have expanded their range and increased their numbers. Prairie-chicken populations tend to fluctuate in response to environmental conditions, and limited hunting seasons have little effect. Consequently, a hunting season was reestablished in 1957 and has been held every year since (Horak, 1987).

Sharp-tailed grouse were relatively common in the northwest quarter of Kansas prior to settlement and existed in the state until the 1930s. Grazing and conversion of prairie to cropland eventually resulted in the demise of this species (Mathews, 1980). Releases of sharptails from North Dakota and Nebraska were carried out in 1982, 1984, 1986, and 1988. These releases have been successful in establishing breeding populations in Rawlins, Osborne, and Rooks counties (Rodgers, 1992).

Other native species of wildlife extirpated from Kansas that have not been reintroduced include the black-footed ferret, the white-tailed jackrabbit, and the common raven. The common raven is largely a carrion feeder and utilizes dead buffalo for food. When the buffalo were eliminated from Kansas, so too was the common raven (Thompson and Ely; 1989, 1992). Black-footed ferrets have not been sighted in Kansas since 1957. These animals usually den in prairie-dog burrows and almost exclusively use prairie dogs for food. As more land was used for agriculture, prairie dogs were poisoned. Because of this, dog towns were reduced in size to the point where they could not sustain black-footed ferrets (Bee et al., 1981). It is probable that black-footed ferrets will never return to Kansas short of allowing extensive prairie-dog towns to develop.

The white-tailed jackrabbit was an inhabitant of native prairie particularly in northwestern Kansas. According to Carter (1939) the white-tailed jackrabbit began to decline in numbers in 1875. It is uncertain whether this decline was caused by converting prairie to cropland, a slight shift in climate, or increased competition with the more arid-adapted black-tailed jackrabbit. Whatever the case, it is doubtful that any whitetails exist in the state, although Bee et al. (1981) believe that they might occur in northwestern Kansas.

Diversity of wildlife generally depends on the variety of habitats available. At the time of settlement there was relatively little habitat diversity, but as settlement proceeded, those few habitats were altered and the changes led to the reduction of some populations, particularly buffalo, antelope, elk, deer, mountain lion, otter, beaver, and populations of such birds as plover, quail, prairie chicken, and turkey. However, the activities of the settlers created new habitats in the form of croplands, weedy fence rows and borrow ditches, and buildings. The weedy fence rows and borrow ditches, in addition to becoming a preferred habitat for a number of species, formed routes of dispersal for other small mammals. They could then penetrate into what had heretofore been hostile environments. Additionally, a great number of trees were planted in western Kansas and these provided habitat for songbirds, forage for deer, and homes for squirrels. This new variety of habitats may even support a greater diversity of species in western Kansas than was present in 1865–79. We can only conjecture, however, because precise lists of the vertebrate fauna present at that time do not exist. Although some species were eliminated from Kansas, none since 1865–79 has become extinct. Furthermore, efforts by environmentalists, sportsmen, game-department personnel, and politicians have been successful in a number of reintroductions.

Many people are unaware of the diversity of wildlife in Kansas and elsewhere on the Great Plains. A large number of species are small and not easily observed. Others are secretive, and some are nocturnal. But the primary reason that the diversity on the Great Plains goes unnoticed is the lack of our sensitization toward wildlife. Most Americans are brought up and educated in cities and have little direct contact with nature. To many of these people the Great Plains is an area merely to be tolerated as they cross in an east-west direction to reach their destination. Few people take the time to leave the four-lane superhighways and truly visit the grasslands. Their exposure to the prairie consists of peering through automobile windows while traveling at sixty-five miles per hour, the sound of the stereo tape deck or compact-disk player filling their ears—a lot like watching television in their living room. They look at the prairie within just feet of their speeding car but do not see it! Those who take the time to aquaint themselves thoroughly with the flora and fauna of the Great Plains may well enjoy a fauna richer than that of 1865.

Reference List

NEWSPAPERS

Commonwealth, The (Topeka, Kans.)
Daily Rocky Mountain News (Denver, Colo.)
Denver (Colo.) *Daily Tribune, The*
Dodge City (Kans.) *Times*
Ellis County News (Hays, Kans.)
Ellis County Star (Hays, Kans.)
Ellsworth (Kans.) *Reporter*
Ford County Globe (Dodge City, Kans.)
Great Bend (Kans.) *Register, The*
Hays (Kans.) *City Sentinel*
Hays (Kans.) *Daily News*
Hutchinson (Kans.) *News, The*
Inland Tribune (Great Bend, Kans.)
Junction City (Kans.) *Union, The*
Junction City (Kans.) *Weekly Union, The*
Kansas City (Mo.) *Star*
Kansas Daily Commonwealth, The (Topeka)
Kinsley Graphic, The (Kirwin, Kans.)
Kirwin (Kans.) *Chief, The*
Larned (Kans.) *Chronoscope, The*
Larned (Kans.) *Optic, The*
Leavenworth (Kans.) *Daily Conservative*
Leavenworth (Kans.) *Weekly Times, The*
Newton (Kans.) *Kansan*
Osborne (Kans.) *County Farmer*
Pawnee County Herald (Larned, Kans.)
Russell (Kans.) *County Record*
Saline County Journal (Salina, Kans.)

Smith County Pioneer (Smith Center, Kans.)
Stockton (Kans.) *News, The*
Topeka (Kans.) *Commonwealth*
Valley Republican, The (Kinsley, Kans.)
White Cloud Kansas Chief
Wichita (Kans.) *City Eagle, The*

DIARIES AND LETTERS

Bill, Arthur C. 1879. The buffalo hunt. Kansas State Historical Society, Topeka.

Clarkson, Matthew. 1867. Diary of Matt Clarkson. Forsythe Library, Fort Hays State University.

Raymond, H. H. 1872–73. Incidents of frontier life. Kansas State Historical Society, Topeka.

Raymond, H. H. 1934. Letter to Mrs. Haley of Austin, Texas. Written on December 6, 1934. Kansas State Historical Society, Topeka.

Watson, Louis. Letters and diaries, 1868–91. Kansas State Historical Society, Topeka.

BOOKS AND ARTICLES

Buffalo hunting. 1867. *Harper's Weekly,* 14 December, pp. 797–98.

Baughman, R. 1980. Antelope update. *Kansas Fish and Game,* 37:15–16.

Bee, J. W., G. E. Glass, R. S. Hoffman, and R. R. Patterson. 1981. *Mammals in Kansas.* University of Kansas, Museum of Natural History, Public Education Series, no. 7.

Brennan, L. A. 1932. Mammal extinction in Kansas, I. The pronghorned antelope. *Aerend,* 1932:231–36.

Carter, F. L. 1939. A study in jackrabbit shifts in range in western Kansas. *Transactions of the Kansas Academy of Science,* 42:431–35.

Choate, J. R. 1987. Post-settlement history of mammals in western Kansas. *Southwestern Naturalist,* 32:157–68.

Choate, J. R., and E. D. Fleharty. 1975. Synopsis of native, recent mammals of Ellis County, Kansas. Occasional Papers, The Museum, Texas Tech University, no. 37. 80 pp.

Cockrum, E. L. 1952. Mammals of Kansas. *University of Kansas Publications, Museum of Natural History,* 7:1–303.

Coffin, M. M. 1976. *Death in early America.* New York: Thomas Nelson.

Coleman, D. 1961. Kansas wildlife. American bison. *Kansas Fish and Game*, 19:9,12.

Collins, J. T. 1993. *Amphibians and Reptiles in Kansas*. 3rd ed. revised. University of Kansas, Museum of Natural History, Public Education Series, no. 13.

Copley, J. 1867. *Kansas and the country beyond*. . . . Philadelphia: J. P. Lippincott.

Dary, David. 1974. *The buffalo book*. Chicago: Swallow Press.

Davis, T. R. 1869. The buffalo range. *Harper's New Monthly Magazine*, 36:147–63.

Dixon, W. H. 1867. *New America*. London: Hurst and Blackett.

Dodge, R. I. 1877. *The hunting grounds of the great west. A description of the plains, game, and Indians of the Great American Desert*. London: Chatto and Windus. *microfiche*.

Dyche, L. L. 1905. The puma or American lion. *Transactions of the Kansas Academy of Science*, 21:165–67.

Fenneman, N. M. 1931. *Physiography of western United States*. New York: McGraw-Hill.

Forsythe, J. 1977. Environmental considerations in the settling of Ellis County, Kansas. *Agricultural History*, 51:38–40.

Frémont, J. C. 1845. *Report of the exploring expedition to the Rocky Mountains in the year 1842, and to Oregon and north California in the years 1843–44*. Ann Arbor, Mich.: University Microfilms.

Funk, T. L. 1988. Pronghorns on the prairie. *Kansas Wildlife and Parks*, 45:2–7.

Gambone, J. 1970. Economic relief in territorial Kansas, 1860–61. *Kansas Historical Quarterly*, 36:149–74.

Gard, W. 1960. *The great buffalo hunt*. Lincoln: University of Nebraska Press.

Greater prairie chicken. 1978. *Kansas Fish and Game*, 35:12–15.

Guild, E. W. 1879. Western Kansas—Its geology, climate, natural history, etc. *Kansas City Review of Science*, 3:461–67.

Greeley, H. 1869. The plains as I crossed them ten years ago. *Harper's New Monthly Magazine*, 38:789–95.

Greene, M. 1856. *The Kansas region*. New York: Fowler and Wells.

Haines, F. D. 1938a. Northward spread of horses among the Plains Indians. *American Anthropologist*, 40:429–37.

Haines, F. D. 1938b. When did the Plains Indians get their horses? *American Anthropologist*, 40:112–17.

Hanzlick, B. 1960. Wild turkeys in Kansas. *Kansas Fish and Game*, 17:7–9.

Harrison, R. 1974. Memoirs of the prairie chicken. *Kansas Fish and Game*, 31:11–14.

Henderson, F. R. 1960. Beaver in Kansas. *University of Kansas, Museum of Natural History Publications*, 26:1–85.

Hill, W. A. 1938. *Historic Hays*. Hays, Kans.: News.

Hlavachick, B. 1964. Antelope in Kansas? *Kansas Fish and Game*, 21:8–9.

Hlavachick, B. 1967. Kansas antelope outlook bright. *Kansas Fish and Game*, 24:3,18.

Horak, G. L. 1987. The prairie bird. *Kansas Wildlife*, 44:8–12.

Johnson, N. 1981. History and management of our most controversial wildlife—the furbearers. *Kansas Wildlife*, 38:9–24.

Kingsley, C. 1874. *South by west*. London: W. Isbister.

Klauber, L. M. 1982. *Rattlesnakes, their habits, life histories, and influence on mankind*. Berkeley: University of California Press.

Kuchler, A. W. 1974. A new vegetation map of Kansas. *Ecology*, 55: 586–604.

Lantz, D. E. 1905. Kansas mammals in their relation to agriculture. *Kansas State College Experment Station Bulletin*, 129:331–404.

Long, S. H. 1823. *Account of an expedition from Pittsburg to the Rocky Mountains. . . .* Philadelphia: H. C. Carey and I. Lea.

Mathews, B. 1980. The sharptail: Will he come home to Kansas? *Kansas Fish and Game*, 37:18–22.

Mathews, B., and K. Sexson. 1989. Twenty-five years of deer management in Kansas. *Kansas Wildlife and Parks*, 46:35–39.

Mead, J. R. 1859–75. *Hunting and trading on the Great Plains, 1859–1875*. Ed. Schuyler Jones. Norman: University of Oklahoma Press.

Miller, R. 1967. Antelope play in Kansas. *Kansas Fish and Game*, 24:12–15.

Miner, H. C. 1986. *West of Wichita: Settling the high plains of Kansas, 1865–1890*. Lawrence: University Press of Kansas.

Modern day deer season. 1965. *Kansas Fish and Game*, 22:8–10, 21–23.

Montei, K. 1986. Update on elk. *Kansas Wildlife*, 43:24–27.

Nelson, E. W. 1925. Status of the pronghorned antelope, 1922–1924. *United States Department of Agriculture Bulletin*, 1346:1–64.

Nichols, R. L. 1980. *Steven Long and American frontier exploration*. Newark: University of Delaware Press.

Palmer, T. S. 1912. *Chronology and index of the more important events in American game protection, 1776–1911*. United States Department of Agriculture, Biological Survey Bulletin 41.

Pike, Z. M. 1810. *Sources of the Mississippi and through the western parts of Louisiana. . . . and a tour through the interior parts of new Spain.* Ann Arbor, Michigan: University Microfilms.

Report of Assistant Surgeon, Fort Larned, 1868. *Fort Larned Records* (Kansas State Historical Society, Topeka).

Richmond, R. W. 1992. *Kansas, a pictorial history.* Lawrence: University Press of Kansas.

Rodgers, R. P. 1992. A technique for establishing sharp-tailed grouse in unoccupied range. *Wildlife Society Bulletin,* 20:101–6.

Self, H. 1978. *Environment and man in Kansas: A geographical analysis.* Lawrence: Regents Press of Kansas.

Sexson, K., B. Hlavachick, and W. van Zwoll. 1985. Kansas deer—resource on the rebound. *Kansas Wildlife,* 42:9–24.

Sexson, M. L. and J. R. Choate. 1981. Historical biogeography of the pronghorn in Kansas. *Transactions of the Kansas Academy of Science,* 84:128–33.

White, R. 1983. *The roots of dependency.* Lincoln: University of Nebraska Press.

LAWS AND GOVERNMENT PUBLICATIONS

Kansas. House Journal, Proceedings of the House of the State of Kansas, 1879.

Kansas. Senate Journal, Proceedings of the Senate of the State of Kansas, 1879.

Kansas. Session Laws of Kansas. 1861. First Session of the Legislature, *Protection of Game,* chap. 39, pp. 163–64.

Kansas. Session Laws of Kansas. 1864. Fourth Session of the Legislature, *Destruction of Wolves,* chap. 130, pp. 243–44.

Kansas. Session Laws of Kansas. 1865. Fifth Session of the Legislature, *Protection of Game,* chap. 41, p. 90.

Kansas. Session Laws of Kansas. 1871a. Eleventh Session of the Legislature, *Fruit Trees—Gopher Scalps,* chap. 87, pp. 204–5.

Kansas. Session Laws of Kansas. 1871b. Eleventh Session of the Legislature, *California Quails—Protection of,* chap. 99, pp. 281–82.

Kansas. Session Laws of Kansas. 1872. Twelfth Session of the Legislature, *Prohibit Hunting—Where,* chap. 157, p. 339.

Kansas. Session Laws of Kansas. 1876. Sixteenth Session of the Legislature, *Game—Protection of,* chap. 82, pp. 183–86.

Kansas. Session Laws of Kansas. 1877a. Seventeenth Session of the Legislature, *Bounty—Wolf, Coyote, Wild-cat, Fox, and Rabbit,* chap. 76, p. 124.

Kansas. Session Laws of Kansas. 1877b. Seventeenth Session of the Legislature, *Fish—Providing for the Protection of,* chap. 117, pp. 164–66.

Kansas. Session Laws of Kansas. 1877c. Seventeenth Session of the Legislature, *Game—Protection of,* chap. 117, pp. 166–68.

Kansas. State Statute. 1868. *Game,* chap. 45, pp. 510–12.

United States. House of Representatives. *Congressional Record,* 44th Cong., 1st sess., 1876 (Feb. 23), pp. 1237–41.

Index

of, 231–32, 234–35, 242–46; reintroduction of, 300
Wolf: attacks on humans, 199–200;
bounty for, 195–96; depredation
by, 191–92; hunting of, 25, 93–94,
98–101; as pet, 140; poisoning of,
69. *See also* Gray wolf
Woodpecker, 20; church steeple at-

tacked by, 182; insects controlled
by, 134; song of, 131; spring sight-
ing, 130
Wren, 20; arrival in western Kansas,
131; hunting of, 122

Zoological park, 128, 155–56